Contents

List of figures

List of tables

Foreword

PRINCE2® is extensively used in more than 150 countries around the world, and its take-up grows daily. It is widely considered as the leading method in project management, with in excess of 20,000 organizations already benefiting from its pioneering and trusted approach.

This updated guidance will help those running projects of any size and in any environment to effectively deliver what is required by appropriately managing the costs, timescales, quality, scope, risks and benefits. Its development has followed widespread consultation and draws upon real-life experiences in both public and private sector organizations.

Today, complex projects often involve several organizations working together in partnership or through contractual arrangements to achieve the objectives. PRINCE2 provides a common language between organizations and with external suppliers. It also allows a focus on the Business Case, providing a mechanism to define what the project is trying to achieve, and the rationale and business justification for it.

This latest version of *Managing Successful Projects with PRINCE2* represents an evolution of the previous manuals. The basic methodology remains, but by building on comments from users, this new manual aims to be more accessible and easier to tailor for specific individual needs.

This new edition covers the principles of PRINCE2, reinforcing the good practices of successful projects. The themes describe aspects of project management that require specific treatment, and the processes describe the progress through a project lifecycle from start-up to closure. It is recommended that you use this manual in conjunction with the companion volume, *Directing Successful Projects with PRINCE2* (TSO, 2009).

The number of people taking PRINCE2 qualifications increases by around 20% year on year, and it remains a key contributor to the successful delivery of projects. It is a vital method for any organization wishing to secure efficient and effective operational outcomes.

Nigel Smith

Chief Executive

Office of Government Commerce

Acknowledgements

The Office of Government Commerce (OGC) has continued to develop and improve the definition and presentation of PRINCE2 within this reference manual. The authoring team are acknowledged for their significant contribution, under contract, to the design and development of this guidance.

Lead author

Andy Murray   Outperform UK Ltd

Authoring team

Nigel Bennett   Sun Microsystems Ltd
John Edmonds   pearcemayfield
Bob Patterson   Fujitsu Services
Sue Taylor   APMG PRINCE2 examiner
Graham Williams   GSW Consultancy Ltd

Lead reviewer and mentor

Colin Bentley   PRINCE2 Chief Examiner 1998-2008

Further contributions

In order to ensure that OGC's *Managing Successful Projects with PRINCE2* (2009) remains a true reflection of current and future trends in the international field of project management best practice, and to produce guidance with lasting value, OGC consulted widely with key stakeholders and experts at every stage in the process. OGC would like to thank the following individuals and their organizations for their contributions to this new guidance:

PRINCE2 reference group

Rob Brace, Department of Work & Pensions; Andrew Bragg, Chief Executive, APM; Prof. Christophe Bredillet, ESC Lille; Terry Cooke Davis, Human Systems; Lynne Crawford, University of Sydney; John Cutting, MOD (DPA – DE&S); Prof. Darren Dalcher, Middlesex University, National Centre for Project Management; Steve Falkenkrog, PMI; Ruth Little, DTI Projects Centre; Dusty Miller, Sun Microsystems Ltd; Bob Patterson, Fujitsu; Philip Rushbrook, Cabinet Office; Beverley Webb, BSI Project Management standard committee; Jens Wandel, Director, UNDP

PRINCE2:2009 project governance

Mike Acaster, OGC, Project Executive; Eddie Borup, BPUG, Senior User; Anne-Marie Byrne, TSO, Project Manager; Janine Eves, TSO, Senior Supplier; Sandra Lomax, BPUG, Senior User; Richard Pharro, APMG, Senior Supplier

Change control panel

Coos Groot, Best Practice User Group (PRINCE2 Italy); Peter Johnson, Peter Johnson PJ Ltd; Sheila Roberts, Cupe Ltd; Martin Rother, Best Practice User Group (PRINCE2 Germany); David Watson, ADt Partnership

Reviewers

Robert Allen, PRS for Music; Adalcir da Silva Angelo, Elumini IT & Business Consulting; Paul Askew, Housing Corporation; Richard Aspden, Pathfinder Project Management; Gareth Atwood, Foster Wheeler Energy; Marc Baetens, Pronohau Ltd; Andrew Ball, Audit Commission; Jim Barker, Curtis & Cartwright Consulting Ltd; Keith Batchelor, Foster Wheeler Energy; Dick Bennett, APMG Chief Assessor; Kate Blackall, APMG PRINCE2 examiner; Johan Bleeker, Standard Bank; Eddie Borup, Ibps solutions; Chris Braithwaite, Wellstream; George Brooke, Oak Lodge Consulting Ltd; Mark Canning, North West Regional Development Agency; Tim Carroll, Standard Chartered Bank; Jacqueline Chadwick, VOSA; Sue Childs, APMG PRINCE2 examiner; Alison Clack, Sean Alison Ltd; Jim Clinch, Clinch Consulting; Brian Coombes, The Projects Group; Arthur Coppens, Getronics Consulting Educational Services; Bjarne Corvinius, Rovsing Management; Anthony Dailey, MWH; Terry Dailey, Deliverables Management Consultants; Bill Duncan, APMG PRINCE2 examiner; Hassan El Meligy, IEEE; Darilyn Evans, Adaptive Frameworks, Alan Ferguson, AFA; Chris Ferguson, Novare Consulting Ltd; Ray Frew, Aspen Management Training; Alvin Gardiner, PR-02 (Scotland) Ltd; Emmanuel Gianquitto, APMG (International); Colin Graham, Aylesbury Vale DC; John Greenwood, CSC; Angelika Hamilton, APMG (Germany); Gary R O Haran Doyle, Swiss Life; Simon Harris, Logical Model

Ltd; Wietse Heidema, Opmaat Consultancy & Training; Luis Herrera, Consultant; Terry Hewins, Land Registry; Emma Jones, APMG PRINCE2 Chief Examiner; Nigel Jones, AJS; Howard Joseph, Home Office; Ravi Joshi, Action For Children; Hans Kemper, APMG (Netherlands); Eddie Kilkelly, ILX Group plc; Lawrie Kirk, Tanner James Management Consultants (Australia); Wieslaw Kosieradzki, P2Ware; Eddie Lamont, Lothian & Borders Police; Tony Levene, Quality Projects; Martin Lewis, Lucid IT; David Lillicrap, London Borough of Ealing; Steve Livingstone, BNFL; Tim Lulham, Network Rail; Maria Maltby, Charnwood Borough Council; Dusty Miller, Sun Microsystems Ltd; Trevor Mirams, Parity; Adrian Newton, Quorum ICT; Bruce Nicholls, Bryan Cave; Helen Nicoll, NHS; Chris Price, Highways Agency; G. Raghunandan, Satyam Computer Services Ltd; Geoff Rankins, Goal Professional Services Pty Ltd; Lizz Robb, Yellowhouse.net pty Ltd; Graham Robertson, Serco; Eileen Roden, PM Professional Learning; Philip Rushbrook, Cabinet Office; Ian Santry, Home Office; Andrew Schuster, Department of Health; Noel Scott, Symantec; John Sherwood, Highways Agency; Joy Shewring, APMG (USA); Jay M. Siegelaub, Impact Strategies LLC; Raed M. Skaf, Oger Systems Ltd; Tim Sneller, Southend-on-Sea Borough Council; Rod Sowden, Aspire Europe Ltd; Phil Stephensen-Payne, Remarc Group; Rob Sucher, Armstrong Webb; Mark Sutton, SCOLL Methods Ltd; Ian Thomas, Liberty Network Consultancy; Dot Tudor, TCC; Bram de Vuyst, Getronics Consulting Management Services; Jens Wandel, United Nations Development Programme; Geoff Ward, APMG PRINCE2 examiner; Sheryl Ward, Skandia; Peter Weaver, Corte-grande; David Whelbourn, Xwave solutions inc; Stephen Wierzbicki, Bristol Management Centre; Jorn Wigh, APMG (Denmark); Gerald Williams, Projectlabs; Philip Wilson, Cabinet Office

Managing Successful Projects with PRINCE2 pilot group

The British Council; Capital Coast District Health Board; Department of Labour (New Zealand); Fishserve; Metropolitan Police; Ministry of Economic Development (New Zealand); Ministry of Education (New Zealand); Staffordshire Metropolitan Borough Council; Standard Bank; Suffolk County Council; Sun Microsystems Ltd; Vietnamese Academy of Social Sciences.

Conventions used in this manual

Throughout this manual, the following terms use title case:

- PRINCE2 themes
- PRINCE2 processes
- PRINCE2 roles
- Defined management products

Activities within PRINCE2 processes will always be referred to using the same key words or phrases, and are not otherwise distinguished, as they should be evident from their context. For example, 'The Project Board will give ad hoc direction in these circumstances.'

Abbreviations and acronyms have largely been avoided; however, where they are used, they will be spelt out in full on first use.

Key points are illustrated like this:

> A PRINCE2 project has continued business justification.

Example techniques are illustrated like this:

> **Example of a prioritization technique – MoSCoW**
>
> Each acceptance criterion is rated as either **M**ust have, **S**hould have, **C**ould have or **W**on't have for now (MoSCoW).
>
> All the 'Must have' and 'Should have' acceptance criteria should be mutually achievable.

Introduction

1 Introduction

1.1 THE PURPOSE OF THIS MANUAL

PRINCE2 (PRojects IN Controlled Environments) is a structured project management method based on experience drawn from thousands of projects – and from the contributions of countless project sponsors, Project Managers, project teams, academics, trainers and consultants. This manual is designed:

- For entry-level project management personnel wishing to learn about project management generally and the PRINCE2 method in particular
- For experienced Project Managers and personnel who wish to learn about the PRINCE2 method
- As a detailed reference source for PRINCE2 practitioners
- As a source of information on PRINCE2 for managers considering whether to adopt the method.

The manual covers the questions frequently asked by people involved in project management and support roles. These questions include:

- What's expected of me?
- What does the Project Manager do?
- What do I do if things don't go to plan?
- What decisions am I expected to make?
- What information do I need or must I supply?
- Who should I look to for support? For direction?
- How can I tailor the use of PRINCE2 for my project?

1.2 THE IMPORTANCE OF PROJECTS

A key challenge for organizations in today's world is to succeed in balancing two parallel, competing imperatives:

- To maintain current business operations – profitability, service quality, customer relationships, brand loyalty, productivity, market confidence etc. What we term 'business as usual'
- To transform business operations in order to survive and compete in the future – looking forward and deciding how business change

can be introduced to best effect for the organization.

As the pace of change (technology, business, social, regulatory etc.) accelerates, and the penalties of failing to adapt to change become more evident, the focus of management attention is inevitably moving to achieve a balance between business as usual and business change.

Projects are the means by which we introduce change – and, while many of the skills required are the same, there are some crucial differences between managing business as usual and managing project work.

1.3 WHAT MAKES PROJECTS DIFFERENT?

A **project** is a temporary organization that is created for the purpose of delivering one or more business products according to an agreed Business Case.

There are a number of characteristics of project work that distinguish it from business as usual:

- **Change** Projects are the means by which we introduce change
- **Temporary** As the definition above states, projects are temporary in nature. Once the desired change has been implemented, business as usual resumes (in its new form) and the need for the project is removed. Projects should have a defined start and a defined end
- **Cross-functional** Projects involve a team of people with different skills working together (on a temporary basis) to introduce a change that will impact others outside the team. Projects often cross the normal functional divisions within an organization and sometimes span entirely different organizations. This frequently causes stresses and strains both within organizations and between, for example, customers and suppliers. Each has a different perspective and motivation for getting involved in the change

- **Unique** Every project is unique. An organization may undertake many similar projects, and establish a familiar, proven pattern of project activity, but each one will be unique in some way: a different team, a different customer, a different location. All these factors combine to make every project unique
- **Uncertainty** Clearly, the characteristics already listed will introduce threats and opportunities over and above those we typically encounter in the course of business as usual. Projects are more risky.

1.4 WHY HAVE A PROJECT MANAGEMENT METHOD?

> **Project management** is the planning, delegating, monitoring and control of all aspects of the project, and the motivation of those involved, to achieve the project objectives within the expected performance targets for time, cost, quality, scope, benefits and risks.

It is the development of the project's deliverables (known as products in PRINCE2) that deliver the project's results. A new house is completed by creating drawings, foundations, floors, walls, windows, a roof, plumbing, wiring and connected services. None of this is project management – so why do we need project management at all? The purpose of project management is to keep control over the specialist work required to create the project's products or, to continue with the house analogy, to make sure the roofing contractor doesn't arrive before the walls are built.

Additionally, given that projects are the means by which we introduce business change, and that project work entails a higher degree of risk than other business activity, it follows that implementing a secure, consistent, well-proven approach to project management is a valuable business investment.

1.5 INTRODUCING PRINCE2

PRINCE2 is a non-proprietary method and has emerged worldwide as one of the most widely accepted methods for managing projects. This is largely due to the fact that PRINCE2 is truly generic: it can be applied to any project regardless of project scale, type, organization, geography or culture.

PRINCE2 achieves this by isolating the management aspects of project work from the specialist contributions, such as design, construction etc. The specialist aspects of any type of project are easily integrated with the PRINCE2 method and, used alongside PRINCE2, provide a secure overall framework for the project work.

Because PRINCE2 is generic and based on proven principles, organizations adopting the method as a standard can substantially improve their organizational capability and maturity across multiple areas of business activity – business change, construction, IT, mergers and acquisitions, research, product development and so on.

1.5.1 What does a Project Manager do?

In order to achieve control over anything, there must be a plan. It is the Project Manager who plans the sequence of activities to build the house, works out how many bricklayers will be required and so on.

It may be possible to build the house yourself – but being a manager implies that you will delegate some or all of the work to others. The ability to delegate is important in any form of management but particularly so (because of the cross-functionality and risks) in project management.

With the delegated work under way, the aim is that it should 'go according to plan', but we cannot rely on this always being the case. It is the Project Manager's responsibility to monitor how well the work in progress matches the plan.

Of course, if work does not go according to plan, the Project Manager has to do something about it, i.e. exert control. Even if the work is going well, the Project Manager may spot an opportunity to speed it up or reduce costs. Whether it is by taking corrective action or implementing measures to improve performance, the aim of PRINCE2 is to make the right information available at the right time for the right people to make the right decisions.

1.5.2 What is it we wish to control?

There are six variables involved in any project, and therefore six aspects of project performance to be managed.

Figure 1.1 Project management

- **Costs** The project has to be affordable and, though we may start out with a particular budget in mind, there will be many factors which can lead to overspending and, perhaps, some opportunities to cut costs
- **Timescales** Allied to this, and probably the next most-frequent question asked of a Project Manager, is: 'When will it be finished?'
- **Quality** Finishing on time and within budget is not much consolation if the result of the project doesn't work. In PRINCE2 terms, the project's products must be fit for purpose
- **Scope** Exactly what will the project deliver? Without knowing it, the various parties involved in a project can very often be talking at cross-purposes about this. The customer may assume that, for instance, a fitted kitchen and/or bathroom is included in the price of the house, whereas the supplier views these as 'extras'. On large-scale projects, scope definition is much more subtle and complex. There must be agreement on the project's scope and the Project Manager needs to have a detailed understanding of what is and what is not within the scope. The Project Manager should take care not to deliver beyond the scope as this is a common source of delays, overspends and uncontrolled change ('scope creep')
- **Risk** All projects entail risks but exactly how much risk are we prepared to accept? Should we build the house near the site of a disused mine, which may be prone to subsidence? If we decide to go ahead, is there something we can do about the risk? Maybe insure against it or have thorough surveys carried out?
- **Benefits** Perhaps most often overlooked is the question, 'Why are we doing this?' It's not enough to build the house successfully on time, within budget and to quality specifications if, in the end, we can't sell or rent it at a profit

or live in it happily. The Project Manager has to have a clear understanding of the purpose of the project as an investment and make sure that what the project delivers is consistent with achieving the desired return.

PRINCE2 is an integrated framework of processes and themes that addresses the planning, delegation, monitoring and control of all these six aspects of project performance.

1.5.3 The structure of PRINCE2

The PRINCE2 method addresses project management with four integrated elements of principles, themes, processes and the project environment (Figure 1.2).

1 The principles (Chapter 2)

These are the guiding obligations and good practices which determine whether the project is genuinely being managed using PRINCE2. There are seven principles and unless all of them are applied, it is not a PRINCE2 project.

2 The themes (Chapters 3 to 10)

These describe aspects of project management that must be addressed continually and in parallel throughout the project. The seven themes explain the specific treatment required by PRINCE2 for various project management disciplines and why they are necessary.

3 The processes (Chapters 11 to 18)

These describe a step-wise progression through the project lifecycle, from getting started to project closure. Each process provides checklists of recommended activities, products and related responsibilities.

4 Tailoring PRINCE2 to the project environment (Chapter 19)

This chapter addresses the need to tailor PRINCE2 to the specific context of the project. PRINCE2 is not a 'one size fits all' solution; it is a flexible framework that can readily be tailored to any type or size of project.

There is a companion guide, *Directing Successful Projects with PRINCE2*, which addresses the PRINCE2 method from the viewpoint of senior personnel, specifically Project Board members.

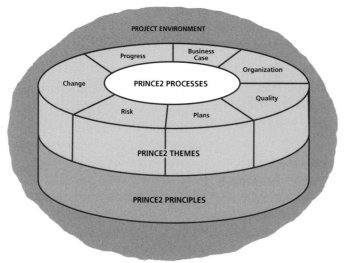

Figure 1.2 The structure of PRINCE2

1.6 RELATED OGC GUIDANCE

PRINCE2 is part of a suite of guidance developed by the UK Office of Government Commerce (OGC), which is aimed at helping organizations and individuals manage their projects, programmes and services consistently and effectively. Figure 1.3 outlines the structure of the set.

Where appropriate, OGC methods and guidance are augmented by qualification schemes, and all aspects are supported by accredited training and consultancy services. Details of these best-practice guides and other relevant guides can be found in Further Information.

1.6.1 What PRINCE2 does not provide

It is not intended (or possible) for PRINCE2 to cover every aspect of project management. There are three broad topic categories which are deliberately considered to be outside the scope of PRINCE2:

■ **Specialist aspects** PRINCE2's strength is in its wide applicability – it is entirely generic. Consequently, industry-specific or type-specific activity is excluded. Engineering models, project lifecycles or specific techniques (such as organizational change management or procurement) can readily be used alongside PRINCE2. PRINCE2 categorizes all these aspects

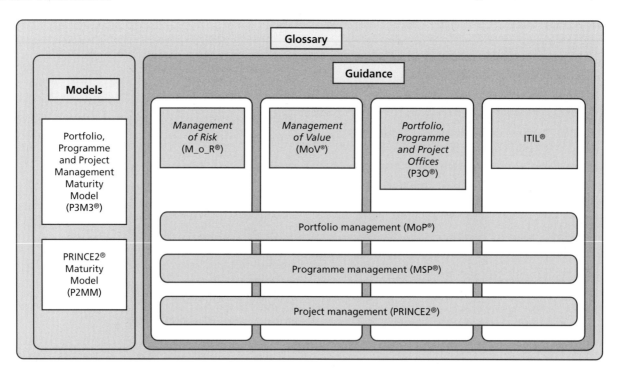

Figure 1.3 OGC best-practice guidance

of project work as 'specialist' (which means that the specialist products concerned need to be identified and included within project scope and plans)

■ **Detailed techniques** There are many proven planning and control techniques that can be used in support of the PRINCE2 themes. Examples are critical path analysis (in planning) and earned value analysis (in progress control). Such techniques are well documented elsewhere. Only techniques that have a specific PRINCE2 approach are described, e.g. the product-based planning and quality review techniques

■ **Leadership capability** Leadership, motivational skills and other interpersonal skills are immensely important in project management but impossible to codify in a method. Leadership styles vary considerably and a style that works in one situation may be entirely inappropriate in another. The fact that it is easy to think of successful leaders who have adopted very different styles – from autocratic to consensus-based – bears this out. For this reason, PRINCE2 cannot address this aspect of project management directly. There are many leadership models and interpersonal-skills training programmes that fulfil this requirement.

1.7 BENEFITS OF PRINCE2

Before introducing the structure of the method, it is worthwhile reviewing the key benefits of adopting PRINCE2:

■ PRINCE2 embodies established and proven best practice and governance for project management

■ It can be applied to any type of project – and can easily be implemented alongside specialist, industry-specific models ('engineering models' or 'development lifecycles')

■ PRINCE2 is widely recognized and understood, and therefore provides a common vocabulary for all project participants – promoting effective communication

■ PRINCE2 provides for the explicit recognition of project responsibilities – so that participants understand each other's roles and needs.

There is a defined structure for accountability, delegation, authority and communication

■ Its product focus clarifies (for all parties) what a project will deliver, why, when, by whom and for whom

■ PRINCE2 plans are carefully designed to meet the needs of the different levels in the management team, improving communication and control

■ It is based on a 'management by exception' framework, providing for the efficient and economic use of management time (whether at corporate, programme, Project Board or project management levels)

■ PRINCE2 ensures that participants focus on the viability of the project in relation to its Business Case objectives – rather than simply seeing the completion of the project as an end in itself

■ It defines a thorough but economical structure of reports

■ It ensures that stakeholders (including sponsors and resource providers) are properly represented in planning and decision making

■ Adopting PRINCE2 promotes learning and continual improvement in organizations

■ PRINCE2 promotes consistency of project work and the ability to reuse project assets; it also facilitates staff mobility and reduces the impact of personnel changes/handovers

■ PRINCE2 is an invaluable diagnostic tool, facilitating the assurance and assessment of project work, troubleshooting and audits

■ There are scores of accredited training and consultancy organizations (ATOs and ACOs) operating worldwide, who can supply expert support for PRINCE2 projects or for organizations planning to adopt PRINCE2.

Principles

2

2 Principles

The purpose of PRINCE2 is to provide a project management method that can be applied regardless of project scale, type, organization, geography or culture. This is possible because PRINCE2 is principles-based. Principles are characterized as:

- Universal in that they apply to every project
- Self-validating in that they have been proven in practice over many years
- Empowering because they give practitioners of the method added confidence and ability to influence and shape how the project will be managed.

The principles on which PRINCE2 is based originate from lessons learned from projects both good and bad. They provide a framework of good practice for those people involved in a project. If a project does not adhere to these principles, it is not being managed using PRINCE2, because the principles are the basis of what defines a PRINCE2 project.

The seven PRINCE2 principles can be summarized as:

- Continued business justification
- Learn from experience
- Defined roles and responsibilities
- Manage by stages
- Manage by exception
- Focus on products
- Tailor to suit the project environment.

It is the adoption of these principles that characterizes whether a project is using PRINCE2, not the adoption of processes and documents alone. The principles facilitate good use of PRINCE2 by ensuring that the method is not applied in an overly prescriptive way or in name only, but applied in a way that is sufficient to contribute to the success of the project.

2.1 CONTINUED BUSINESS JUSTIFICATION

A PRINCE2 project has continued business justification.

A requirement for a PRINCE2 project is that:

- There is a justifiable reason to start it
- The justification should remain valid throughout the life of the project
- The justification is documented and approved.

In PRINCE2, the justification is documented in a Business Case. As a project is inextricably linked to its business justification, it drives the decision-making processes to ensure that the project remains aligned to the business objectives and benefits being sought.

Organizations that lack rigour in developing Business Cases may find that some projects proceed even where there are few real benefits or where a project has only tentative associations with corporate strategy. Poor alignment with corporate strategies can also result in organizations having a portfolio of projects that have mutually inconsistent or duplicated objectives.

Even projects that are compulsory (for example, to comply with new legislation) require justification of the option chosen, as there may be several options available that yield different costs, benefits and risks.

Although the justification should remain valid, it may change. It is therefore important that the project and evolving justification remain consistent.

If, for whatever reason, the project can no longer be justified, the project should be stopped. Stopping a project in these circumstances is a positive contribution to an organization as its funds and resources can be reinvested in other more worthwhile projects.

2.2 LEARN FROM EXPERIENCE

> PRINCE2 project teams learn from previous experience: lessons are sought, recorded and acted upon throughout the life of the project.

Projects involve a temporary organization for a finite timescale for a specific business purpose. A common characteristic is that the project includes an element of uniqueness such that it cannot be managed by existing line management or functional units. It is this element of uniqueness that makes projects challenging as the temporary team may not have experience of a project like the one being undertaken.

In PRINCE2, learning from experience permeates the method:

- **When starting a project** Previous or similar projects should be reviewed to see if lessons learned could be applied. If the project is a 'first' for the people within the organization, then it is even more important to learn from others and the project should consider seeking external experience
- **As the project progresses** The project should continue to learn. Lessons should be included in all reports and reviews. The goal is to seek opportunities to implement improvements during the life of the project
- **As the project closes** The project should pass on lessons. Unless lessons provoke change, they are only lessons identified (not learned).

It is the responsibility of everyone involved with the project to **seek** lessons learned rather than waiting for someone else to provide them.

2.3 DEFINED ROLES AND RESPONSIBILITIES

> A PRINCE2 project has defined and agreed roles and responsibilities within an organization structure that engages the business, user and supplier stakeholder interests.

Projects involve people. No amount of good planning or control will help if the wrong people are involved, if the right people are not involved, or if people involved do not know what's expected of them or what to expect of others.

A project is typically cross-functional, may involve more than one organization, and may involve a mixture of full-time and part-time resources. The management structures of the parties involved in the project are likely to be different – with different priorities, objectives and interests to protect. The day-to-day line management structures may not be designed for, or suited to, project work.

To be successful, projects must have an explicit project management team structure consisting of defined and agreed roles and responsibilities for the people involved in the project and a means for effective communication between them.

All projects have the following primary stakeholders:

- 'Business' sponsors who endorse the objectives and ensure that the business investment provides value for money
- 'Users' who, after the project is completed, will use the products to enable them to gain the intended benefits
- 'Suppliers' who provide the resources and expertise required by the project (these may be internal or external).

Therefore, all three stakeholder interests need to be represented effectively in the project management team – two out of three is not enough. If the project costs outweigh the benefits, the project will fail. Equally, if the outcome of the project does not meet the users' or operational needs, or cannot feasibly be delivered by the suppliers, failure is inevitable.

The defined project management team structure unites the various parties in the common aims of the project. For all those people involved, a defined project management team structure provides the answer to the question, 'What is expected of me?'

2.4 MANAGE BY STAGES

> A PRINCE2 project is planned, monitored and controlled on a stage-by-stage basis.

Management stages provide senior management with control points at major intervals throughout the project. At the end of each stage, the project's status should be assessed, the Business Case and plans reviewed to ensure that the project remains viable, and a decision made as to whether to proceed.

Breaking the project into a number of stages enables the extent of senior management control over projects to be varied according to the business priority, risk and complexity involved. Shorter stages offer more control, while longer stages reduce the burden on senior management.

Planning can only be done to a level of detail that is manageable and foreseeable. A great deal of effort can be wasted on attempts to plan beyond a sensible planning horizon. For example, a detailed plan to show what each team member is doing for the next 12 months will almost certainly be inaccurate after just a few weeks. A detailed Team Plan for the short term and an outline plan for the long term is a more effective approach.

PRINCE2 overcomes the planning horizon issue by:

- Dividing the project into a number of management stages
- Having a high-level Project Plan and a detailed Stage Plan (for the current stage)
- Planning, delegating, monitoring and controlling the project on a stage-by-stage basis.

PRINCE2 requires there to be a minimum of two management stages: one initiation stage and one or more further management stages.

2.5 MANAGE BY EXCEPTION

> A PRINCE2 project has defined tolerances for each project objective to establish limits of delegated authority.

PRINCE2 enables appropriate governance by defining distinct responsibilities for **directing**, **managing** and **delivering** the project and clearly defining accountability at each level. Accountability is established by:

- Delegating authority from one management level to the next by setting tolerances against six objectives for the respective level of the plan:
  - **Time** Plus or minus an amount of time on the target completion dates
  - **Cost** Plus or minus an amount of the planned budget
  - **Quality** Plus or minus degrees off a quality target (e.g. a product that weighs a target 300 g, with an allowed –5 g to +10 g tolerance)
  - **Scope** Permissible variation of the plan's products (e.g. mandatory requirements plus or minus desirable requirements)
  - **Risk** Limits on the plan's aggregated risks (e.g. cost of aggregated threats to remain less than 10% of the plan's budget) or limits on any individual threat (e.g. a threat to operational service)
  - **Benefit** Plus or minus degrees off an improvement goal (e.g. 30–40% cost reduction)
- Setting up controls so that if those tolerances are forecast to be exceeded, they are immediately referred up to the next management layer for a decision on how to proceed
- Putting an assurance mechanism in place so that each management layer can be confident that such controls are effective.

This implementation of 'management by exception' provides for very efficient use of senior management time as it reduces senior managers' time burden without removing their control by ensuring decisions are made at the right level in the organization.

2.6 FOCUS ON PRODUCTS

> A PRINCE2 project focuses on the definition and delivery of products, in particular their quality requirements.

A successful project is output-oriented not activity-oriented. An output-oriented project is one that agrees and defines the project's products prior to undertaking the activities required to produce them. The set of agreed products defines the scope of a project and provides the basis for planning and control.

The purpose of a project is to fulfil stakeholder expectations in accordance with the business justification, and to do this there must be a common understanding of the products required and the quality expectations for them. The purpose of a project can be interpreted in many different ways unless there is an explicit understanding of the products to be produced and the criteria against which they will be individually approved.

A PRINCE2 project uses Product Descriptions to provide such clarity by defining each product's purpose, composition, derivation, format, quality criteria and quality method. They provide the means to determine effort estimates, resource requirements, dependencies and activity schedules.

The 'product focus' supports almost every aspect of PRINCE2: planning, responsibilities, status reporting, quality, change control, scope, configuration management, product acceptance and risk management.

Without a product focus, projects are exposed to several major risks such as acceptance disputes, rework, uncontrolled change ('scope creep'), user dissatisfaction and underestimation of acceptance activities.

2.7 TAILOR TO SUIT THE PROJECT ENVIRONMENT

> PRINCE2 is tailored to suit the project's environment, size, complexity, importance, capability and risk.

The value of PRINCE2 is that it is a universal project management method that can be applied regardless of project type, organization, geography or culture. It can be used by any project because the method is designed to be tailored to its specific needs.

If PRINCE2 is not tailored, it is unlikely that the project management effort and approach are appropriate for the needs of the project. This can lead to 'robotic' project management at one extreme (the method is followed without question) or 'heroic' project management at the other extreme (the method is not followed at all).

The purpose of tailoring is to:

- Ensure the project management method relates to the project's environment (e.g. aligning the method to the business processes that may govern and support the project, such as human resources, finance and procurement)
- Ensure that project controls are based on the project's scale, complexity, importance, capability and risk (e.g. the reporting and reviewing frequency and formality).

Tailoring requires the Project Manager and the Project Board to make an active decision on how the method will be applied, for which guidance is provided. When tailoring PRINCE2, it is important to remember that it requires information (not necessarily documents) and decisions (not necessarily meetings).

To ensure that all those people involved with the project understand how PRINCE2 is to be used, the Project Initiation Documentation should state how the method is being tailored for that particular project.

Introduction to PRINCE2 themes

3

3   Introduction to PRINCE2 themes

3.1   WHAT ARE THE THEMES?

The PRINCE2 themes describe aspects of project management that must be addressed continually. Any Project Manager who gives thorough attention to these themes will fulfil the role in a professional manner.

However, the strength of PRINCE2 is the way in which the seven themes are integrated, and this is achieved because of the **specific PRINCE2 treatment**

of each theme, i.e. they are carefully designed to link together effectively.

The PRINCE2 processes address the chronological flow of the project – with actions relating to different themes mixed together. Here, the logical thread that runs through each theme is highlighted and more detailed guidance is provided in order to amplify the process activities. Table 3.1 lists the seven PRINCE2 themes and the relevant chapter.

Table 3.1   The PRINCE2 themes

Theme	Description	Answers	Chapter
Business Case	The project starts with an idea which is considered to have potential value for the organization concerned. This theme addresses how the idea is developed into a viable investment proposition for the organization and how project management maintains the focus on the organization's objectives throughout the project.	Why?	4
Organization	The organization sponsoring the project needs to allocate the work to managers who will be responsible for it and steer it through to completion. Projects are cross-functional so the normal line function structures are not suitable. This theme describes the roles and responsibilities in the temporary PRINCE2 project management team required to manage the project effectively.	Who?	5
Quality	The initial idea will only be understood as a broad outline. This theme explains how the outline is developed so that all participants understand the quality attributes of the products to be delivered – and then how project management will ensure that these requirements are subsequently delivered.	What?	6
Plans	PRINCE2 projects proceed on the basis of a series of approved plans. This theme complements the Quality theme by describing the steps required to develop plans and the PRINCE2 techniques that should be applied. In PRINCE2, the plans are matched to the needs of the personnel at the various levels of the organization. They are the focus for communication and control throughout the project.	How? How much? When?	7
Risk	Projects typically entail more risk than stable operational activity. This theme addresses how project management manages the uncertainties in its plans and in the wider project environment.	What if?	8
Change	This theme describes how project management assesses and acts upon issues which have a potential impact on any of the baseline aspects of the project (its plans and completed products). Issues may be unanticipated general problems, requests for change or instances of quality failure.	What's the impact?	9
Progress	This theme addresses the ongoing viability of the plans. The theme explains the decision-making process for approving plans, the monitoring of actual performance and the escalation process if events do not go according to plan. Ultimately, the Progress theme determines whether and how the project should proceed.	Where are we now? Where are we going? Should we carry on?	10

3.2 APPLYING THE THEMES

All seven themes must be applied in a project but they should be **tailored** according to the scale, nature and complexity of the project concerned.

Themes can be tailored 'up' or 'down', i.e. additional detailed documentation and process discipline can be introduced for complex or high-risk projects, whereas concise bullet-point presentations and more informal processes may be adequate for simple, low-risk projects.

3.3 FORMAT OF THE THEMES

Each of the themes chapters are structured as follows:

- **Purpose** Why it is important to the successful delivery of the project
- **Theme defined** Terms and definitions used
- **The PRINCE2 approach to the theme** The specific treatment of the particular aspect of project management required for the PRINCE2 processes to be fully effective
- **Responsibilities** Specific to the key theme for each PRINCE2 role.

Business Case

4

4 Business Case

4.1 PURPOSE

The purpose of the Business Case theme is to establish mechanisms to judge whether the project is (and remains) desirable, viable and achievable as a means to support decision making in its (continued) investment.

It is a PRINCE2 principle that a project must have continued business justification.

The business justification is the reason for the project. Without it no project should start. If business justification is valid at the start of a project, but disappears once it is under way, the project should be stopped or changed.

In PRINCE2, the business justification is documented in a Business Case describing the reasons for the project based on estimated costs, risks and the expected benefits.

The reasons for undertaking the project must drive decision making. When projects face changes or risks, the impact analysis should focus on the Business Case, remembering that the project is only a means to an end and not the end itself.

The ongoing and ever-present decision regarding the Business Case is whether the project can (still) be justified. This is based on whether the project is desirable (the cost/benefit/risk balance), viable (the project can deliver the products) and achievable (the products can provide the benefits).

The Senior User(s) is responsible for specifying the benefits and subsequently realizing the benefits through the use of the products provided by the project. The Executive is responsible for ensuring that those benefits specified by the Senior User(s) represent value for money, are aligned to corporate objectives, and are capable of being realized.

In PRINCE2, the Business Case is developed at the beginning of the project and maintained throughout the life of the project, being formally verified by the Project Board at each key decision point, such as end stage assessments, and the benefits are confirmed as they start to accrue. In some cases the project may be initiated with a pre-existing Business Case (from corporate or programme management), in which case it will be refined during initiation.

4.2 BUSINESS CASE DEFINED

4.2.1 What is a Business Case?

The Business Case presents the optimum mix of information used to judge whether the project is (and remains) desirable, viable and achievable, and therefore worthwhile investing in.

The Project Board and stakeholders must have confidence at all times that the project remains viable. In PRINCE2, the Business Case provides the vital test of the viability of the project. It provides the answer to the question: is the investment in this project still worthwhile?

Since this viability question is ongoing, the Business Case is not static. It should not be used only to gain initial funding for a project, but should be actively maintained throughout the life of the project and be continually updated with current information on costs, risks and benefits.

When making investment decisions, it is important to ascertain what benefits can be gained when, with what degree of risk and from what level of investment. Projects should be evaluated on how well they will contribute to corporate objectives. Such analysis enables one project to be compared with another so that the organization can choose to invest in the best set of projects.

4.2.2 Outputs, outcomes and benefits
In PRINCE2:

- A project's **output** is any of the project's specialist products (whether tangible or intangible)
- An **outcome** is the result of the change derived from using the project's outputs
- A **benefit** is the measurable improvement resulting from an outcome that is perceived as an advantage by one or more stakeholders.

> **Example of output, outcome and benefits**
>
> Output: New sales system
>
> Outcome: Sales orders are processed more quickly and accurately
>
> Benefits: Costs are reduced by 10%, volume of sales orders increased by 15% and revenue increased by 10% annually.

As the project's outcomes and benefits are often only realized after the project has closed, it is unfortunately easy for projects to become focused solely on creating products (the outputs). The link from the project's outputs to outcomes and benefits should be clearly identified and made visible to those involved, otherwise the original purpose of the project can get lost (Figure 4.1).

4.2.3 Types of Business Case

The reasons for undertaking projects vary enormously and are largely driven by their environment. The nature of the project will determine the objectives that will be used to verify the desirability of the project and later to confirm that the project's products have met those objectives. Such objectives will be measured differently depending on the type of project, for example:

■ Compulsory project
■ Not-for-profit project
■ Evolving project

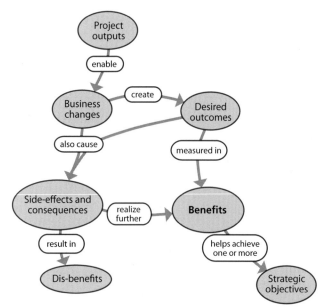

Figure 4.1 Relationship between outputs, outcomes and benefits

■ Customer/supplier project
■ Multi-organization project.

Some of these projects may be measured principally on 'return on investment', but others (particularly the compulsory or not-for-profit projects) may be measured on other non-financial benefits.

Regardless of the type of measure being used, the question remains: for this level of investment, are the anticipated benefits more desirable, viable and achievable than the other options available? For more details on how the project environment affects the Business Case, see Chapter 19.

4.3 THE PRINCE2 APPROACH TO THE BUSINESS CASE

In PRINCE2, the Business Case is **developed** at the beginning of the project and **maintained** throughout the life of the project, being formally **verified** by the Project Board at each key decision point, such as end stage assessments, and **confirmed** throughout the period that the benefits accrue.

In this context:

■ **Develop** means getting the right information upon which decisions can be made
■ **Verify** means assessing whether the project is (still) worthwhile
■ **Maintain** means to update the Business Case with actual costs and benefits and current forecasts for costs and benefits
■ **Confirm** means assessing whether the intended benefits have been (or will be) realized. Confirming benefits will mostly take place post-project.

The Business Case is at the centre of any impact assessment of risks, issues and changes by asking the question: how will this risk, issue or change affect the viability of the Business Case and the business objectives and benefits being sought?

4.3.1 Developing the Business Case

In PRINCE2 the Executive is responsible for the Business Case. It does not necessarily mean that the Executive writes the Business Case, merely that the Executive is responsible for ensuring that the Business Case is written and approved.

Development of the Business Case may be delegated, for example, to a business analyst or

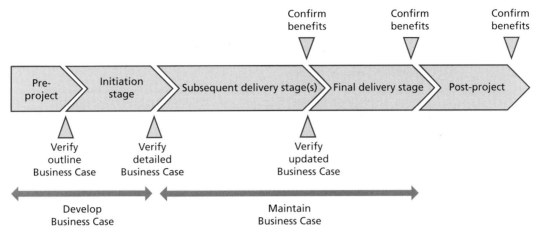

Figure 4.2 The development path of the Business Case

perhaps even to the Project Manager. In some cases, programme management will provide an approved Business Case as part of the Project Brief. Whoever is given the task of developing the Business Case, it is important to ensure that they have the appropriate business skills required (for example, understanding the difference between a cash-flow forecast, a profit-and-loss account and a balance sheet). If not, then the Project Board should consider using Project Assurance to assist with the development of the Business Case.

The outline Business Case is derived from the project mandate and developed pre-project in the Starting up a Project process in order to gain approval by the Project Board in the Directing a Project process to initiate the project.

The detailed Business Case is derived from the outline Business Case, the Project Plan (costs, timescale, products) and the Risk Register. Due to the inputs required to develop a Business Case, its development will be iterative. There needs to be an initial justification to proceed with the project, but until the project is planned in detail, the outline Business Case is based on costs and timescales that are, at best, approximate. Once the costs and timescales are better understood, it may increase or decrease the desirability, viability and achievability of the project and could therefore change the project approach, leading to some replanning.

4.3.2 Verifying and maintaining the Business Case

The Business Case drives all decision making by ensuring that the project remains justified and that the business objectives and benefits being sought can be realized.

To drive the decision making, the Business Case should be reviewed:

- At the end of the Starting up a Project process by the Project Board in order to authorize project initiation based on a reasonable justification
- At the end of the Initiating a Project process by the Project Board in order to authorize the project
- As part of any impact assessment by the Project Manager of any new or revised issues or risks
- In tandem with an Exception Plan by the Project Board, in order to authorize the revised stage and the continuation of the project
- At the end of each stage by the Project Manager to determine whether any of the costs, timescales, risks or benefits need to be updated
- At the end of each stage by the Project Board, to authorize the next stage and the continuation of the project
- During the final stage by the Project Manager, to assess the project's performance against its requirements and the likelihood that the outcomes will provide the expected benefits
- As part of the benefits review (possibly by corporate or programme management), to determine the success of the project outcomes in realizing their benefits.

It is the responsibility of the Executive to assure the project's stakeholders that the project remains desirable, viable and achievable at all times. The Executive should not rely on end stage assessments alone to make this judgement and should use Project Assurance to assist.

The investment appraisal section of the Business Case provides the Project Board with the source of information to verify that the Business Case justifies the authorization or continuation of the project.

Example of an unverified Business Case

A project to build a tourist attraction in London was justified on the basis of attracting 12 million visitors in its first year. The projected number of visitors determined the revenue for the exhibition and, with the project team under pressure to build a 'world class exhibition', the project budget was set at a level that was break-even with 11 million visitors. The projected 12 million visitors was an untested assumption and significantly higher than the actual 4.5 million visitors. In project terms it was a success – the exhibition opened on time, was within 5% of cost budget and had all the facilities that were requested (so therefore met the acceptance criteria). However, the shortfall of visitors significantly reduced revenue, which meant that the necessary government grant increased from £399 million to £628 million. It was a commercial and public relations disaster, illustrating that delivering a project on time, within budget and to specification based on unsound benefit assumptions negates the successful project delivery.

4.3.3 Confirming the benefits

The approach to confirming benefits is to:

- Identify the benefits
- Select objective measures that reliably prove the benefits
- Collect the baseline measures (from which the improvements will be quantified)
- Decide how, when and by whom the benefit measures will be collected.

The Senior User(s) specifies the benefits and is held to account by demonstrating to corporate or programme management that the forecast benefits that formed the basis of project approval are in fact realized. This may involve a commitment beyond the life of the project as it is likely that many benefits will not be realized until after it has closed.

This poses a dilemma because, once the project closes, the 'temporary organization' is disbanded along with the framework (and in particular the funding and resources) to carry out any measurement activities.

PRINCE2 overcomes this dilemma through defining a Benefits Review Plan. The project's Benefits Review Plan will use the detailed Business Case to define the scope, timing and responsibility of a number of reviews based on the timing and nature of the expected benefits.

By default, the Executive is responsible for ensuring that benefits reviews are planned and executed, but there are circumstances where this may not always be the case:

- For projects in a programme environment, the project's Benefits Review Plan may be produced and executed by the programme, as one of the roles of the programme is to coordinate the realization of the benefits of its projects
- If the corporate organization has a centre of excellence or some form of performance monitoring unit, it may undertake the responsibility for measuring benefits of all projects within the organization
- For post-project measurement activities, the responsibility for benefits reviews will transfer from the Executive to corporate or programme management as the project closes (as the reviews will need to be funded and resourced).

The Benefits Review Plan is first created by the Project Manager in the initiation stage and is submitted to the Project Board for approval when seeking project authorization. If corporate or programme management are to manage or participate in the benefits reviews, the Project Board may need to seek approval from corporate or programme management. The Benefits Review Plan is updated towards the end of each stage with actual benefits achieved, and a revised plan is created for any remaining reviews whether within or beyond the life of the project.

As the Benefits Review Plan may be managed by the project, corporate or programme management, PRINCE2 recommends that it is kept separate from the Project Plan and Stage Plans.

The benefits that can be measured during the life of a project should be reported by the Project Manager in the End Stage Report. Any residual benefits should be re-examined and their forecast updated as part of the Managing a Stage Boundary process.

The post-project benefits review(s) will involve corporate or programme management holding the Senior User(s) to account by asking them to provide evidence of how the individual benefits allocated to them have been gained in comparison to those benefits promised to justify the cost and risk of the project when it was authorized. The post-project benefits review(s) will also review the performance of the project's products in operational use and identify whether there have been any side-effects (beneficial or adverse) that may provide useful lessons for other projects.

4.3.4 The contents of a Business Case

The Business Case should describe the reasons for the project based on estimated costs, risks and expected benefits. It typically contains:

- An executive summary
- Reasons
- Business options
- Expected benefits
- Expected dis-benefits
- Timescale
- Costs
- Investment appraisal
- Major risks.

The Product Description for a Business Case can be found in Appendix A. The following sections provide further guidance for some of the Business Case content.

4.3.4.1 Reasons

The Business Case should explain the reasons **why** the project is required. Ideally, it should be linked to the organizational context and should explain how the project will enable the achievement of corporate strategies and objectives.

The reasons are likely to be defined in the project mandate. If not, clarification should be sought. For example, the reason for relocating an office may be because of changing demographics or increasing leasing costs, because the firm has outgrown its current office or to meet new legislation, such as disability access.

4.3.4.2 Business options

There are three basic business options concerning any investment:

- Do nothing
- Do the minimum
- Do something.

'Do nothing' should always be the starting option to act as the basis for quantifying the other options – the difference between 'do nothing' and 'do the minimum'/'do something' is the benefit that the investment will buy.

The analysis of each option provides the Project Board and the project's stakeholders with sufficient information to judge which option presents the best value for the organization. It provides the answer to the question: for this level of investment, are the anticipated benefits more desirable, viable and achievable than the other options available?

The Business Case for the chosen option should be continually assessed for desirability, viability and achievability as any new risks and/or changes may make one of the other options more justifiable.

4.3.4.3 Expected benefits

The Business Case should list each benefit that it is claimed would be achieved by the project's outcome (for the selected business option). It is important to define the current status of each benefit in quantifiable terms so that measurable improvements can be assessed after the project has been completed. The Business Case should outline how and when the measurement of the improvement can be made. For example, one of the benefits of relocating the office could be a saving in hotel conferencing costs, but only if the new site has more conference rooms.

Benefits can be financial and non-financial (sometimes referred to as cashable and non-cashable). Regardless of whether they are financial or non-financial, benefits should be:

- Aligned to corporate objectives and strategy
- Mapped from the outputs and outcomes provided by the project
- Quantified (with tolerance)
- Measurable
- Assigned.

Clear responsibility for benefits, collectively and individually, is a key requirement for successful benefits realization. The Senior User(s) is responsible for the set of benefits within their respective areas, but responsibility for individual benefits should be assigned to an appropriate person, ideally from within the group of users affected by that benefit.

The list of expected benefits will influence the set of products that the project will provide. The project should not include any products that do not directly or indirectly enable the sought-after benefits to be achieved. Mapping products to outcomes and subsequently to benefits aids decision making in the planning and control of the project. Such mapping enables decisions to be made based on the impact of the realization of the expected benefits, i.e. the justification for undertaking the project.

Wherever possible, benefits should be expressed in tangible ways. The Senior User or Executive may define many benefits as intangible (for example, 'happier staff'). It is worth making the effort to think carefully about intangible benefits to see whether they can be expressed in measurable ways. In this example, 'happier staff' may translate into reduced staff turnover and/or less time off for stress-related problems. Both of these can be converted into a likely monetary saving.

The quantification of benefits enables benefits tolerance to be set (e.g. a 10–15% increase in sales) and the measurability of the benefits ensures that they can be proven. If the project includes benefits that cannot be proven, then it is impossible to judge whether the project:

- Has been a success
- Has provided value for money
- Should be (or have been) initiated.

There are many ways to verify the expected benefits. For example, sensitivity analysis can be used to determine whether the Business Case is heavily dependent on a particular benefit. If it is, this may affect project planning, monitoring and control activities, and risk management, as steps would need to be taken to protect that specific benefit.

Another example is to define three views of the achievement of the benefits, i.e. what are we really expecting, what might we achieve if things went well, and what might be the worst-case scenario?

The last might be affected by building into the costs an allowance for estimating inaccuracies, changes and risks. This analysis usually reveals whether benefit expectations are reasonable or overoptimistic. The result of this analysis can lead to revision of the decision to go ahead with the project, which in turn would form a basis for setting any benefit tolerance.

Once the benefits are defined, the activities to establish and collect the measures should be described in the Benefits Review Plan.

4.3.4.4 Expected dis-benefits

A dis-benefit is an outcome perceived as negative by one or more stakeholders. Dis-benefits are actual consequences of an activity whereas, by definition, a risk has some uncertainty about whether it will materialize.

For example, a decision to merge two elements of an organization onto a new site may have benefits (e.g. better joint working), costs (e.g. expanding one of the two sites) and dis-benefits (e.g. drop in productivity during the merger). These would all need to be considered and valued as part of the investment appraisal.

4.3.4.5 Timescale

Corporate and/or programme management will wish to know:

- Over what period the project costs will be incurred
- Over what period the cost/benefits analysis will be based
- When the organization can expect to accrue benefits
- What the earliest/latest feasible start date is
- What the earliest/latest feasible completion date is.

Identifying the timescale requirement for a project can help identify tolerances and timings for benefits reviews.

4.3.4.6 Costs

The Business Case should summarize the costs derived from the Project Plan together with the assumptions upon which they are based. The costs should also include details of the ongoing operations and maintenance costs and their funding arrangements.

4.3.4.7 Investment appraisal

With the information in the Business Case, it is possible and necessary to compare the development, operations and maintenance costs with the value of the benefits over a period of time (often referred to as an investment appraisal). The investment appraisal period may be a fixed number of years or the useful life of the products. The commissioning authority may have prescribed accounting rules defining how the investment will be appraised.

The investment appraisal should cover both the project costs (to produce the required products and the project management costs) and the ongoing operations and maintenance costs. For example, the estimated costs for office relocation could cover the project costs for the relocation activities, new stationery costs, penalties for terminating service agreements on the current premises, and the increase in rent/rates and service costs for the new premises.

4.3.4.8 Major risks

Any opportunity is likely to be offset by an element of risk. Therefore in order to make the judgement of 'business justification', the Project Board needs to understand not only the benefits and the project costs, but the set of risks that may either reduce/enhance the benefits or reduce/increase the cost.

The Business Case should include a summary of the aggregated risks (and it is suggested that this is in the form of a summary risk profile) and highlight the major risks that will have an effect on the business objectives and benefits (therefore covering both the project delivery and the ongoing operations and maintenance). For example, the risks for the office relocation could include unforeseen moving costs (e.g. asbestos removal) or impact on business continuity (e.g. loss of key staff unwilling to relocate).

4.4 RESPONSIBILITIES

Table 4.1 outlines the responsibilities relevant to the Business Case theme. Refer to Appendix C for further details of project management team roles and their associated responsibilities.

Investment appraisal techniques

Investment appraisal techniques include:

Through-life costs Analysing the total cost of implementation and any incremental operations and maintenance costs

Net benefits Analysing the total value of the benefits less the cost of implementation and ongoing operation calculated over a defined period

Return on investment (ROI) Profits or savings resulting from investments (this is the same as net benefits if the benefits were only financial)

Payback period Calculating the period of time required for the ROI to 'repay' the sum of the original investment

Discounted cash flow A means of expressing future benefits based on the current value of money. Sometimes discounted cash flows include risk adjustments as the business may not be confident that all the benefits will materialize

Net present value The total value of discounted future cash inflows less the initial investment. For example, if inflation is at 6%, the value of money halves approximately every 12 years. If a project is forecasting a £500,000 benefit to materialize in year 12, then it is only worth £250,000 in today's money

Sensitivity analysis Business Cases are based on uncertain forecasts. In order to identify how robust the Business Case is, it is useful to understand the relationship between input factors (e.g. project costs, timescale, quality, scope, project risk) and output (e.g. operations and maintenance costs, business benefits and business risk). Sensitivity analysis involves tweaking the input factors to model the point at which the output factors no longer justify the investment. For example, the project is worthwhile if it can be done in four months, but ceases to be worthwhile if it were to take six months.

Table 4.1 Responsibilities relevant to the Business Case

Role	Responsibilities
Corporate or programme management	Provide the project mandate and define any standards to which the Business Case needs to be developed.
	Hold the Senior User(s) to account for realizing the post-project benefits enabled by the project's products.
	Responsible for the Benefits Review Plan (post-project).
Executive	Responsible for the Business Case for the duration of the project.
	Responsible for the Benefits Review Plan (for the duration of the project) unless being managed by corporate or programme management.
	Oversee the development of a viable Business Case, ensuring that the project is aligned with corporate strategies, and secure the funding for the project.
Senior User(s)	Responsible for specifying the benefits upon which the Business Case is approved.
	Ensure the desired outcome of the project is specified.
	Ensure that the project produces products which deliver the desired outcomes.
	Ensure that the expected benefits (derived from the project's outcomes) are realized.
	Provide actual versus forecast benefits statement at the benefits reviews.
Senior Supplier(s)	Responsible for the supplier Business Case(s) (if they exist) – see section 19.6.1.1.
	Confirm that the products required can be delivered within the expected costs and are viable.
Project Manager	Prepare the Business Case on behalf of the Executive.
	Conduct impact analysis of any new or revised issues or risks that affect the project's desirability, viability or achievability against the original basis for approving the project.
	Assess and update the Business Case at the end of each management stage.
	Assess and report on project performance at project closure.
Project Assurance (business assurance responsibilities)	Assist in the development of the Business Case.
	Verify and monitor the Business Case against external events and project progress.
	Ensure the project fits with overall programme or corporate strategy.
	Monitor project finance on behalf of the customer.
	Ensure the value-for-money solution is constantly reassessed.
	Monitor changes to the Project Plan to identify any impact on the needs of the business or the Business Case.
	Review the impact assessment of potential changes on the Business Case and Project Plan.
	Verify and monitor the Benefits Review Plan for alignment to corporate or programme management.
Project Support	The Business Case should have a baseline and therefore be under configuration management. Project Support should advise the Project Manager of any proposed or actual changes to products that affect the Business Case.

Organization 5

5 Organization

5.1 PURPOSE

> The purpose of the Organization theme is to define and establish the project's structure of accountability and responsibilities (the who?).

PRINCE2 is based on a customer/supplier environment. It assumes that there will be a customer who will specify the desired result and probably pay for the project, and a supplier who will provide the resources and skills to deliver that result.

Every project needs effective direction, management, control and communication. Establishing an effective project management team structure and strategy for communication at the beginning of a project, and maintaining these throughout the project's life, are essential elements of a project's success.

One of the principles of PRINCE2 is that all projects must have a defined organizational structure to unite the various parties in the common aims of the project and to enable effective project governance and decision making.

A successful project management team should:

- Have business, user and supplier stakeholder representation
- Ensure appropriate governance by defining responsibilities for directing, managing and delivering the project and clearly defining accountability at each level
- Have reviews of the project roles throughout the project to ensure that they continue to be effective
- Have an effective strategy to manage communication flows to and from stakeholders.

5.2 ORGANIZATION DEFINED

5.2.1 Project

PRINCE2 defines a project as 'a temporary organization that is created for the purpose of delivering one or more business products according to an agreed Business Case'. It needs to be flexible and is likely to require a broad base of skills for a comparatively short period of time.

5.2.2 Programme

A project can be run as a stand-alone entity or can be part of a programme of related projects. A programme is a temporary flexible organizational structure created to coordinate, direct and oversee the implementation of a set of related projects and activities, in order to deliver outcomes and benefits related to the organization's strategic objectives. It is likely to have a longer life than a single project. A project which forms part of a programme may be impacted by the programme structure and reporting requirements.

5.2.3 Corporate organization

A project may or may not form part of a programme. It will, however, exist within the wider context of a corporate organization. Corporate organizational structures can vary from 'traditional' functional structures, where staff are organized by type of work (for example, marketing, finance, sales etc., where there are clear reporting lines), to project-focused corporate organizations, which work with project teams as a norm, to variations in between.

5.2.4 Roles and jobs

In order to be flexible and meet the needs of different environments and different project sizes, PRINCE2 does not define management **jobs** to be allocated to people on a one-to-one basis. It defines **roles**, each of which is defined by an associated set of responsibilities. Roles might be shared or combined according to the project's needs but the responsibilities must always be allocated. When combining roles, consideration should be given to any conflicts of responsibilities, whether one person has the capacity to undertake the combined responsibilities, and whether any bottlenecks might be created as a result.

5.2.5 Three project interests

The PRINCE2 principle of defined roles and responsibilities states that a PRINCE2 project will always have three primary categories of stakeholder, and the interests of all three must be satisfied if the project is to be successful. Figure 5.1 shows the three primary interests which make up the Project Board. PRINCE2 recommends that for completeness the Project Board should include representation from each of the business, user and supplier interests at all times.

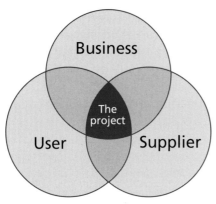

Figure 5.1 The three project interests

- **Business** The products of the project should meet a business need which will justify the investment in the project. The project should also provide value for money. The business viewpoint therefore should be represented to ensure that these two prerequisites exist before a project commences and remain in existence throughout the project. The Executive role is defined to look after the business interests

- **User** PRINCE2 makes a distinction between the business interests and the requirements of those who will use the project's outputs. The user viewpoint should represent those individuals or groups for whom some or all of the following will apply:
  - They will use the outputs of the project to realize the benefits after the project is complete
  - They will operate, maintain or support the project's outputs
  - The outputs of the project will impact them

  The user presence is needed to specify the desired outputs and ensure that the project delivers them. The Senior User(s) will represent this stakeholder interest on the Project Board

- **Supplier** The creation of the project's outputs will need resources with certain skills. The supplier viewpoint should represent those who will provide the necessary skills and produce the project product. The project may need to

use both in-house and external supplier teams to construct the project product. The Senior Supplier(s) will represent this stakeholder interest on the Project Board.

The level of overlap between the interests of the business, user and supplier will change according to the type of corporate organization and project. For example, if a project uses an in-house supplier, the business and supplier interests will be more likely to have overlapping interests than if an external supplier is used.

Note the term 'customer' is also used in PRINCE2, normally in the context of a commercial customer/supplier relationship. 'Customer' can usually be interpreted as a collective term for the business and user interests. However, one example of an exception to this broad rule would be where an organization is developing a new product to bring to market. In this case, the business interest is aligned with that of the supplier and 'customer' equates simply with 'users'. Where the user interest is external to the organization sponsoring the development, as in this example, it still needs to be represented in some way – perhaps by the sales/marketing function.

As well as the primary categories of business, user and supplier interests which should be represented on the Project Board, there will be a wider range of stakeholders which may affect, or be affected by, the project. These stakeholders may be internal or external to the corporate organization and may support, oppose or be indifferent to the project. Effective engagement with these stakeholders is key to a project's success (see section 5.3.5).

5.3 THE PRINCE2 APPROACH TO ORGANIZATION

5.3.1 Levels of organization

The level of management required to make decisions and commitments may be too busy to be involved on a day-to-day basis with the project. But projects need day-to-day management if they are to be successful. PRINCE2 separates the direction and management of the project from the delivery of the project's outputs, concentrating on the former and using the principle of management by exception.

The project management structure has four levels, three of which represent the project management team and the fourth which sits outside of the

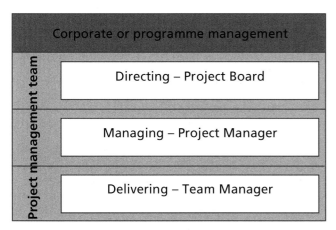

Figure 5.2 The four levels of management within the project management structure

project. Figure 5.2 illustrates these four levels of management.

The four levels of management are:

■ **Corporate or programme management** This level sits outside the project management team but will be responsible for commissioning the project, including identifying the Executive and defining the project-level tolerances within which the Project Board will work. This

information should, if possible, be documented in the project mandate

■ **Directing** The Project Board is responsible for the overall direction and management of the project within the constraints set out by corporate or programme management. The Project Board is accountable for the success of the project. As part of directing the project, the Project Board will:
- Approve all major plans and resources
- Authorize any deviation that exceeds or is forecast to exceed stage tolerances
- Approve the completion of each stage and authorize the start of the next stage
- Communicate with other stakeholders

■ **Managing** The Project Manager is responsible for the day-to-day management of the project within the constraints set out by the Project Board. The Project Manager's prime responsibility is to ensure that the project produces the required products in accordance with the time, cost, quality, scope, risk and benefit performance goals

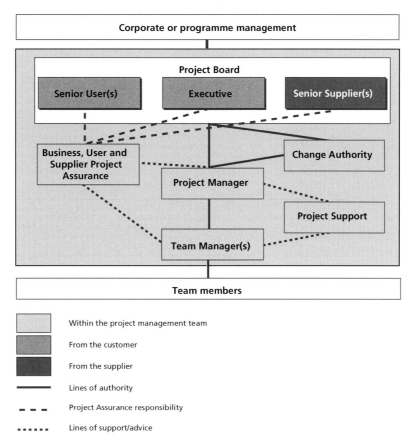

Figure 5.3 Project management team structure

■ **Delivering** While the Project Manager is responsible for the day-to-day management of the project, team members are responsible for delivering the project's products to an appropriate quality within a specified timescale and cost. Depending on the size and complexity of the project, the authority and responsibility for planning the creation of certain products and managing a team of specialists to produce those products may be delegated to a Team Manager.

5.3.2 The project management team

5.3.2.1 Project management team structure

A project management team is a temporary structure specifically designed to manage the project to its successful conclusion. The structure allows for channels of communication to decision-making forums and should be backed up by role descriptions that specify the responsibilities, goals, limits of authority, relationships, skills, knowledge and experience required for all roles in the project management team. Figure 5.3 illustrates the structure of the project management team and its reporting lines.

The Executive (representing the business viewpoint) and Senior User (representing the user viewpoint) roles can often be combined. In such cases, to avoid any conflict of interest, two individuals could be appointed to carry out Project Assurance, one looking after the user interests and the other representing the business interests.

Some of the PRINCE2 responsibilities cannot be shared or delegated if they are to be undertaken effectively. For example:

■ The Project Manager and Executive roles cannot be shared. The Executive cannot also be the Project Manager and there cannot be more than one Executive or Project Manager
■ The Project Manager and Project Board decision-making accountability cannot be delegated.

PRINCE2 provides role description outlines in Appendix C, which should be tailored to the needs of the specific project and each specific appointment.

5.3.2.2 Project Board

Together, the Executive, Senior User(s) and Senior Supplier(s) make up the Project Board. The Project Board has authority and responsibility for the project within the instructions (initially contained in the project mandate) set by corporate or programme management.

PRINCE2 defines the duties of the Project Board as:

■ Being accountable for the success or failure of the project in terms of the business, user and supplier interests
■ Providing unified direction to the project. As one of the key responsibilities of the Project Board is to provide direction to the Project Manager, it is important that all members have a unified view as to what the direction should be
■ Delegating effectively, using the PRINCE2 organizational structure and controls designed for this purpose
■ Facilitating integration of the project management team with the functional units of the participating corporate or external organizations
■ Providing the resources and authorizing the funds necessary for the successful completion of the project
■ Ensuring effective decision making
■ Providing visible and sustained support for the Project Manager
■ Ensuring effective communication both within the project team and with external stakeholders.

Further guidance on these duties can be found in OGC's *Directing Successful Projects with PRINCE2* (TSO, 2009).

A good Project Board should display four key characteristics:

■ **Authority** The members of the Project Board should be senior enough within the corporate organization to make strategic decisions about the project. As the Project Board is accountable for the project, the individuals chosen must have sufficient authority to make these decisions and to provide resources to the project, such as personnel, cash and equipment. The managerial level required to fill the roles will depend on factors such as the budget, scope and importance of the project

- **Credibility** The credibility of the Project Board members within the corporate organization will affect their ability to direct the project
- **Ability to delegate** A key part of the Project Board's role is to ensure that the Project Manager is given enough 'space' to manage the project by keeping Project Board activity at the right level. Project Board members should not be involved in the detail of how the project is managed, nor in the specialist content of the project
- **Availability** Project Board members who meet all the above characteristics are of little value to the project if they are not available to make decisions and provide direction to the Project Manager.

Project Board members are often from senior management positions, and their Project Board responsibilities will be in addition to their normal responsibilities. The concept of management by exception allows the Project Manager to keep them regularly informed of project progress but only requires decision making at key points in the project.

The frequency and detail of communication required by the Project Board during a project should be documented in the Communication Management Strategy. Project Board members may require more detailed or frequent information at the start of the project. As the project progresses, and the Project Board becomes more comfortable with the progress being achieved, the requirement for frequent or detailed Highlight Reports may reduce. It is important to review the level and frequency of reporting for each stage during the Managing a Stage Boundary process.

Executive

Although the Project Board is responsible for the project, the Executive (supported by the Senior User(s) and Senior Supplier(s)) is ultimately accountable for the project's success and is the key decision maker. The Project Board is not a democracy controlled by votes.

The Executive's role is to ensure that the project is focused throughout its life on achieving its objectives and delivering a product that will achieve the forecasted benefits. The Executive has to ensure that the project gives value for money, ensuring a cost-conscious approach to the project, balancing the demands of the business, user and supplier.

The Executive is appointed by corporate or programme management during the pre-project process of Starting up a Project. The role of the Executive is vested in one individual, so that there is a single point of accountability for the project. The Executive will then be responsible for designing and appointing the rest of the project management team, including the other members of the Project Board. If the project is part of a programme, corporate or programme management may appoint some or all Project Board members.

Throughout the project, the Executive is responsible for the Business Case.

Senior User

The Senior User(s) is responsible for specifying the needs of those who will use the project's products, for user liaison with the project management team and for monitoring that the solution will meet those needs within the constraints of the Business Case in terms of quality, functionality and ease of use.

The role represents the interests of all those who will use the project's products (including operations and maintenance), those for whom the products will achieve an objective, or those who will use the products to deliver benefits. The Senior User role commits user resources and monitors products against requirements. This role may require more than one person to cover all the user interests. For the sake of effectiveness the role should not be split between too many people.

The Senior User(s) specifies the benefits and is held to account by demonstrating to corporate or programme management that the forecasted benefits that were the basis of project approval are in fact realized. This is likely to involve a commitment beyond the end of the project's life.

Senior Supplier

The Senior Supplier(s) represents the interests of those designing, developing, facilitating, procuring and implementing the project's products.

This role is accountable for the quality of products delivered by the supplier(s) and is responsible for the technical integrity of the project. This role will include providing supplier resources to the project and ensuring that proposals for designing and developing the products are feasible and realistic.

In most cases, the Senior Supplier also represents the interests of those who will maintain the specialist products of the project after closure, e.g. engineering maintenance and support. Exceptions to this do occur, e.g. when an external supplier is delivering products to a customer who will maintain them in service/operation – in this instance the operations and maintenance interests are more likely to be represented by a Senior User. In fact, the distinction is not really important; what matters is that operations, service and support interests are represented appropriately from the outset.

If necessary, more than one person may be required to represent the suppliers.

5.3.2.3 Project Assurance

The Project Board is responsible, via its Project Assurance role, for monitoring all aspects of the project's performance and products independently of the Project Manager.

Project Board members are responsible for the aspects of Project Assurance aligned to their respective areas of concern – business, user or supplier. If they have sufficient time available, and the appropriate level of skills and knowledge, they may conduct their own Project Assurance tasks, otherwise they may appoint separate individuals to carry these out.

The Project Board may also make use of other members of the corporate organization taking specific Project Assurance roles, such as appointing the corporate quality manager to monitor the quality aspects of the project. Project Board members are accountable for the Project Assurance actions aligned to their area of interest, even if they delegate these to separate individuals.

Project Assurance is not just an independent check, however. Personnel involved in Project Assurance are also responsible for supporting the Project Manager, by giving advice and guidance on issues such as the use of corporate standards or the correct personnel to be involved in different aspects of the project, e.g. quality inspections or reviews.

Where Project Assurance tasks are shared between Project Board members and other individuals, it is important to clarify each person's responsibilities. Anyone appointed to a Project Assurance role reports to the Project Board member overseeing

the relevant area of interest, and must be independent of the Project Manager. The Project Board should not assign any Project Assurance roles to the Project Manager.

As part of its function to monitor all aspects of the project's performance and products independently of the Project Manager, Project Assurance should be involved in all of the PRINCE2 processes.

5.3.2.4 Change Authority

One consideration at project initiation should be who is permitted to authorize requests for change or off-specifications. It is the Project Board's responsibility to agree to each potential change before it is implemented. In a project where few changes are envisaged, it may be reasonable to leave this authority in the hands of the Project Board. But projects may be in a dynamic environment, where there are likely to be, for example, many requests to change the initial agreed scope of the project. Technical knowledge may also be needed to evaluate potential changes.

If it has not already been determined within Starting up a Project, the Project Board needs to decide before the project moves out of the initiation stage if it wishes to delegate some authority for approving or rejecting requests for change or off-specifications.

To facilitate this, the Project Board should define in the Configuration Management Strategy a scale of severity ratings for requests for change. Depending on the severity, the request for change could be handled by:

- Corporate or programme management
- The Project Board
- Delegating to a Change Authority
- Delegating to the Project Manager.

These delegated authorities must be written into the appropriate role descriptions. For projects that exist within a programme, the programme management should define the level of authority that the Project Board will have in order to be able to approve changes.

The Project Manager and/or the people with delegated Project Assurance responsibilities may act as the Change Authority. Refer to Chapter 9 for more information on changes.

Example of a Change Authority

A Project Manager is given authority to approve changes to individual products only if the changes would:

■ Cost less than a pre-arranged limit

■ Impact the project timescales by no more than one week

■ Not require any changes to the Project Product Description or any other product.

Any changes that fall outside of these limits would have to be escalated to the Project Board.

5.3.2.5 Size of the Project Board

The Executive, supported by the Project Manager, is responsible for agreeing a suitable team structure and tailoring it to the project's size, risk and complexity. The Project Board needs to represent all of the interested parties in the corporate organization, and involve any suppliers (internal or external) that have been identified.

On a large project, tailoring the project management team could mean breaking the PRINCE2 roles into multiple appointments – for example, several Senior Users or Senior Suppliers could be appointed. However, it is good practice to keep the size of the Project Board as small as possible while still representing all business, user and supplier interests. To avoid enlarging the Project Board, user or supplier groups could be used to maintain broad-ranging senior management involvement in those projects that impact on a large user or supplier community. These groups discuss user or supplier issues and risks, and pass recommendations to the Senior User(s) or Senior Supplier(s) on the Project Board. If a user or supplier group is involved, it is important to define at the outset who is authorized to represent its collective view and how this will operate. It may also be appropriate to appoint members of these groups to user or supplier Project Assurance; multiple individuals can fulfil Project Assurance roles. The commercial context will also affect the project's organizational structure (e.g. if a prime contractor is appointed).

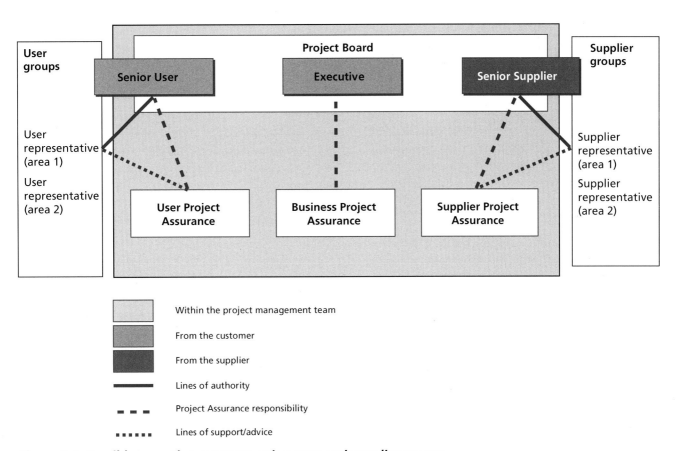

Figure 5.4 Possible reporting structure using user and supplier groups

Figure 5.4 shows a potential project-reporting structure which includes user and supplier groups.

Producing a matrix of stakeholders against the project's products also helps split the project stakeholders (who need to be engaged as part of the Communication Management Strategy) from the project decision makers (who need to be on the Project Board).

The decision on whether to include external suppliers on the Project Board may be a cultural one based on fear of divulging commercial or financial information. Leaving them out of the Directing a Project process could cause delays due to the lack of supplier resources to deal with change and to address specialist issues. It is the Executive's decision as to how this dilemma is solved practically.

5.3.2.6 Project Manager

The Project Manager is the single focus for day-to-day management of a project. This person has the authority to run the project on behalf of the Project Board within the constraints laid down by the Project Board. In a PRINCE2 environment the Project Manager role should not be shared.

The Project Manager will normally come from the customer corporate organization, but there may be projects where the Project Manager comes from the supplier. Refer to Chapter 19 for more information on customer/supplier relationships.

The Project Manager is responsible for the work of all the PRINCE2 processes except for the Directing a Project process, and appointing the Executive and the Project Manager in the pre-project process Starting up a Project. The Project Manager also delegates responsibility for the Managing Product Delivery process to the Team Manager(s).

The Project Manager manages the Team Managers and Project Support, and is responsible for liaison with Project Assurance and the Project Board. In projects with no separate individual allocated to a Team Manager role, the Project Manager will be responsible for managing work directly with the team members involved. In projects with no separate Project Support role, the support tasks also fall to the Project Manager, although they may be shared with team members.

As the single focus for the day-to-day management of a project, there are many different aspects to the Project Manager role. Figure 5.5 shows some of these different facets.

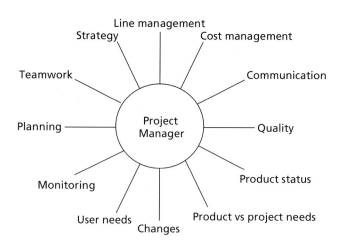

Figure 5.5 The many facets of the Project Manager role

5.3.2.7 Team Manager

The Team Manager's primary responsibility is to ensure production of those products allocated by the Project Manager. The Team Manager reports to, and takes direction from, the Project Manager.

The Team Manager role may be assigned to the Project Manager or a separate person. There are many reasons why the Project Manager may decide to appoint other people to be Team Managers rather than undertake the role themselves. Among these are the size of the project, the particular specialist skills or knowledge needed for certain products, geographical location of some team members and the preferences of the Project Board. The Project Manager should discuss the need for separate individuals as Team Managers with the Project Board and, if required, should plan the role at the start of the project during the Starting up a Project process, or for each stage in the Managing a Stage Boundary process.

PRINCE2 uses Work Packages to allocate work to Team Managers or team members. They can be used formally or informally depending on the needs of the project. In addition to the information included in Appendix A, a Work Package can include items such as resource costs, accounting codes, allocated resources and other management information. Defining the deliverables at the appropriate level will also assist new Team Managers in becoming more effective as it is clear what has to be produced, and with the definition of reporting frequency and method, the feedback from the Team Manager can be clearly controlled.

If the Team Manager comes from the supplier corporate organization, there could be a reporting line to a Senior Supplier. It is vital that any such links are understood to avoid conflicts of interest and any undermining of the Project Manager's authority.

The structure of the project management team does not necessarily reflect line function or seniority but represents roles on the project. A Team Manager, for example, may be more senior in the corporate organization than the Project Manager, or may be a senior representative from an external supplier. In the context of the project, however, the Team Manager reports to, and takes direction from, the Project Manager.

5.3.2.8 Project Support

Project Support is the responsibility of the Project Manager. If required, the Project Manager can delegate some of this work to a Project Support role: this may include providing administrative services or advice and guidance on the use of project management tools or configuration management. It could also provide specialist functions to a project such as planning or risk management. Unless performed by a corporate or programme management function, Project Support is typically responsible for administering any configuration management procedure and tools as defined in the Configuration Management Strategy.

It is important to stress that the role of Project Support is not optional, but the allocation of a separate individual or group to carry out the required tasks is. The role defaults to the Project Manager if it is not otherwise allocated.

Some corporate organizations may have a project office (a temporary office set up to support the delivery of a specific project) or similar structure, which can fulfil some or all of the Project Support role. Refer to OGC's Portfolio, Programme and Project Offices (P3O®) for further information on the use of a project office.

Project Support and Project Assurance roles should be kept separate in order to maintain the independence of Project Assurance.

5.3.2.9 Dealing with changes to the project management team

Ideally, the Project Manager and Project Board members should stay with the project throughout its life. In practice, however, this may not always be possible and the project management team may change during the project. A clearly defined team structure, together with comprehensive role descriptions outlining the responsibilities for each role, should help to alleviate disruption caused by project management team changes.

The use of management stages also allows a smooth transition for changes to the project management team. Project roles should be reviewed for the next stage during the Managing a Stage Boundary process. The use of End Stage Reports and Stage Plans can help to ensure that any handover procedure is thorough and well documented. Although ideally the Project Executive and Project Manager should stay with the project throughout its lifecycle, a stage boundary provides an opportunity to hand over the role during the project if this is necessary.

> **Example of changes to the project management team**
>
> A project may include a procurement stage, during which a supplier is selected to develop some of the project's products. Before the supplier has been selected, a senior representative from the procurement department may represent the Senior Supplier on the project. After the supplier has been selected and the project moves to the development stage, a senior representative from the selected supplier's organization could be included on the team as a Senior Supplier.

5.3.3 Working with the project team

5.3.3.1 Balancing the project, team and individual

People are crucial to the success of a project. It is not enough to have the required processes and systems in place: if the people on a project do not work effectively together, then the chances of the project's success are severely restricted. Knowledge of different types of personalities and how these work together can help the Project Manager to structure balanced teams that can work together effectively during a project.

Different people have different characteristics, and certain types of people are more suited to certain roles. In a given environment, some combinations of personality types work better than others.

Example of team building using different personalities

Some people are very sociable and enthusiastic, generating many different ideas. Others are more analytical, skilled in detailed work and ensuring no tasks get missed. While it is not usually possible to change people's characteristics, it is possible to balance a team so that it has an appropriate mix of personality types to enable tasks to be completed effectively. Project Managers who know the natural roles of the team members can use that knowledge to build effective teams during the Starting up a Project process for the management team and the Initiating a Project process when identifying team members. It is important to achieve the correct balance: for example, a team consisting of only 'ideas' people risks losing focus on the detail of tasks which need to be performed. Conversely, a team made up of only 'detailed' people may lack a strategic overview of a solution.

5.3.3.2 Training needs for project teams

At the start of the project, team members may need training. This could include training on any processes and standards to be used on the project (such as configuration management procedures, quality methods, progress reporting and other project-specific areas), or it could be an introduction to the project and its goals designed to motivate the team members. Project Board members may also need training on their roles, including what is expected of them and the procedures needed to carry out their responsibilities. Training on PRINCE2 processes and terminology may also be required for Team Managers and other members of the project management team.

During a project, team members may also need specialist training to enable them to complete their assigned tasks. The Project Manager should ensure that training needs are built into the appropriate plans.

5.3.3.3 Part-time teams

Project teams are brought together for the duration of a project and then return to their routine work. The manager of a small project is therefore likely to find that team members are working on the project on a part-time basis. Part-time team members suffer more absences and diversions, as a percentage of their working time, than full-time team members. The Project Manager should allow for this when designing a plan – either by negotiating guaranteed availability or greater tolerance.

If individuals are tasked with working on too many projects, they will simply stand still on all of the projects, expending a lot of effort but making no forward progress. Solutions include undertaking fewer projects in parallel or, where possible, allocating staff full time to projects for limited periods.

5.3.4 Working with the corporate organization

5.3.4.1 Line management/functional management

In a strongly functional environment, Project Managers can find difficulties when managing cross-functional projects due to the inability to agree overall leadership from within the various groups. As a result, the Project Board may need to be involved more closely to lead, direct and prioritize work and resolve issues. Whatever the environment, the Project Manager will have to adapt to, and work within, the corporate organization and this will affect the level of management required for the team members.

Example of a Project Manager's responsibilities to line/functional management

The Project Manager may be responsible for carrying out performance appraisals as part of a project, or may provide input to the appraisal undertaken by the functional area of the corporate organization responsible for the team member.

Understanding and working within the wider corporate organization can be challenging for the Project Manager, particularly if working part-time or on a contract basis. Setting up clear project controls at the start of the project, and agreeing these with the Project Board, will help to ensure that the Project Manager understands the level of interaction and support to expect during the project and is given appropriate exposure to other areas of the corporate organization.

5.3.4.2 Centre of excellence

The concept of a centre of excellence is that of a central standards unit, which defines standards (such as processes, templates and tools), and provides skills, training and possibly independent assurance functions to a number of projects.

> **Example of a centre of excellence**
>
> An organization has established a centre of excellence that provides:
>
> - A central filing system for all projects
> - A configuration management system
> - Expertise for estimating techniques
> - Advice on the preparation of plans
> - A historical database of how long specific activities take (metrics) and an analysis of productivity
> - PRINCE2 expertise and advice
> - Consolidated reports summarizing the status of all the projects in the portfolio.

A centre of excellence can be useful where:

- Resource shortages, either in numbers or skills, make it difficult to supply people to perform project administration for each current project
- There are a number of small projects of a diverse nature that individually require only limited support from Project Support
- There is a large programme, requiring coordination of individual projects
- A large project requires several resources to handle Project Support roles.

Refer to OGC's guidance *Portfolio, Programme and Project Offices* (TSO, 2008) for further information on the centre of excellence and its relationship to projects.

5.3.5 Working with stakeholders

5.3.5.1 Types of stakeholder

In addition to the stakeholders in the project management team, there are likely to be individuals or groups who are not part of the project management team, but who may need to interact with the project or who may be affected by the project's outcome. Such people may:

- Support or oppose the project
- Gain or lose as a result of project delivery
- See the project as a threat or enhancement to their position
- Become active supporters or blockers of the project and its progress.

It is important to analyse who these stakeholders are and to engage with them appropriately.

> **Example of stakeholder analysis**
>
> Stakeholder analysis identified the following stakeholders for a project to relocate a chemical factory:
>
> - A number of unions
> - An environmental pressure group
> - An industry regulator
> - The programme's quality assurance function
> - A number of corporate management functions (e.g. internal audit, finance, legal)
> - The external contractor
> - Some members of the public affected by the project.
>
> Note that some of these were external to the project management team but internal to the corporate or programme management organization.

5.3.5.2 Stakeholder engagement

Stakeholder engagement is the process of identifying and communicating effectively with those people or groups who have an interest or influence on the project's outcome. It is usually carried out at the programme level. All projects need to have some level of some stakeholder engagement, particularly if not part of a programme.

Parties external to the project management team can exert a powerful influence on a project. Effective communication with key stakeholders, both internal and external to the corporate organization, is essential to the project's success.

Example of stakeholder engagement

OGC's Managing Successful Programmes (MSP®) identifies a six-step procedure for stakeholder engagement:

- **Identifying stakeholders (Who?)** Identifying the individual stakeholders involved in, or affected by, the project and perhaps grouping similar stakeholders together so that key messages can be targeted effectively
- **Creating and analysing stakeholder profiles (What?)** Gaining an understanding of the influences, interests and attitudes of the stakeholders towards the project and the importance and power of each stakeholder. For instance, is a particular group likely to be negative, irrespective of the message, and therefore require particular care? Stakeholders' influence and interests, whether rational or emotional, must all be taken into account. They have the potential to affect the success of the project. Perceptions may be mistaken, but they must be addressed. The stakeholder's perception of the benefits should be quantified where possible
- **Defining the stakeholder engagement strategy (How?)** Defining how the project can effectively engage with the stakeholders, including defining the responsibilities for communication and the key messages that need to be conveyed. For each interested party, agree the:
  - Information the party needs from the project
  - Method, format and frequency of communication
  - Sender and recipient of the communication
- **Planning the engagements (When?)** Defining the methods and timings of the communications. These are best planned after defining how the project will engage with the different stakeholders. When selecting the senders of information, it is important to select communicators who have the respect and trust of the audience. Their position in the corporate organization and expertise in the subject matter will greatly influence their credibility. Many projects have a formal commencement meeting to introduce the project and its aims to the corporate organization. If this type of meeting is used, it is important that the members of the Project Board attend to show their support and commitment to the project
- **Engaging stakeholders (Do)** Carrying out the planned engagements and communications. The first two steps in stakeholder engagement – identifying and analysing – also engage stakeholders to some degree
- **Measuring effectiveness (Results)** Checking the effectiveness of the engagements. Project Assurance could be involved in checking all the key stakeholders, their information needs and that the most appropriate communication channels are covered.

5.3.5.3 The Communication Management Strategy

The Communication Management Strategy contains a description of the means and frequency of communication to parties both internal and external to the project. It facilitates engagement with stakeholders through the establishment of a controlled and bi-directional flow of information. Where the project is part of a programme, the Communication Management Strategy should also define what information the programme needs and how this is to be communicated.

If a formal stakeholder engagement procedure has been completed, such as that described earlier, this should also be documented as part of the Communication Management Strategy. Refer to Appendix A for more details of the suggested content for the Communication Management Strategy.

The Project Manager should be responsible for documenting the Communication Management Strategy during the Initiating a Project process. It is also important to review and possibly update the Communication Management Strategy at each stage boundary in order to ensure that it still includes all the key stakeholders. When planning the final stage of the project it is also important to review the Communication Management Strategy to ensure it includes all the parties who need to be advised that the project is closing.

During a project, corporate or programme management retains control by receiving project information as defined in the Communication Management Strategy and taking decisions on project-level exceptions escalated by the Project Board.

If a project forms part of a programme, there will need to be consistency and communication between the project and programme levels of management. Refer to Chapter 19 for more detailed information on programme roles and how they may interact with project roles.

5.4 RESPONSIBILITIES

Table 5.1 outlines the responsibilities relevant to the Organization theme. Refer to Appendix C for further details of project management team roles and their associated responsibilities.

Table 5.1 Responsibilities relevant to the Organization theme

Role	Responsibilities
Corporate or programme management	Appoint the Executive and (possibly) the Project Manager.
	Provide information to the project as defined in the Communication Management Strategy.
Executive	Appoint the Project Manager (if not done by corporate or programme management).
	Confirm the appointments to the project management team and the structure of the project management team.
	Approve the Communication Management Strategy.
Senior User	Provide user resources.
	Define and verify user requirements and expectations.
Senior Supplier	Provide supplier resources.
Project Manager	Prepare the Communication Management Strategy.
	Review and update the Communication Management Strategy.
	Design, review and update the project management team structure.
	Prepare role descriptions.
Team Manager	Manage project team members.
	Advise on project team members and stakeholder engagement.
Project Assurance	Advise on selection of project team members.
	Advise on stakeholder engagement.
	Ensure that the Communication Management Strategy is appropriate and that planned communication activities actually take place.
Project Support	Provide administrative support for the project management team.

Quality

6

6 Quality

6.1 PURPOSE

> The purpose of the Quality theme is to define and implement the means by which the project will verify products that are fit for purpose.

The Quality theme defines the PRINCE2 approach to ensuring that the project's products:

- Meet business expectations
- Enable the desired benefits to be achieved subsequently.

The 'product focus' principle is central to PRINCE2's approach to quality. It provides an explicit common understanding of what the project will create (the scope) and the criteria against which the project's products will be assessed (the quality). Without this understanding, the project would be exposed to major risks (such as acceptance disputes, rework, uncontrolled change, user dissatisfaction) that could weaken or invalidate the Business Case.

Only after establishing the quality criteria for the products and the quality management activities that have to be included in the project's plans can the full project costs and timescales be estimated. Underestimating or omitting quality management activities is likely to lead to slippages, overspends and/or poor quality results. The Quality theme addresses the quality methods and responsibilities not only for the specification, development and approval of the project's products, but also for the management of the project.

The Quality theme also covers the implementation of continuous improvement during the project – for example, looking for ways to introduce more efficiency or effectiveness into the management of the project and the project's products. Capturing and acting on lessons contributes to the PRINCE2 quality approach, as it is a means of achieving continuous improvement.

6.2 QUALITY DEFINED

Terms used in a quality context are sometimes interpreted differently or interchangeably by various people. This can lead to misunderstandings. For the purposes of PRINCE2, the terminology used is derived from the ISO 9000 standards but is aimed specifically at project work.

6.2.1 Quality

PRINCE2 defines quality as the totality of features and inherent or assigned characteristics of a product, person, process, service and/or system that bear on its ability to show that it meets expectations or satisfies stated needs, requirements or specification. In PRINCE2, a product can also be a role description, process, service and/or system, so the focus of quality is on a product's ability to meet its requirements.

6.2.2 Scope

The scope of a plan is the sum total of its products. It is defined by the product breakdown structure for the plan and its associated Product Descriptions.

6.2.3 Quality management and quality management systems

Quality management is defined as the coordinated activities to direct and control an organization with regard to quality. A quality management system is the complete set of quality standards, procedures and responsibilities for a site or organization.

In the project context, 'sites' and 'organizations' should be interpreted as the permanent or semi-permanent organization(s) sponsoring the project work, i.e. they are 'external' to the project's temporary organization. A programme, for instance, can be regarded as a semi-permanent organization that sponsors the project, and may have a documented quality management system.

It is frequently the case that more than one permanent organization will be involved in a project – for example, separate customer and supplier businesses – and it follows that each may have its own quality management system. Alternatively, if the project has a single key sponsoring organization, or is part of a programme, a single established quality management system is more likely to apply. These various circumstances must be addressed when determining the project's approach to quality.

6.2.4 Quality planning

To control anything, including quality, there must be a plan. Quality planning is about defining the products required of the project, with their respective quality criteria, quality methods (including effort required for quality control and product acceptance) and the quality responsibilities of those involved.

6.2.5 Quality control

Quality control focuses on the operational techniques and activities used by those involved in the project to:

- Fulfil the requirements for quality (for example, by quality inspections or testing)
- Identify ways of eliminating causes of unsatisfactory performance (for example, by introducing process improvements as a result of lessons learned).

6.2.6 Quality assurance

It is good practice to arrange for quality assurance independent of the project management team. Quality assurance provides a check that the project's direction and management are adequate for the nature of the project and that it complies with relevant corporate or programme management standards and policies. Quality assurance activities are outside the scope of PRINCE2 as it is the responsibility of the corporate or programme organization.

Quality assurance is about independently checking that the organization and processes are in place for quality planning and control (i.e. not actually performing the quality planning or control, which will be undertaken by the project management team). It provides the project's stakeholders with confidence that the quality requirements can be fulfilled.

The term 'quality assurance' is used in two senses:

- As the function within an organization (or site or programme) that establishes and maintains the quality management system
- As the activity of reviewing a project's organization, processes and/or products to assess independently whether quality requirements will be met.

Note that, in both senses of the term, quality assurance involves contributions that are independent of the project management team, whereas quality planning and quality control are undertaken by the project. Nevertheless, it is a project management responsibility to ensure that adequate quality assurance is arranged.

Quality assurance should not be confused with Project Assurance. Project Assurance refers specifically to the Project Board's accountability

Table 6.1   The relationship between Project Assurance and quality assurance

	Project Assurance	Quality assurance
What they do	Provide assurance to the project's stakeholders that the project is being conducted appropriately and properly.	Provide assurance to the wider corporate or programme organization that the project is being conducted appropriately, properly and complies with relevant corporate or programme management standards and policies.
How they differ	Must be independent of the Project Manager, Project Support, Team Managers and project teams.	Performed by personnel who are independent of the project (i.e. not a member of the project management team).
	Responsibility of the Project Board, therefore undertaken from **within the project**.	Responsibility of the corporate or programme management organization, therefore **external to the project**.
How they relate	Quality assurance as a corporate or programme management function could be used by the Project Board as part of its Project Assurance regime (for example, having quality assurance perform a peer review).	Quality assurance would look for (or require) effective Project Assurance as one of the indicators that the project is being conducted properly.

for assuring that the project is conducted properly in all respects. This is, therefore, a responsibility within the project management team. Although Project Assurance is independent of the Project Manager, unlike quality assurance it is not independent of the project. However, Project Assurance and quality assurance do overlap, as illustrated in Table 6.1.

6.3 THE PRINCE2 APPROACH TO QUALITY

The specific treatment for quality in PRINCE2 is the focus on products from the outset, requiring systematic activities to:

■ Identify all the project's products (i.e. to the level at which the project intends to exert control)

■ Define them in Product Descriptions – including the quality criteria by which they will be assessed; the quality methods to be used in designing, developing and accepting them; and the quality responsibilities of those involved

■ Implement and track the quality methods employed throughout the project.

The first two of these are covered by **quality planning** (section 6.3.1) and the last is covered by **quality control** (section 6.3.2) and **quality assurance** (section 6.2.6).

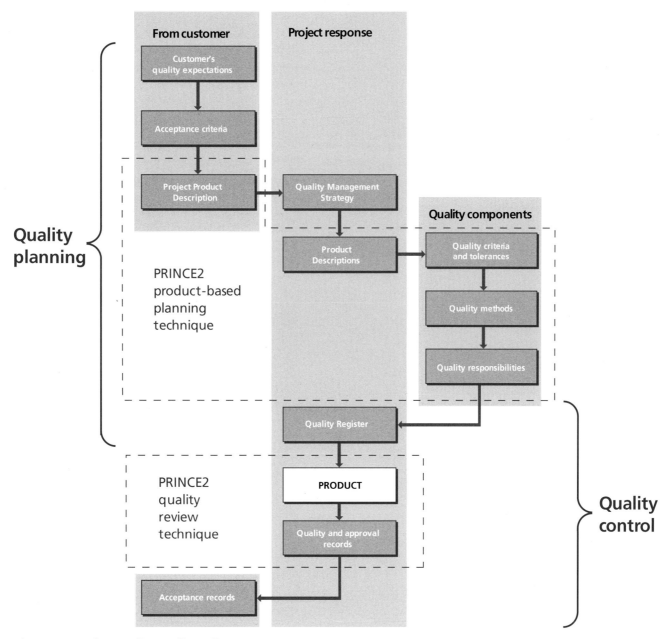

Figure 6.1   The quality audit trail

The PRINCE2 approach to quality can be summarized simply by the quality audit trail depicted in Figure 6.1. The terms used in the diagram are explained in the remainder of this section.

6.3.1 Quality planning

The purpose of quality planning is to provide a secure basis for:

■ **Project Board agreement** on the overall quality expectations, the products required with their associated quality criteria (including corporate and other standards to be observed), the means by which quality will be achieved and assessed and, ultimately, the acceptance criteria by which the project's product will be judged

■ **Communicating** these agreements unambiguously so that all the project stakeholders have a common understanding of what the project is setting out to achieve

■ **Control**, i.e. establishing an effective baseline for the project's quality controls (including the quality tolerances) and a secure means of achieving products that are fit for purpose.

When these aspects of planning are neglected, the people involved in the project may have conflicting views on the scope of the solution, on what constitutes a successful result, on the approach to be adopted, on the extent of the work required, on who should be involved, and on what their roles should be.

Quality planning comprises:

■ Understanding the customer's quality expectations (section 6.3.1.1)

■ Defining the project's acceptance criteria (section 6.3.1.2)

■ Documenting the customer's quality expectations and the project's acceptance criteria in the Project Product Description (section 6.3.1.3)

■ Formulating a Quality Management Strategy (section 6.3.1.4)

■ Writing clear Product Descriptions containing quality criteria, quality tolerances, quality method and quality responsibilities (section 6.3.1.5)

■ Setting up the Quality Register (section 6.3.1.6).

6.3.1.1 The customer's quality expectations

The customer's quality expectations are a statement about the quality expected from the project product. They are defined and agreed early in the Starting up a Project process. The expectations are captured in discussions with the customer and then refined for inclusion in the Project Product Description.

To avoid misinterpretations and inaccurate assumptions about the project's quality requirements, the customer's quality expectations should cover:

■ The key quality requirements for the project product

■ Any standards and processes that will need to be applied to achieve the specified quality requirements, including the extent to which the customer's and/or supplier's quality management system should be used

■ Any measurements that may be useful to assess whether the project product meets the quality requirements (for example, existing customer satisfaction measures).

The key quality requirements will drive the choice of solution and, in turn, influence the time, cost, scope, risk and benefit performance targets of the project.

Examples of quality expectation

The quality expectation for a water pump in a remote village is that it is robust enough to 'last a lifetime', whereas because the oil pump in a racing car needs to be as light as possible, it may only need to last the duration of one race.

The customer's quality expectations are often expressed in broad terms as a means to gain common understanding of general quality requirements. They are then used to identify more detailed acceptance criteria, which should be specific and precise.

Where possible, the customer's quality expectations should be prioritized as they will be used as inputs to define quality tolerances for the project's products.

The customer's quality expectations should be reviewed at the end of each management stage in case any external factors have changed them.

6.3.1.2 Acceptance criteria

The project's acceptance criteria form a prioritized list of measurable definitions of the attributes required for a set of products to be acceptable to key stakeholders. Examples are ease of use, ease of support, ease of maintenance, appearance, major functions, development costs, running costs, capacity, availability, reliability, security, accuracy, and performance.

Acceptance criteria should be prioritized as this helps if there has to be a trade-off between some criteria – high quality, early delivery and low cost, for example, may not be compatible and one of them may need to be sacrificed in order to achieve the other two.

> **Example of a prioritization technique – MoSCoW**
>
> Each acceptance criterion is rated as either **M**ust have, **S**hould have, **C**ould have or **W**on't have for now (MoSCoW).
>
> All the 'Must have' and 'Should have' acceptance criteria should be mutually achievable.

When the project can demonstrate that all the acceptance criteria have been met, the project's obligations are fulfilled and the project can be closed.

The acceptance criteria should be agreed between the customer and supplier during the Starting up a Project process and documented as part of the Project Product Description. It is important to recognize that little may be understood about the project's products at this early point. Consequently, it is often the case that acceptance criteria will be refined and agreed during the Initiating a Project process and reviewed at the end of each management stage. Once finalized in the Project Product Description, acceptance criteria are subject to change control and can only be changed with the approval of the Project Board.

In considering acceptance criteria, it is useful to select proxy measures that will be accurate and reliable indicators of whether benefits will subsequently be achieved.

> **Example of acceptance criteria**
>
> If a customer's quality expectation for a water pump is that it 'lasts a lifetime', the acceptance criteria should focus on those measures that provide sufficient indication or confidence that the pump is capable of lasting a lifetime (defined as a specific number of years). This may include complying with certain engineering standards relating to product durability.

Identifying the acceptance methods is crucial because they address the question: how do we prove whether and when the project product has been completed and is it acceptable to the customer?

6.3.1.3 The Project Product Description

The Project Product Description is created in the Starting up a Project process as part of the initial scoping activity and may be refined during the Initiating a Project process when creating the Project Plan. It is subject to formal change control and should be checked at stage boundaries (during Managing a Stage Boundary) to see if any changes are required. It is used by the Closing a Project process as part of the verification that the project has delivered what was expected of it and that the acceptance criteria have been met.

The Project Product Description includes:

- The overall purpose of the product
- Its composition (i.e. the set of products it needs to comprise)
- The customer's quality expectations
- Acceptance criteria, method and responsibilities
- Project-level quality tolerances.

The approved Project Product Description is included as a component of the Project Brief and is used to help select the project approach. The Project Product Description defines what the customer is expecting the project to deliver and the project approach defines the solution or method to be used by the supplier to create the project product.

The Project Product Description is a special form of Product Description in that it includes the customer's quality expectations and, at this level, the quality criteria and quality methods constitute the acceptance criteria and acceptance methods for the project overall.

6.3.1.4 The Quality Management Strategy

The Quality Management Strategy is prepared during the Initiating a Project process and approved subsequently by the Project Board. It augments the project approach and can be regarded as the project management team's proposals in response to the customer's quality expectations and acceptance criteria.

The Quality Management Strategy describes how the quality management systems of the participating organizations will be applied to the project and confirms any quality standards, procedures, techniques and tools that will be used. Where models and standards are to be tailored, the tailoring should also be outlined in the Quality Management Strategy for approval.

The Quality Management Strategy also provides a means by which the levels of formality to be applied in the quality plans and controls can be scaled and agreed according to the particular needs of the project.

It should outline the arrangements for quality assurance, including independent audits where these are required by the policies of the participating organizations.

Key responsibilities for quality should be defined (both within and outside the project management team), including a summary of the approach to Project Assurance.

Where there is already an established quality management system for projects, for example in a programme, only the measures specific to this project may need to be documented.

The Quality Management Strategy is maintained, subject to change control, throughout the life of the project.

6.3.1.5 Product Descriptions

Once detailed planning gets underway, Product Descriptions should be created for all of the project's products. Product Descriptions are not optional. They govern the development of the products and their subsequent review and approval.

The level of detail in a Product Description is a matter of judgement, with the primary aim being to select a level that provides a secure and appropriate measure of control sufficient to fulfil the customer's quality expectations.

The content of a Product Description is described fully in Appendix A. The 'purpose' section of the Product Description should clearly state who needs the product, why they need it and what it will do. In addition to the 'purpose', the sections specific to quality are: quality criteria, quality tolerances, quality methods, quality skills required and quality responsibilities. These define the quality controls that must be applied during product development and in the review and approval procedures for the completed product.

Care should be taken not to write Product Descriptions in too much detail. They exist to help support the planning, development, quality and approval methods. Product Descriptions that are too detailed can lead to an unnecessary increase in the cost of quality for the project. Incomplete or inaccurate Product Descriptions can lead to acceptance disputes if the delivered results do not match the customer's expectations. Where necessary, the Product Description should reference supporting information, such as any applicable standards or specialist design documents.

The time needed to create good Product Descriptions will depend on factors such as how important, complex and unique the product is, how many stakeholders will review and approve the product, and whether the organization has a library of standard Product Descriptions for reuse. Product Description libraries are frequently implemented by PRINCE2 users, to promote consistency and reuse.

Quality criteria

The Product Description should include the quality specifications that the product must meet, and the quality measurements that will be applied by those inspecting the finished product.

The quality criteria should be of sufficient detail and clarity to enable those reviewing a product to unambiguously confirm whether the product meets its requirements.

Quality tolerances

Quality tolerances for a product can be specified in quality criteria by defining an acceptable range of values. For example: 'Is the duration of the presentation 30 minutes (plus or minus 5 minutes)?', 'Is temperature maintained in the range of 1 to 5°C?'

Example of quality criteria

Consider a project to design and manufacture a new camera. One quality criterion is that the camera and its packaging must weigh no more than 1 kg. The product breakdown structure identifies a user guide product. It follows that the size and weight of the user guide is an important factor and not, for example, the number of pages.

Questions to be asked include: What is the target market for the camera? Does this also imply that the manual needs to be written in several languages? Will that mean it gets heavier? Or will a CD-ROM-based manual suffice? This could reduce the weight of the manual and allow the camera itself to be heavier.

Considering quality criteria often highlights connections and factors such as these which inform the subsequent planning process.

Quality methods

The quality methods section of the Product Description is used to specify the quality activities to be implemented during the development of a product, for review and approval on completion. Where specialized skills are implicit in the quality

methods, these should also be specified. There are two primary types of quality methods: in-process methods and appraisal methods (see section 6.3.2.1).

Quality responsibilities

To avoid doubt, the quality responsibilities for a product should be specified. The responsibilities will fall into one of three categories:

- **Producer** The person or group responsible for developing a product
- **Reviewer(s)** A person or group independent of the producer who assesses whether a product meets its requirements as defined in its Product Description
- **Approver(s)** The person or group, for example a Project Board, who is identified as qualified and authorized to approve a product as being complete and fit for purpose.

6.3.1.6 The Quality Register

The Quality Register is effectively a diary of the quality events planned and undertaken (for example, workshops, reviews, inspections, testing, pilots, acceptance and audits). It is created during the Initiating a Project process as the products and quality control measures are being defined. It is then maintained (in line with the current baseline plans) throughout the project.

Table 6.2 Example of a Quality Register

Quality Activity ID	Product ID	Product	Quality Method	Producer	Reviewer(s)	Approver(s)	Target Review Date	Actual Review Date	Target Approval Date	Actual Approval Date	Result
1	121	Test Plan	Inspection	Ali	Paulo	John, Rita	14-Feb	21-Feb	21-Feb	28-Feb	Pass
2	124	Water Pump	Performance Test	Paulo	Ali, Bob	John	20-Mar	20-Mar	27-Mar	NA	Fail
3	124	Water Pump	Maintenance Test	Paulo	Ali, Amir	Rita	21-Mar	21-Mar	27-Mar	27-Mar	Pass
.	.	.	.	.	.	.	.	.	.	.	.
.	.	.	.	.	.	.	.	.	.	.	.
9	124	Water Pump	Performance Test	Paulo	Ali, Bob	John	14-Jun		21-Jun		

As the project progresses and records of the quality activities are received, the Quality Register is updated to reflect (in summary form) the actual results from the quality activities. The Quality Register provides key audit and assurance information, relating what was planned and agreed (in the Quality Management Strategy and Product Descriptions) to the quality activities actually performed.

The amount of information included in the Quality Register can vary considerably, depending on the extent to which quality metrics (e.g. 'defect counts') need to be analysed for process improvement purposes. An example of a Quality Register is shown in Table 6.2.

6.3.2 Quality control

Quality control is achieved by implementing, monitoring and recording the quality methods and responsibilities defined in the Quality Management Strategy and Product Descriptions (and subsequently agreed to in Work Packages).

Quality control comprises:

- Carrying out the quality methods (section 6.3.2.1)
- Maintaining quality and approval records (sections 6.3.2.2 and 6.3.2.3)
- Gaining acceptance (section 6.3.2.4).

6.3.2.1 Quality methods

The cost of correcting flaws in products increases the longer they remain undetected. It is much easier and cheaper to correct a design document early in the project than to correct a design fault that is only discovered when the finished product is being tested or, worse, when the product is already in operational use. It follows that quality inspections, implemented early in the design and development process, are potentially the most cost-effective quality methods available.

There are two types of quality methods:

- **'In-process' methods** These are the means by which quality can be 'built into' the products as they are developed. These might involve the use of specialist methods and/or techniques, including calibrated process controls, automation (e.g. robotics, software tools), piloting exercises, workshops, surveys and consultation, or, more simply, the use of

quality inspections during the course of product development as well as upon completion
- **Appraisal methods** These are the means by which the finished products are assessed for completeness and fitness for purpose. There are, in essence, two types of appraisal methods, depending on the extent to which it is possible to define objective quality criteria: **testing** (if the quality criteria are truly objective and quantifiable) or **quality inspection** (if some subjective judgement is required).

A quality inspection is a systematic, structured assessment of a product conducted in a planned, documented and organized fashion. A systematic but flexible approach to quality inspection can be used:

- During the development of products of this type, whether formally (i.e. in line with what was agreed during quality planning) or informally (simply as a means of assessing the quality of a 'work in progress')
- To mark the completion and approval of products
- To complement testing, e.g. simply for checking test results.

Quality inspection techniques are particularly applicable when professional judgement is required to assess the product's fitness for purpose. The techniques can be used within the project, as quality controls, and by independent experts, as part of quality assurance. Peer and gateway reviews are examples of quality assurance activities that can be implemented by using or adapting a generic inspection technique. Used as a project management team control, conducting systematic quality inspections can also have valuable team-building side-benefits.

Even when testing is the primary appraisal method, it is often the case that someone has to check that the test results meet the criteria for success and so a simple inspection is still required.

There are a variety of systematic inspection techniques, some being specific to certain industries or types of product. PRINCE2 accommodates the use of these techniques, but also provides a useful quality review technique, which complements the use of PRINCE2 Product Descriptions.

The PRINCE2 quality review technique

Objectives

- To assess the conformity of a product which takes the form of a document (or similar item, e.g. a presentation or test results) against set criteria
- To involve key interested parties in checking the product's quality and in promoting wider acceptance of the product
- To provide confirmation that the product is complete and ready for approval
- To baseline the product for change control purposes.

Review team roles

- **Chair** This role is responsible for the overall conduct of the review
- **Presenter** This role introduces the product for review and represents the producer(s) of the product. The presenter also coordinates and tracks the work after the review, i.e. applying the changes to the product agreed by the team
- **Reviewer** This role reviews the product, submits questions and confirms corrections and/or improvements
- **Administrator** This role provides administrative support for the chair and records the result and actions.

The minimum form of review (used for simple inspections, e.g. of test results) involves only two people: one taking the chair and reviewer roles, the other taking the presenter and administrator roles.

Note: quality review is a generic technique which can be used outside the project context. Thus the quality review roles have no specific relationship to roles in the project management team structure. However, team-building benefits can be realized where Project and Team Managers regularly chair reviews. Chairing quality reviews requires competence in facilitation and independence of the product being reviewed (the primary responsibility is to ensure that the review is undertaken properly).

Review preparation

- Make the administrative arrangements for the review (chair/administrator)

- Check the product is ready for review and confirm the availability of the reviewers (chair)
- Distribute copies of the product and the relevant Product Description to the review team, allowing sufficient time for reviewers to prepare (presenter)
- Review the product in line with the quality criteria in the associated Product Description (reviewers)
- Submit a question list to the chair and presenter ahead of the review (reviewers)
- Annotate the product copy where there are spelling/grammar mistakes and return to the presenter (reviewers)
- Produce a consolidated question list (chair) and send to the presenter in advance of the meeting.

Review meeting agenda

- **Personal introductions,** if necessary (chair)
- **Product introduction** (presenter) A very brief summary, covering the product's purpose: who needs it, why they need it and what it will do
- **Major/global questions** (chair) Invite each reviewer to contribute any major or global questions with the product. Global questions are ones that appear repeatedly throughout the product. The review team agrees any action on each question as it is raised. The administrator records the actions and responsibilities
- **Product 'talk-through'** (presenter) Lead the review team through the product section by section or page by page, as appropriate, by reviewing the consolidated question list and inviting clarification where required. The review team agrees actions on each question as it is raised. The administrator records the actions and responsibilities
- **Read back actions** (administrator) Confirm the actions and responsibilities
- **Determine the review result** (chair) Lead the review team to a collective decision. The options are:
  - **Complete** (the product is fit for purpose, as is)
  - **Conditionally complete** (the product is fit for purpose subject to the actions)

- ● **Incomplete** (the product requires another quality review cycle)
- ■ **Close the review** (chair)
- ■ **Inform interested parties of the result** (chair).

Review follow-up

- ■ Coordinate the actions (presenter)
- ■ Sign off individual actions (reviewers, as agreed at the meeting)
- ■ Once all actions are complete, sign off that the product is now complete (chair)
- ■ Communicate the quality review outcome to appropriate managers/support personnel (administrator)
- ■ Store the quality records (administrator)
- ■ Request approval for the product (presenter).

Hints and tips

- ■ **Reviewers** Review the product **not** the person. This means avoid personalizing issues ('You …') and operate as a team ('We …')
- ■ **Reviewers** Operate as a team but defer to specialist areas of expertise. Some reviewers may be selected to address specific aspects of the product and their comments may be considered to carry more weight in those areas
- ■ **Reviewers** Do not introduce trivia at reviews (spelling, punctuation etc.) unless it is a major/global issue (e.g. if the document will be communicated to an important audience, such as the public)
- ■ **Chair** Encourage the presenter to maintain a steady pace during the product talk-through. The reviewers must have the opportunity to introduce their issues but allowing too much time invites comments that would not otherwise be made. The presenter should not be opening discussions unnecessarily
- ■ **Chair** Resolve each point as it is raised by getting a decision from the review team. Does the product have to be changed or not? Do not allow discussions to drift. Remember, the purpose of the review is to identify defects, not to design solutions to them. Avoid the temptation to formulate and agree solutions. These should be done post-review
- ■ **Chair** Focus on this product. Do not allow discussion to drift onto other related

products. If it appears that there may be a problem associated with a related product, handle it outside the meeting as an issue

- ■ **Chair** Make sure the reviewers contribute effectively. It is your responsibility to ensure that the approved product is fit for purpose
- ■ **Chair** If a reviewer cannot attend the review, accept the question list from them and either raise the questions on their behalf, accept a delegate or replace the reviewer
- ■ **Presenter** It may be that a follow-up action is not feasible to implement or cannot be done within agreed tolerances, in which case an issue should be raised to the Project Manager
- ■ **Approver** If the person (or group) who will approve the product participates in the quality review, it may be possible to approve the product as part of the review.

The formal approval of a product may or may not result from a quality review. Products that have been signed off as complete at an inspection or review may still have to be submitted to a separate authority for approval.

The PRINCE2 quality review technique (and other quality inspection techniques) can yield substantial side-benefits, particularly in terms of:

- ■ **Stakeholder engagement** Quality inspections are opportunities for effective cross-functional communication. Many important stakeholders may only have direct contact with the project through these reviews, so they provide a 'window' into the project. This is particularly true for users. Structured quality inspections are among the most effective ways of encouraging buy-in to the project. Generally, the more systematic and effective the reviews, the better the impression for the stakeholders
- ■ **Leadership** In many circumstances a focus on quality (as in 'fitness for purpose') elicits a better response from review team members (and users) than simply focusing on budgets and schedules. Quality inspection techniques often provide excellent tips and 'soft guidance' on effective behaviour and decision making in meetings

- **Team building** Formal and informal quality inspections are opportunities to focus on building an effective project team, where members understand each other's contributions, needs and priorities
- **Developing individuals** New starters learn from more experienced personnel and spot omissions that others take for granted. Experienced personnel learn from the fresh perspectives brought by newcomers
- **Quality documentation** Consistent and familiar quality records make for improvements in communication and in the analysis of quality metrics
- **Quality culture** The PRINCE2 quality review technique is generic. It can be employed on programmes, projects and services throughout an organization, resulting in a positive and familiar 'quality culture'.

6.3.2.2 Quality records

It is important that evidence is gathered to demonstrate that the planned quality activities have been carried out. The records support entries in the Quality Register by providing the Project Manager and the Project Board with assurance that:

- Products really are complete (and consequently that the related activities are finished)
- Products have met their associated quality criteria and are fit for their intended purposes (alternatively there are records of any quality failures and corrective action)
- The agreed processes have been observed
- Approval authorities and key product stakeholders are satisfied
- Planned audits have been conducted and reported.

Quality records should include references to the quality inspection documentation, such as a test plan; details of any 'defect' statistics and actions required to correct errors and omissions of the products inspected; and any quality-related reports (for example, an audit). When these records are received by Project Support, the Quality Register entries for the relevant products can be completed. During the project and at project closure, the quality records provide a valuable source of information for analysis in accordance with the PRINCE2 principle that projects should learn from

experience. For example, quality metrics, such as defect types and trends, can be used as a source for lessons learned and process improvements.

6.3.2.3 Approval records

While quality records provide evidence that each product has met its requirements as specified in its Product Description, it is good practice to obtain a record that the product has been approved.

PRINCE2 does not specify the format or composition of approval records as these will depend on the level of formality required, the customer/supplier relationship and the quality management system of the organizations involved. The format for approval records could include, for example, a note in the minutes of a meeting, an email, a letter, a signature on a document, or a certificate.

6.3.2.4 Acceptance records

Products are approved throughout the life of the project and ownership may even be transferred to the customer as part of a phased handover. But, during the Closing a Project process, it is important to check that all forms of approval have been obtained and records kept for audit and/or contractual purposes.

PRINCE2 uses the term 'acceptance' to describe the ultimate approval of the project's product. Acceptance is frequently required from more than one set of stakeholders, e.g. those using the project's products and those maintaining them (in which case both categories of stakeholder should have been involved in defining the relevant products, participating in quality inspections and granting approval during the course of the project).

Acceptance may be qualified, and documented 'concessions' can be granted (e.g. if there are faults in the solution or some performance criteria have not been fully achieved). Where concessions have been granted by the Project Board, it may be necessary to recommend follow-on actions for later improvements or remedies for the products concerned.

6.4 RESPONSIBILITIES

Table 6.3 outlines the responsibilities relevant to the Quality theme. Refer to Appendix C for further details of project management team roles and their associated responsibilities.

Table 6.3 Responsibilities relevant to the Quality theme

Role	Responsibilities
Corporate or programme management	Provide details of the corporate or programme quality management system.
	Provide quality assurance.
Executive	Approve the Project Product Description.
	Approve the Quality Management Strategy.
	Confirm acceptance of the project product.
Senior User	Provide the customer's quality expectations and acceptance criteria.
	Approve the Project Product Description.
	Approve the Quality Management Strategy.
	Approve Product Descriptions for key user products.
	Provide resources to undertake user quality activities and product approval.
	Provide acceptance of the project product.
Senior Supplier	Approve the Project Product Description (if appropriate).
	Approve the Quality Management Strategy.
	Approve the quality methods, techniques and tools adopted in product development.
	Provide resources to undertake supplier quality activities.
	Approve Product Descriptions for key specialist products.
Project Manager	Document customer's quality expectations and acceptance criteria.
	Prepare the Project Product Description (with users).
	Prepare the Quality Management Strategy.
	Prepare and maintain the Product Descriptions.
	Ensure that Team Managers implement the quality control measures agreed in Product Descriptions and Work Packages.
Team Manager	Produce products consistent with Product Descriptions.
	Manage quality controls for the products concerned.
	Assemble quality records.
	Advise the Project Manager of product quality status.
Project Assurance	Advise the Project Manager on the Quality Management Strategy.
	Assist the Project Board and Project Manager by reviewing the Product Descriptions.
	Advise the Project Manager on suitable quality reviewers/approvers.
	Assure Project Board members on the implementation of the Quality Management Strategy, i.e. the proper conduct of the project management and quality procedures.
Project Support	Provide administrative support for quality controls.
	Maintain the Quality Register and the quality records.
	Assist Team Managers and members with the application of the project's quality processes.

Plans

7

7 Plans

7.1 PURPOSE

> The purpose of the Plans theme is to facilitate communication and control by defining the means of delivering the products (the where and how, by whom, and estimating the when and how much).

Effective project management relies on effective planning as without a plan there is no control. Planning provides all personnel involved in the project with information on:

- What is required
- How it will be achieved and by whom, using what specialist equipment and resources
- When events will happen
- Whether the targets (for time, cost, quality, scope, risk and benefits) are achievable.

The development and maintenance of credible plans provides a baseline against which progress can be measured. They enable planning information to be disseminated to stakeholders in order to secure any commitments which support the plan.

The very act of planning helps the project management team to think ahead to 'mentally rehearse the project'. It is such rehearsal that enables omissions, duplication, threats and opportunities to be identified and managed.

The Plans theme provides a framework to design, develop and maintain the project's plans (Project Plan, Stage Plans and Team Plans).

7.2 PLANS DEFINED

7.2.1 What is a plan?

When asked to describe a plan, many people think of a chart showing timescales.

A PRINCE2 plan is more comprehensive. It is a document describing how, when and by whom a specific target or set of targets is to be achieved. These targets will include the project's products, timescales, costs, quality and benefits.

A plan must therefore contain sufficient information and detail to confirm that the targets are achievable.

Plans are the backbone of the management information system required for any project. It is important that plans are kept in line with the Business Case at all times. A plan requires the approval and commitment of the relevant levels of the project management team.

7.2.2 What is planning?

Planning is the act or process of making and maintaining a plan. The term is also used to describe the formal procedures used in this exercise, such as the creation of documents and diagrams. Planning is essential, regardless of the type or size of the project; it is not a trivial exercise but is vital to the success of the project.

Without effective planning, the result of complex projects cannot be predicted in terms of scope, quality, risk, timescale, cost and benefits. Those involved in providing resources cannot optimize their operations.

Poorly planned projects cause frustration, waste and rework. It is therefore essential to allocate sufficient time for the planning stage.

PRINCE2 requires a product-based approach to planning.

7.2.3 Levels of plan

All aspects of planning become more difficult the further into the future they extend. The period of time for which it is possible to plan accurately is known as the planning horizon. Because of this, it is seldom desirable, or possible, to plan an entire project in detail at the start. Therefore plans need to be produced at different levels of scope and detail (see section 2.4).

PRINCE2 recommends three levels of plan to reflect the needs of the different levels of management involved in the project, stage and team. A Product Description for a plan can be found in Appendix A.

PRINCE2's planning levels are illustrated in Figure 7.1.

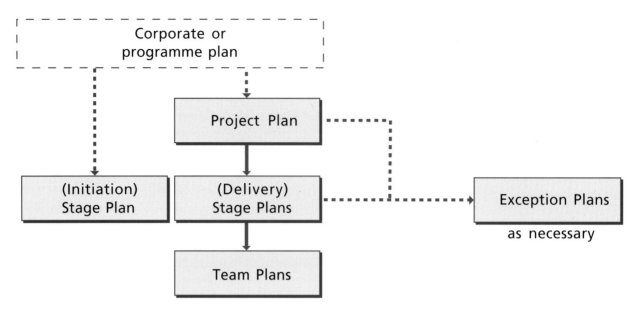

Figure 7.1 PRINCE2's planning levels

The Project Plan is created by the Initiating a Project process.

The Initiation Stage Plan is created by the Starting up a Project process and each subsequent Stage Plan is created by the Managing a Stage Boundary process. Note that since the Initiation Stage Plan is created prior to the Project Plan, it is influenced by the corporate or programme plan (or equivalent) from the organization commissioning the project.

Team Plans are created by the Managing Product Delivery process.

The only other plan in PRINCE2 is the Benefits Review Plan (see Chapter 4 for more details). This covers activities during and after the project and therefore may be part of a corporate or programme plan. The Benefits Review Plan covers corporate, project and stage levels.

7.2.4 The Project Plan

The Project Plan provides a statement of how and when a project's time, cost, scope and quality performance targets are to be achieved, by showing the major products, activities and resources required for the project. The Project Plan:

- Provides the Business Case with planned project costs and timescales, and identifies the major control points, such as management stages and milestones
- Is used by the Project Board as a baseline against which to monitor project progress stage by stage

- Should align with the corporate or programme management's plan.

7.2.5 Stage Plans

A Stage Plan is required for each management stage. The Stage Plan is similar to the Project Plan in content, but each element will be broken down to the level of detail required to be an adequate basis for day-to-day control by the Project Manager.

Each Stage Plan for the next management stage is produced near the end of the current management stage. This approach allows the Stage Plan to:

- Be produced close to the time when the planned events will take place
- Exist for a much shorter duration than the Project Plan (thus overcoming the planning horizon issue)
- Be produced with the knowledge of the performance of earlier management stages.

See Chapter 10 for further guidance on partitioning a project into management stages.

7.2.6 Team Plans

A Team Plan is produced by a Team Manager to facilitate the execution of one or more Work Packages. Team Plans are optional; their need and number will be determined by the size and complexity of the project and the number of resources involved.

PRINCE2 does not prescribe the format or composition of a Team Plan. There may be more than one team on a project and each team may come from separate organizations following different project management standards (not necessarily PRINCE2). In some customer/supplier contexts it could even be inappropriate for the Project Manager to see the details of a supplier's Team Plan; instead, summary information would be provided sufficient for the Project Manager to exercise control. Therefore the formality of the Team Plan could vary from simply appending a schedule to the Work Package to a fully formed plan in similar style to a Stage Plan.

The Team Manager(s) may create their Team Plans in parallel with the Project Manager creating the Stage Plan for the management stage.

7.2.7 Exception Plans

An Exception Plan is a plan prepared for the appropriate management level to show the actions required to recover from the effect of a tolerance deviation. If approved, the Exception Plan will replace the plan that is in exception and it will become the new baselined Project Plan or current Stage Plan, as appropriate.

If a Stage Plan is being replaced, this needs the approval of the Project Board. Replacement of a Project Plan should be referred by the Project Board to corporate or programme management if it is beyond the authority of the Project Board.

An Exception Plan is prepared to the same level of detail as the plan it replaces. It picks up from the current plan actuals and continues to the end of that plan. Exception Plans are not produced for Work Packages. Should a Team Manager forecast that the assigned Work Package may exceed tolerances, they will notify the Project Manager by raising an issue. If the issue relating to the Work Package can be resolved within stage tolerances, the Project Manager will take corrective action by updating the Work Package or issuing a new Work Package(s) and instructing the Team Manager(s) accordingly.

For more explanation of the types and the use of tolerance in PRINCE2, see Chapter 10.

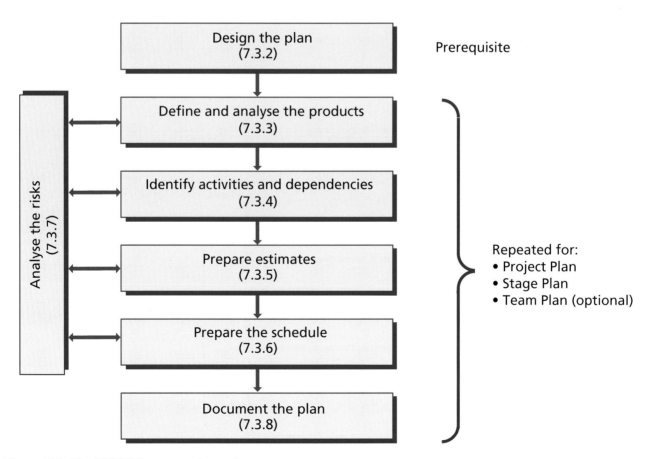

Figure 7.2 The PRINCE2 approach to plans

7.3 THE PRINCE2 APPROACH TO PLANS

7.3.1 Philosophy

The philosophy behind producing plans in PRINCE2 is that the products required are identified first, and only then are the activities, dependencies and resources required to deliver those products identified. This is known as **product-based planning** and is used for the Project Plan, the Stage Plan and, optionally, the Team Plan. Figure 7.2 illustrates the steps required in producing a PRINCE2 plan.

Each step in the planning procedure may need to be revisited on completion of later steps (for example, in preparing the schedule if additional activities or dependencies are identified).

7.3.2 Prerequisites for planning – design the plan

Decisions need to be made about how the plan can best be presented, given the audience for the plan and how it will be used, together with the presentation and layout of the plan, planning tools, estimating methods, levels of plan, and monitoring methods to be used for the project. This will include the use of diagrams versus text and will be driven, in part, by any standards adopted by the project.

Where the project is part of a programme, the programme may have developed a common approach to project planning. This may cover standards – for example, level of planning – and tools. These will be the starting point for designing any Project Plan. Any project-specific variations should be highlighted and the agreement of programme management sought. There may also be a company standard for planning and control aids, or the customer may stipulate the use of a particular set of tools. The choice of planning tool may depend on the complexity of the project – hence the choice may need to be deferred until the level of complexity is known.

The estimating methods to be used in the plan may affect the plan design, so decisions on the methods should be made as part of the plan design itself.

The use of planning tools is not obligatory, but it can save a great deal of time if the plan is to be regularly updated and changed. A good tool can also validate that the correct dependencies have been built in and have not been corrupted by any plan updates.

7.3.3 Define and analyse the products

PRINCE2 uses a technique known as product-based planning to identify, define and analyse the plan's products, as shown in Figure 7.3.

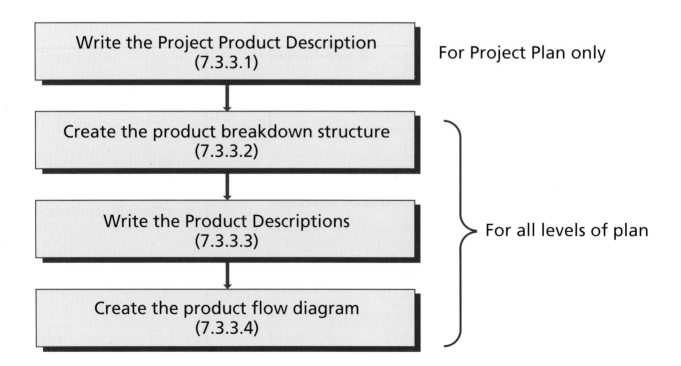

Figure 7.3 Product-based planning technique

Product-based planning is likely to be iterative. In the case of Product Descriptions, this means that at first it may comprise simply a title and a statement of purpose. Therefore, in the following note, 'write' (as in 'write a Product Description') should be interpreted as meaning 'commence to write, and proceed to complete as fully as appropriate as soon as convenient'.

The format and presentation of the product breakdown structure and product flow diagram is determined by personal preference. See Appendix D for examples.

The benefits of product-based planning include:

- Clearly and consistently identifying and documenting the plan's products and the interdependencies between them. This reduces the risk of important scope aspects being neglected or overlooked
- Removing any ambiguity over expectations
- Involving users in specifying the product requirements, thus increasing buy-in and reducing approval disputes
- Improving communication: the product breakdown structure and product flow diagram provide simple and powerful means of sharing and discussing options for the scope and approach to be adopted for the project
- Clarifying the scope boundary: defining products that are in and out of the scope for the plan and providing a foundation for change control, thus avoiding uncontrolled change or 'scope creep'
- Identifying products that are external to the plan's scope but are necessary for it to proceed, and allocating them to other projects or organizations
- Preparing the way for the production of Work Packages for suppliers
- Gaining a clear agreement on production, review and approval responsibilities.

7.3.3.1 Write the Project Product Description

The first task of product-based planning is to write the Project Product Description. Although the Senior User is responsible for specifying the project product, in practice the Project Product Description is often written by the Project Manager in consultation with the Senior User and Executive. Every effort should be made to make this Product Description as complete as possible at the outset.

See Appendix A for the suggested composition of the Project Product Description.

7.3.3.2 Create the product breakdown structure

The plan is broken down into its major products, which are then further broken down until an appropriate level of detail for the plan is reached. A lower-level product can be a component of only one higher-level product. The resultant hierarchy of products is known as a product breakdown structure.

When creating a product breakdown structure, consider the following:

- It is usual to involve a team of people in the creation of a product breakdown structure, perhaps representing the different interests and various skill sets involved in the plan's output
- It is common to identify products by running a structured brainstorming session (for example, using sticky notes or a whiteboard) to capture each product as it is identified
- When a team is creating a product breakdown structure, there is likely to be discussion on the way in which to break down the products. For example, if the output of the plan is a computerized accounts system, users might want to separate the system into Accounts Payable, Accounts Receivable, General Ledger etc. The suppliers, however, may prefer Screens, Reports, Databases etc. Neither breakdown is wrong, but the project management team must reach a consensus on which approach will be used in the product breakdown structure (and hence the plan)
- It is useful to identify any **external products** required by the plan. External products already exist or are being created or updated outside of the scope of the plan and are required in order to create one or more of the plan's products. For example, a procurement project would show the bidders' tender responses as external products. The Project Manager is not accountable for the creation of external products as they will be supplied by parties external to the project management team. For each external product there should be a corresponding entry on the Risk Register detailing the threat to the plan if they are late or not to the required specification. Consider whether external products require Product

Descriptions to reduce the likelihood of them not providing what's expected of them

- When using product-based planning, it is important to consider whether to include different **states** of a particular product. An example of product states is 'dismantled machinery, moved machinery and reassembled machinery'. It could be appropriate to identify the different states as separate products, where each state would require its own Product Description with different quality criteria and quality controls. This may be particularly useful when the responsibility for creating each state will pass from one team to another. Alternatively, a single Product Description could be used with a set of quality criteria that the product needs to meet in order to gain approval for each state

- When presenting the product breakdown structure, consider the use of different shapes, styles or colours for different types of product. For example, a rectangle could be used in a product breakdown structure to represent most types of product, but it may be helpful to use different shapes such as ellipses or circles to distinguish external products. Colours could be used to indicate which team is responsible for the product or in which stage the product will be created

- If the project is broken down into several stages, the products for each stage are extracted from the project product breakdown structure to form the stage product breakdown structure. These may be expanded to more levels of detail and thus 'extra products' may be added to give the detail required of the Stage Plan. Care must be taken to use the same names in the Stage Plan diagrams as were used in the Project Plan. The creation of Stage Plan diagrams may cause rethinking that requires further modification of the Project Plan's diagrams in order to retain consistency

- In some cases, the organization's lifecycle model may have a preset product breakdown structure and product flow diagram for common types of projects and a library of Product Description outlines for common products. In such cases the steps in the PRINCE2 product-based planning technique should not be skipped but used to verify the completeness of any library material. As every project is unique, there may be additional product requirements for this project

or subtle differences in the quality criteria; the locations may be different, or the people and responsibilities involved may be different. Moreover, lifecycle models frequently address only one aspect of a project's scope.

7.3.3.3 Write the Product Descriptions

A Product Description is required for all the identified products. When creating a Product Description, consider the following:

- Product Descriptions should be written as soon as possible after the need for the product has been identified. Initially, these may only be 'skeletons' with little more than the title and identifier as information. They will be refined and amended as the product becomes better understood and the later planning steps are done

- A Product Description should be baselined when the plan containing the creation of that product is baselined. If the product is later changed, the Product Description must also pass through change control

- Although the responsibility for writing Product Descriptions rests officially with the Project or Team Manager, it is wise to involve representatives from the area with expertise in the product and those who will use the product in question. The latter should certainly be consulted when defining the quality criteria for the product

- Successful Product Descriptions may be reused for other projects within that programme or organization. For this to happen, a library of Product Descriptions for reuse will need to be established and a mechanism for Product Descriptions to be placed in the library will also need to be implemented. The Project Manager should therefore refer to the library in order to see if any of the Product Descriptions within it are suitable for reuse and/or modification for the project

- If a detailed requirements specification for a product is already available, this may be used as a substitute for the Product Description as long as the requirements specification covers the components and meets the quality criteria expected of a Product Description. Alternatively a Product Description should be created referencing the requirements specification contents where appropriate

- For a small project, it may only be necessary to write the Project Product Description
- Quality criteria, aimed at separating an acceptable product from an unacceptable one, need careful thought. One way of testing quality criteria is by asking the question: how will I know when work on this product is finished as opposed to stopped?

7.3.3.4 Create the product flow diagram

A product flow diagram needs to be created to identify and define the sequence in which the products of the plan will be developed and any dependencies between them.

The product flow diagram also identifies dependencies on any products outside the scope of the plan. It leads naturally into consideration of the activities required, and provides the information for other planning techniques, such as estimating and scheduling.

When creating a product flow diagram, consider the following:

- Although the Project or Team Manager is responsible for the creation of the product flow diagram, it is sensible to involve those who are to develop or contribute to the products contained in the plan
- Rather than preparing the product flow diagram once the product breakdown structure has been drawn, some planners prefer to create the product flow diagram in parallel with the product breakdown structure
- A product flow diagram needs very few symbols. Each product to be developed within the plan in question is identified (for example, it may be enclosed in a rectangle), and the sequence in which they are to be created is shown (the rectangles may be connected by arrows, for example). Any products that already exist or that come from work outside the scope of the plan should be clearly identified as external products (for example, they may be enclosed in a different shape, such as an ellipse)
- It may be useful to add a starting point in the product flow diagram from which all entry points are attached. There is always one exit on a product flow diagram but when there are many entrances, such a place marker prevents

any from being overlooked. The symbol becomes the predecessor for all entry points and would be the only symbol on a product flow diagram that is not on the product breakdown structure.

7.3.4 Identify activities and dependencies

7.3.4.1 Activities

Simply identifying products may be insufficient for scheduling and control purposes. The activities required to create or change each of the planned products need to be identified to give a fuller picture of the plan's workload.

There are several ways to identify activities, including:

- Making a separate list of the activities, while still using the product flow diagram as the source of the information
- Taking the products from the product breakdown structure and creating a work breakdown structure to define the activities required.

The activities should include management and quality-checking activities as well as the activities needed to develop the specialist products. The activities should include any that are required to interact with external parties – for example, obtaining a product from an outside source or converting external products into something that the plan requires.

Guard against a proliferation of activities beyond the detail appropriate to the level of the plan. If in doubt, keep things simple.

7.3.4.2 Dependencies

Any dependencies between activities (and products) should also be identified. There are two types of dependency: **internal** and **external**. An example of an internal dependency is that activity C cannot start until activities A and B have been completed. External dependencies may, for example, be:

- The delivery of a product required by this project from another project
- The provision of a purchase order by the user
- A decision from programme management.

Examples of estimating techniques

- **Top-down estimating** Once a good overall estimate has been arrived at for the plan (by whatever means), it can be subdivided through the levels of the product breakdown structure. By way of example, historically development may be 50% of the total and testing may be 25%. Subdivide development and testing into their components and apportion the effort accordingly
- **Bottom-up estimating** Each individual piece of work is estimated on its own merit. These are then summed together to find the estimated efforts for the various summary level activities and overall plan
- **Top-down and bottom-up approach** An overall estimate is calculated for the plan. Individual estimates are then calculated, or drawn from previous plans, to represent the relative weights of the tasks. The overall estimate is then apportioned across the various summary and detailed-level tasks using the bottom-up figures as weights
- **Comparative estimating** Much data exist about the effort required and the duration of particular items of work. Over time an organization may build up its own historical data regarding projects that it has undertaken (previous experience or lessons learned). Where such data exists, it may be useful to reference it for similar projects and apply that data to the estimates
- **Parametric estimating** Basing estimates on measured/empirical data where possible (for example, estimating models exist in the construction industry that predict materials, effort and duration based on the specification of a building)
- **Single-point estimating** The use of sample data to calculate a single value which is to serve as a 'best guess' for the duration of an activity
- **Three-point estimating** Ask appropriately skilled resource(s) for their best-case, most likely and worst-case estimates. The value that the Project Manager should choose is the weighted average of these three estimates

- **Delphi technique** This relies on obtaining group input for ideas and problem solving without requiring face-to-face participation. It uses a series of questionnaires interspersed with information summaries and feedback from preceding responses to achieve an estimate.

7.3.5 Prepare estimates

A decision about how much time and resource are required to carry out a piece of work to acceptable standards of performance must be made by:

- Identifying the type of resource required. Specific skills may be required depending on the type and complexity of the plan. Requirements may include non-human resources, such as equipment, travel or money
- Estimating the effort required for each activity by resource type. At this point, the estimates will be approximate and therefore provisional.

Estimating cannot guarantee accuracy but, when applied, provides a view about the overall cost and time required to complete the plan. Estimates will inevitably change as more is discovered about the project.

Estimates should be challenged, as the same work under the same conditions can be estimated differently by various estimators or by the same estimator at different times.

Basic rules for estimating

Many books and software packages include some basic rules to help ensure that an accurate and realistic estimate is produced. Examples of such planning rules include:

- Assume that resources will only be productive for, say, 80% of their time
- Resources working on multiple projects take longer to complete tasks because of time lost switching between them
- People are generally optimistic and often underestimate how long tasks will take
- Make use of other people's experiences and your own
- Ensure that the person responsible for creating the product is also responsible for creating the effort estimates

- Always build in provision for problem solving, meetings and other unexpected events
- Cost each activity rather than trying to cost the plan as a whole
- Communicate any assumptions, exclusions or constraints you have to the user(s).

7.3.6 Prepare the schedule

A plan can only show the ultimate feasibility of achieving its objectives when the activities are put together in a schedule that defines when each activity will be carried out. There are many different approaches to scheduling. Scheduling can either be done manually or by using a computer-based planning and control tool.

7.3.6.1 Define activity sequence

Having identified the activities, their dependencies and estimated their duration and effort, the next task is to determine the optimal sequence in which they can be performed.

This is an iterative task as the assigning of actual resources may affect the estimated effort and duration.

The amount of time that an activity can be delayed without affecting the completion time of the overall plan is known as the **float** (sometimes referred to as the **slack)**. Float can either be regarded as a provision within the plan, or as spare time.

The critical path(s) through the diagram is the sequence of activities that have zero float. Thus, if any activity on the critical path(s) finishes late, then the whole plan will also finish late (for example, if task 4 in Figure 7.4 is delayed, then completion of the plan will be delayed).

Identifying a plan's critical path enables the Project Manager to monitor those activities:

- That must be completed on time for the whole plan to be completed to schedule
- That can be delayed for a time period if resources need to be re-allocated to catch up on missed activities.

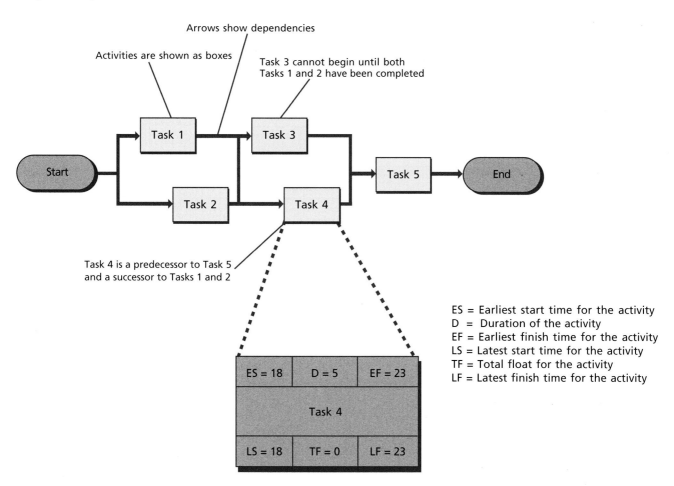

Figure 7.4   Simple activity-on-node diagram

Example of activity-on-node technique

An activity-on-node diagram (sometimes called an arrow diagram) can be used to schedule dependent activities within a plan. It helps a Project Manager to work out the most efficient sequence of events needed to complete any plan and enables the creation of a realistic schedule.

The activity-on-node diagram displays interdependencies between activities through the use of boxes and arrows. Arrows pointing into an activity box come from its predecessor activities, which must be completed before the activity can start. Arrows pointing out of an activity box go to its successor activities, which cannot start until at least this activity is complete. A simple activity-on-node diagram is shown in Figure 7.4.

7.3.6.2 Assess resource availability

The number of people who will be available to do the work (or the cost of buying in resources) should be established. Any specific information should be noted (for example, names, levels of experience, percentage availability, available dates).

7.3.6.3 Assign resources

Using the resource availability and the information from the activity sequence allows the Project Manager to assign resources to activities. The result will be a schedule that shows the loading of work on each person, and the use of non-human resources.

A useful approach is to allocate resources to those activities with zero slack first (by definition they are on the critical path). Those activities with the greatest slack are the lowest priority for resource allocation.

It is important that task owners be defined. If a group needs to complete a task, ask one person from the group to be accountable to the group for that task.

If any of the task owners do not participate in creating the schedule, make sure you check with them first on their availability and willingness to own the task. Do not assume that putting their names on a plan or schedule will automatically get the work done. Collaborate, communicate and follow up with each task owner to make sure that they understand what it means to complete the task.

When assigning resources, it is important to re-check the critical path as actual resources assigned may be more or less productive than the assumption made when calculating activity effort and duration.

7.3.6.4 Level resource usage

The first allocation of resources may lead to uneven resource usage or over-utilization of some resources. It may therefore be necessary to rearrange resources – this is called **levelling**.

Activities may be reassigned, or they may have start dates and durations changed within the slack available.

The end result is a final schedule with all activities assigned and resource utilization equating to resource availability.

The critical chain technique

The critical chain method of planning puts more emphasis on the resources required to execute the plan and their availability. This is in contrast to traditional methods, which emphasize task order and rigid scheduling. A critical chain network will tend to keep the resources levelly loaded, but will require them to be flexible in their start times and to switch quickly between tasks and task chains to keep the whole plan on schedule.

7.3.6.5 Agree control points

The draft schedule enables the control points to be confirmed by the Project Board.

Activities relating to the end of a management stage (for example, preparing the End Stage Report and the next Stage Plan) should be added to the activity network and the schedule revised.

One common mistake when creating a schedule is not to allow time for approvals of products or releases.

7.3.6.6 Define milestones

A milestone is an event on a schedule which marks the completion of key activities. This could be the completion of a Work Package, a technical stage or a management stage. In a commercial environment, reaching a milestone may be the trigger for a payment to a supplier.

Breaking the plan into intervals associated with a milestone allows the Project Manager to have an early indication of issues associated with the schedule itself, and also a better view of the activities whose completion is critical to the timeline of the plan.

While there is no 'correct' number of milestones or duration between them, they lose their value when there are too many or too few. There should be far fewer milestones than deliverables or Work Packages, but there should be enough milestones at major intervals to gauge whether or not the plan is proceeding as expected.

7.3.6.7 Calculate total resource requirements and costs

The resource requirements can be tabulated, and the cost of the resources and other costs calculated to produce the plan's budget.

The budget should include:

- Costs of the activities to develop and verify the specialist products, and the cost of the project management activities
- Risk budget (see Chapter 8)
- Change budget (see Chapter 9)
- Cost tolerances.

The use of risk budgets and change budgets is optional.

7.3.6.8 Present the schedule

A schedule is best presented in a graphical form. There are a number of ways of presenting a schedule and the choice of format will depend on the scale and complexity of the plan and the needs of the people who will receive it. Most planning tools will offer a choice of formats to view the schedule.

7.3.7 Analyse the risks

This planning activity will typically run parallel with the other steps, as risks may be identified at any point in the creation or revision of a plan.

Each resource and activity, and all the planning information, should be examined for its potential risk content. All identified risks should be entered into the Risk Register (or the Daily Log when planning the initiation stage).

Examples of presentation formats for the schedule

Gantt charts

A Gantt chart is a graphical representation of the duration of tasks against the progression of time. It allows the Project Manager to:

- Assess how long a plan should take
- Lay out the order in which tasks need to be carried out
- Manage the dependencies between tasks
- See what should have been achieved at a certain point in time
- See how remedial action may bring the plan back on course.

Critical path diagram

A critical path diagram highlights those tasks which cannot be delayed without causing the plan to be delayed, and those tasks that can be delayed without affecting the end date of the plan. It helps with monitoring and communication.

Spreadsheets

It is possible to create a list of tasks 'down' the spreadsheet and a timeline 'across' it, then colour in the cells to represent where the tasks will occur in the timeline, and progress to date. For simple projects where the timeline is unlikely to change, this may be adequate. For large or complex projects, the timeline may change frequently. This means that the Project Manager may spend a significant amount of time changing the schedule while neglecting the day-to-day tasks required in order to manage the project.

Product checklist

A product checklist is a list of the major products of a plan, plus key dates in their delivery. An example of a product checklist is shown in the Product Description outline for a plan in Appendix A.

Once the plan has been produced, it should still be considered a draft until the risks inherent in the plan have been identified, assessed and the plan possibly modified.

See Chapter 8 for more details on identifying and analysing risks.

Examples of planning risks

- Omission of plans at the appropriate management level(s)
- Lots of resources joining the project at the same time can slow progress and cause communication issues (plotting an S-curve for the resource profile over time can identify this – steep curves should be avoided)
- The plan includes unnamed resources, causing the productivity of the actual resource to differ from the estimated productivity in the plan
- The plan contains a high proportion of external dependencies
- The plan uses untested suppliers or is dependent on new technologies
- There is a high proportion of activities on the critical path – a delay to any one of them will delay the plan
- The plan does not allow for sufficient management decision points such as stage boundaries
- There is not much float in the plan (creating a histogram showing the number of activities by amount of float is a useful way of identifying this risk)
- A large number of products are to be completed at the same time
- The plan is time-bound by fiscal boundaries (e.g. the budget cannot be transferred from this year to the next) or by calendar boundaries (e.g. millennium bug projects were calendar-bound)
- The schedule shows many paths narrowly paralleling the critical path are likely to become critical themselves if there is a minor slip.

7.3.8 Document the plan

Having completed the schedule satisfactorily, the plan, its costs, the required controls and its supporting text need to be consolidated in accordance with the plan design.

Narrative needs to be added to explain the plan, any constraints on it, external dependencies, assumptions made, any monitoring and control required, the risks identified and their required responses.

It is a good discipline to keep plans as simple as is appropriate. Consider summary diagrams if the plan is to be presented to the Project Board.

It may be sensible to have one plan format for presentation in submissions seeking approval, and a more detailed format for day-to-day control purposes. Also consider different levels of presentation of the plan for the different levels of readership. Most planning software packages offer such options.

See Appendix A for the suggested composition of a plan.

7.4 RESPONSIBILITIES

Table 7.1 outlines the responsibilities relevant to the Plans theme. Refer to Appendix C for further details of project management team roles and their associated responsibilities.

Table 7.1 Responsibilities relevant to the Plans theme

Role	Responsibilities
Corporate or programme management	Set project tolerances and document them in the project mandate.
	Approve Exception Plans when project-level tolerances are forecast to be exceeded.
	Provide the corporate or programme management planning standards.
Executive	Approve the Project Plan.
	Define tolerances for each stage and approve Stage Plans.
	Approve Exception Plans when stage-level tolerances are forecast to be exceeded.
	Commit business resources to Stage Plans (e.g. finance).
Senior User	Ensure that Project Plans and Stage Plans remain consistent from the user perspective.
	Commit user resources to Stage Plans.
Senior Supplier	Ensure that Project Plans and Stage Plans remain consistent from the supplier perspective.
	Commit supplier resources to Stage Plans.
Project Manager	Design the plans.
	Prepare the Project Plan and Stage Plans.
	Decide how management and technical stages are to be applied.
	Instruct corrective action when Work Package-level tolerances are forecast to be exceeded.
	Prepare an Exception Plan to implement corporate management, programme management or the Project Board's decision in response to Exception Reports.
Team Manager	Prepare Team Plans.
	Prepare schedules for each Work Package.
Project Assurance	Monitor changes to the Project Plan to see whether there is any impact on the needs of the business or the project Business Case.
	Monitor stage and project progress against agreed tolerances.
Project Support	Assist with the compilation of Project Plans, Stage Plans and Team Plans.
	Contribute specialist expertise (for example, planning tools).
	Baseline, store and distribute Project Plans, Stage Plans and Team Plans.

8

Risk

8 Risk

8.1 PURPOSE

The purpose of the Risk theme is to identify, assess and control uncertainty and, as a result, improve the ability of the project to succeed.

Risk taking in projects is inevitable since projects are enablers of change and change introduces uncertainty, hence risk.

Management of risk should be systematic and not based on chance. It is about the proactive identification, assessment and control of risks that might affect the delivery of the project's objectives.

The project should establish and maintain a cost-effective risk management procedure. The aim is to support better decision making through a good understanding of risks – their causes, likelihood, impact, timing, and the choice of responses to them.

Management of risk is a continual activity, performed throughout the life of the project. Without an ongoing and effective risk management procedure it is not possible to give confidence that the project is able to meet its objectives and therefore whether it is worthwhile for it to continue. Hence effective risk management is a prerequisite of the continued business justification principle.

8.2 RISK DEFINED

8.2.1 What is a risk?

A risk is an uncertain event or set of events that, should it occur, will have an effect on the achievement of objectives. It consists of a combination of the probability of a perceived threat or opportunity occurring, and the magnitude of its impact on objectives, where:

- **Threat** is used to describe an uncertain event that could have a negative impact on objectives
- **Opportunity** is used to describe an uncertain event that could have a favourable impact on objectives.

8.2.2 What is at risk?

In the context of a project, it is the project's objectives that are at risk. These will include completing the project to a number of targets, typically covering time, cost, quality, scope, benefits and risk.

For more information on these targets, see section 2.5.

8.2.3 What is risk management?

The term risk management refers to the systematic application of procedures to the tasks of identifying and assessing risks, and then planning and implementing risk responses. This provides a disciplined environment for proactive decision making.

For risk management to be effective, risks need to be:

- **Identified** This includes risks being considered that could affect the achievement of the project's objectives, and then described to ensure that there is a common understanding of these risks
- **Assessed** This includes ensuring that each risk can be ranked in terms of estimated likelihood, impact and immediacy, and understanding the overall level of risk associated with the project
- **Controlled** This includes identifying appropriate responses to risks, assigning risk owners, and then executing, monitoring and controlling these responses.

Risk management applies from the strategic, operational, programme and project perspectives. The approach to the management of risk can be common across all of these perspectives but risk management procedures should be tailored to suit each one. See Figure 8.1 for organizational perspectives.

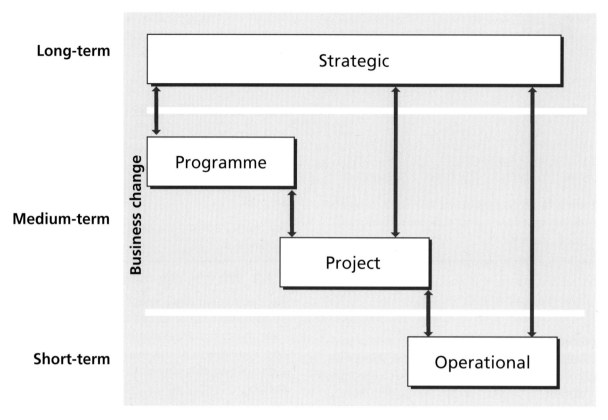

Figure 8.1 Organizational perspectives

8.3 THE PRINCE2 APPROACH TO RISK

8.3.1 Management of Risk (M_o_R®) principles

PRINCE2's approach to the management of risk is based on OGC's publication *Management of Risk: Guidance for Practitioners* (TSO, 2007). Management of risk is based on a number of risk management principles, of which the following are appropriate within a project context:

- Understand the project's context
- Involve stakeholders
- Establish clear project objectives
- Develop the project risk management approach
- Report on risks regularly
- Define clear roles and responsibilities
- Establish a support structure and a supportive culture for risk management
- Monitor for early warning indicators
- Establish a review cycle and look for continual improvement.

8.3.2 Risk management in projects

A starting point for all projects will be to identify whether there are any corporate or programme policies and processes that need to be applied. This information may be in the form of a risk management policy and/or a risk management process guide (or similar documents).

- An organization's risk management policy should communicate how risk management will be implemented throughout the organization to support the realization of its strategic objectives. This will include information such as the organization's risk appetite (an organization's unique attitude towards risk taking that in turn dictates the amount of risk that it considers acceptable), risk tolerances, procedures for escalation and defined roles and responsibilities
- An organization's risk management process guide should describe the series of steps and their respective associated activities necessary to implement risk management. This guide

should provide a best-practice approach that will support a consistent method of risk management across the organization.

Where the project forms part of the programme, the project's approach to risk management will be determined by the programme's Risk Management Strategy.

PRINCE2 recommends that every project should have its own Risk Management Strategy (defining the project procedures for risk management from identification through to implementation) and a means of control, i.e. the Risk Register.

For more information on the risk management policy and process guide documents, see OGC's *Management of Risk: Guidance for Practitioners* (TSO, 2007).

8.3.3 Risk Management Strategy

Having reviewed the organizational- and programme-level documents, and before embarking on any risk management activities, a Risk Management Strategy should be developed for the project. The purpose of this strategy is to describe how risk management will be embedded in the project management activities.

A key decision that needs to be recorded within the Risk Management Strategy is the Project Board's attitude towards risk taking, which in turn dictates the amount of risk that it considers acceptable. This information is captured in the form of risk tolerances, which represent the levels of exposure that, when exceeded, will trigger an Exception Report to bring the situation to the attention of the Project Board.

Example of risk tolerance

A large electrical retailer would not tolerate any unnecessary disruption to its support systems during the peak trading period, which extends from the middle of November through to the end of January. Projects are not permitted to introduce any changes to the support systems during this period. Therefore any risks in the Risk Register that mean the support systems would change in this peak trading window would need to be escalated to the Project Board.

See Appendix A for the Product Description of a Risk Management Strategy.

8.3.4 Risk Register

The purpose of the Risk Register is to capture and maintain information on all of the identified threats and opportunities relating to the project. Each risk on the Risk Register is allocated a unique identifier as well as details such as:

- Who raised the risk
- When it was raised
- The category of risk
- The description of the risk (cause, event, effect)
- Probability, impact and expected value
- Proximity
- Risk response category
- Risk response actions
- Risk status
- Risk owner
- Risk actionee.

Project Support will typically maintain the Risk Register on behalf of the Project Manager. The Risk Management Strategy will describe the procedure for registering risks and maintaining the risk register.

See Appendix A for the Product Description of a Risk Register.

8.3.5 Risk management procedure

PRINCE2 recommends a risk management procedure comprising the following five steps:

- Identify (context and risks)
- Assess (i.e. Estimate and Evaluate)
- Plan
- Implement
- Communicate.

The first four steps are sequential, with the 'Communicate' step running in parallel because the findings of any of the other steps may need to be communicated prior to the completion of the overall process. All of the steps are iterative in nature in that when additional information becomes available, it is often necessary to revisit earlier steps and carry them out again to achieve the most effective result.

Figure 8.2 shows the elements of the risk management procedure, which are described in sections 8.3.5.1–8.3.5.5.

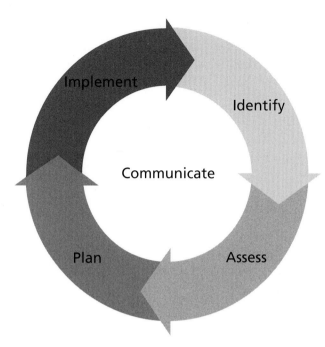

Figure 8.2 The risk management procedure

8.3.5.1 Identify

Identify context

The primary goal of the 'Identify context' step is to obtain information about the project in order to understand the specific objectives that are at risk and to formulate the Risk Management Strategy for the project. The Risk Management Strategy describes how risks will be managed during the project. It is created during the initiation stage and then reviewed and possibly updated at the end of each stage. The project's Risk Management Strategy should be based on the corporate risk management policy or on the programme's Risk Management Strategy.

The following will have an influence on the project's Risk Management Strategy:

- Customer's quality expectations
- Number of organizations involved and the relationship between them
- The needs of the stakeholders involved with the project
- The importance, complexity and scale of the project
- What assumptions have been made
- The organization's own environment (e.g. legislative or governance requirements)
- The organization's approach to risk management as described by its risk management policy.

This information will be derived from the project mandate, the Project Brief and the Project Product Description. The Risk Management Strategy will include decisions on the:

- Risk management procedure
- Tools and techniques to be used
- Records to be kept
- Risk reporting
- Timing of risk management activities
- Roles and responsibilities for the risk management procedure
- Risk scales to be used (for probability, impact, proximity)
- Any categorization of risks (and possibly the risk breakdown structure to use)
- Risk response categories to be used
- Early warning indicators
- Any risk tolerances
- Whether a risk budget will be established and, if so, how it will be controlled.

The early warning indicators (relevant to the project) will provide advanced warning that one or more of the project's objectives could be at risk. Early warning indicators could include progress performance data (see Chapter 10) such as:

- Percentage of Work Packages accomplished/not accomplished to schedule
- Percentage of approvals accomplished/not accomplished to schedule
- Number of issues being raised (per week/ month)
- Percentage of issues that remain unresolved
- Average number of days that issues remain unresolved
- Average number of defects captured in quality inspections
- Adherence to budget (e.g. rate of spend behind or ahead of planned spend)
- Adherence to schedule (e.g. days behind or ahead of schedule).

Other early warning indicators could include non-project data such as customer satisfaction, absenteeism levels, staff attrition rates etc., if they are relevant to the project. It is also useful to analyse and report on the direction of travel of these early warning indicators (i.e. are they improving/deteriorating) as that can be of more significance than their snapshot value.

Risk identification techniques

Risks can be identified using a number of techniques, such as:

- **Review lessons** Risks are driven by uncertainty, so one of the most effective ways to reduce uncertainty is to review similar previous projects to see what threats and opportunities affected them
- **Risk checklists** These are in-house lists of risks that have either been identified or have occurred on previous similar projects. Risk checklists are useful aids to ensure that risks identified on previous projects are not overlooked
- **Risk prompt lists** These are publicly available lists that categorize risks into types or areas and are normally relevant to a wide range of projects. Risk prompt lists are useful aids to help stimulate thinking about sources of risk in the widest context
- **Brainstorming** This enables group thinking, which can be more productive than individual thinking. However, it is important to avoid criticism during the brainstorm as this can stop people contributing. In addition to identifying risks, brainstorming can also be used to understand the stakeholders' views of the risks identified
- **Risk breakdown structure** This is a hierarchical decomposition of the project environment assembled to illustrate potential sources of risk. Each descending level represents an increasingly detailed definition of sources of risk to the project. The structure acts as a prompt and an aid to support the project management team in thinking through the potential sources of risk to the objectives. There are numerous ways to break down risk and it may be useful to do more than one list. For example, a risk breakdown structure could be broken down by PESTLE (political, economical, sociological, technological, legal/legislative, environmental), product breakdown structure, stage, benefits/objectives etc. Figure 8.3 shows a risk breakdown structure relating to financial risk. These structures will help to identify appropriate risk owners to develop responses.

Identify risks

The primary goal of the 'Identify risks' step is to recognize the threats and opportunities that may affect the project's objectives.

PRINCE2 recommends the following actions:

- Capture identified threats and opportunities in the Risk Register
- Prepare early warning indicators to monitor critical aspects of the project and provide information on the potential causes of risk
- Understand the stakeholders' view of the specific risks captured.

An effective way of identifying risks is to use a risk workshop. This is a group session designed to identify threats and opportunities. The session should be facilitated by someone who is able to use a range of identification techniques, such as those listed in the boxed example. Workshops should lead to the identification of a broad range of risks and possible risk owners.

An important aspect of identifying risks is being able to provide a clear and unambiguous expression of each one. A useful way of expressing risk is to consider the following aspects of each risk:

- **Risk cause** This should describe the source of the risk, i.e. the event or situation that gives rise to the risk. These are often referred to as risk drivers. They are not risks in themselves, but the potential trigger points for risk. These may be either internal or external to the project
- **Risk event** This should describe the area of uncertainty in terms of the threat or the opportunity
- **Risk effect** This should describe the impact(s) that the risk would have on the project objectives should the risk materialize.

The cause, event and effect relationship is shown in Figure 8.4.

The cause, event and effect relationship could also be expressed in a sentence, for example:

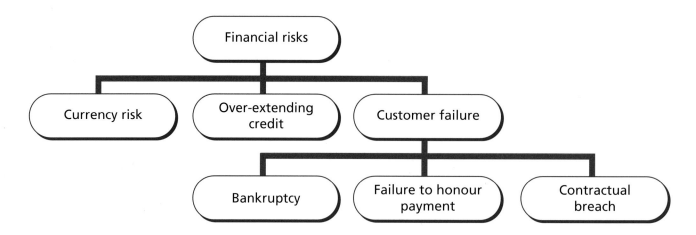

Figure 8.3 Example of a risk breakdown structure

- **Threat** Because it has been raining heavily (risk cause), there is a threat that the river flowing through the farmer's field might overflow (risk event), which would severely damage the farmer's crop (risk effect)
- **Opportunity** Because the weather has been particularly mild this winter (risk cause), there is an opportunity that fewer people will be hospitalized with influenza (risk event), which will mean that there will be less disruption to planned routine operations (risk effect).

8.3.5.2 Assess

Estimate

The primary goal of the 'Estimate' step is to assess the threats and the opportunities to the project in terms of their probability and impact. The risk proximity will also be of interest to gauge how quickly the risk is likely to materialize if no action were taken.

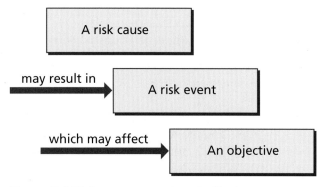

Figure 8.4 Risk cause, event and effect

Risk estimation techniques

Risks can be estimated using a number of techniques, such as:

- **Probability trees** These are graphical representations of possible events resulting from given circumstances. A probability tree can be used to predict an outcome in a qualitative way when historical data is used to populate the likelihood of each circumstance happening. Probability trees assist in communicating to project participants or decision makers the likelihood of the different possible outcomes to a set of circumstances

- **Expected value** This technique quantifies risk by combining the cost of the risk impact with the probability of the risk occurring. Expected value is useful when a tangible measure of risk is required to enable risks to be prioritized. For example, if the cost of a risk was £160,000 and its likelihood of occurrence was estimated at 25%, then the expected value would be £40,000

- **Pareto analysis** This technique ranks or orders risks once they have been assessed to determine the order in which they should be addressed. Pareto analysis can be used to focus management effort on those risks that have the potential to have the greatest impact on the project objectives

- **Probability impact grid** This grid contains ranking values that may be used to rank threats and opportunities qualitatively. The probability scales are measures of probability derived from percentages, and the impact scales are selected to reflect the level of impact on project objectives. The values within the grid cells are the combination of a particular probability and impact, and are determined by multiplying the probability by the impact. A probability impact grid can be used to provide an assessment of the severity of a risk and enable risks to be ranked so that management time and effort can be prioritized. For example, the Project Board may set their risk tolerance at any risk with a value of greater than 0.18, and they may require a proactive response for any risk with a value of greater than 0.045, as depicted by the dark shading shown in Figure 8.5.

PRINCE2 recommends that the following is understood:

■ The probability of the threats and opportunities in terms of how likely they are to occur

■ The impact of each threat and opportunity in terms of the project objectives. For example, if the objectives are measured in time and cost, the impact should also be measured in units of time and cost

■ The proximity of these threats and opportunities with regard to when they might materialize

■ How the impact of the threats and opportunities may change over the life of the project.

A useful way of summarizing the set of risks and their estimations is to plot them onto a summary risk profile, an example of which is shown in Figure 8.6. This profile represents a situation at a specific point in time, i.e. a snapshot of the risk environment. The numbered markers in the matrix represent unique risk identifiers used in the Risk Register on which this is based. The risks above and to the right of the dotted risk tolerance line represent those that the organization will not tolerate except under special circumstances. In the depicted case, the Project Manager would refer risks 1, 3 and 4 to the Project Board.

The summary risk profile can also be used to show trends. For example, risk 6 may have previously been recorded as 'low probability, high impact', indicating that its likelihood of occurring is increasing.

Evaluate

The primary goal of the 'Evaluate' step is to assess the net effect of all the identified threats and opportunities on a project when aggregated together. This will enable an assessment to be made of the overall severity of the risks facing the project, to determine whether this level of risk is within the risk tolerance set by the Project Board and whether the project has continued business justification.

Risk evaluation techniques

Risks can be evaluated by using techniques such as:

■ **Risk models** Take, for example, the Monte Carlo analysis. This model enables simulation of 'what if' scenarios using random numbers to determine whether each risk within a given range occurs or not. The simulations are repeatedly run to predict the 'average' level of risk to the project's time or cost. The scenarios can also be used to model extreme cases (e.g. if nearly all the risks occur)

■ **Expected monetary value** This technique takes the expected values of a number of risks and sums them to arrive at an overall value. It provides a quick and easy assessment of a group of risks to understand their combined effect. An example is shown in Table 8.1.

Table 8.1 Example of the expected monetary value technique

Risk ID	Likelihood (%)	Impact (£)	Expected value (£)
1	60	20,000	12,000
2	30	13,000	3,900
3	10	4,000	400
4	5	10,000	500
Expected monetary value			16,800

8.3.5.3 Plan

The primary goal of the 'Plan' step is to prepare specific management responses to the threats and opportunities identified, ideally to remove or reduce the threats and to maximize the opportunities. Attention to the Plan step ensures as far as possible that the project is not taken by surprise if a risk materializes.

Probability			Impact				
0.9	Very high 71–90%		0.045	0.09	0.18	0.36	0.72
0.7	High 51–70%		0.035	0.07	0.14	0.28	0.56
0.5	Medium 31–50%		0.025	0.05	0.10	0.20	0.40
0.3	Low 11–30%		0.015	0.03	0.06	0.12	0.24
0.1	Very low up to 10%		0.005	0.01	0.02	0.04	0.08
			Very low	Low	Medium	High	Very high
			0.05	0.1	0.2	0.4	0.8
					Impact		

Figure 8.5 Probability impact grid

The Plan step involves identifying and evaluating a range of options for responding to threats and opportunities. It is important that the risk response is proportional to the risk and that it offers value for money. A key factor in the selection of responses will be balancing the cost of implementing the responses against the probability and impact of allowing the risk to occur. Any chosen responses should be built into the appropriate level of plan, with a provision made for any fallback plans.

The various types of response for threats and opportunities are summarized in Figure 8.7.

The types of response are explained further in Table 8.2.

Risk responses do not necessarily remove the inherent risk in its entirety, leaving residual risk. If the inherent risk was significant and the risk response was only partially successful, the residual risk can be considerable. It may be appropriate to select more than one risk response.

In some cases, implementing a risk response will reduce or remove other related risks. It is also possible that the responses to risks, once implemented, will change some aspect of the project. This in turn may lead to secondary risks, i.e. risks that may occur as a result of invoking a risk response. It is essential that these are identified, assessed and controlled in the same way as the inherent risk.

It is advisable to review lessons from previous similar projects when planning risk responses. This will help in identifying the range of responses available and in evaluating how effective they are likely to be.

Prob. / Impact	Very low	Low	Medium	High	Very high
Very high				❶❸	
High	⑪				❹
Medium		❽		❻	
Low		❿		❼	
Very low	❾		❷		❺

- - - - - Risk tolerance line

Figure 8.6 Summary risk profile

Threat responses	Opportunity responses
Avoid	Exploit
Reduce (probability and/or impact) Fallback (reduces impact only) Transfer (reduces impact only, and often only the financial impact)	Enhance
Share	
Accept	Reject

Figure 8.7 Threat and opportunity responses

Consideration should also be given to the effect the possible responses could have on:

- The Project Plan, Stage Plan and Work Packages
- The Business Case
- Corporate and/or programme management.

8.3.5.4 Implement

The primary goal of the 'Implement' step is to ensure that the planned risk responses are actioned, their effectiveness monitored, and corrective action taken where responses do not match expectations.

An important part of the Implement step is to ensure that there are clear roles and responsibilities allocated to support the Project Manager in the management of project risks. The main roles in this respect are:

- **Risk owner** A named individual who is responsible for the management, monitoring and control of all aspects of a particular risk assigned to them, including the implementation of the selected responses to address the threats or to maximize the opportunities

- **Risk actionee** An individual assigned to carry out a risk response action or actions to respond to a particular risk or set of risks. They support and take direction from the risk owner.

Example of a risk owner and risk actionee

There is a risk that a key supplier may go bankrupt. The commercial director has been appointed as the risk owner. A number of risk responses have been identified and selected. One of the risk responses (fallback) is to identify possible alternative suppliers who have the capacity to undertake the affected Work Packages at short notice, and to obtain some quotes from them. The Procurement Manager is the risk actionee for this particular risk response.

In many cases, the risk owner and risk actionee are likely to be the same person. The risk owner should be the person most capable of managing the risk. Allocating too many risks to any one individual should be avoided.

Table 8.2 Risk responses

Response	Definition	Example
Avoid (threat)	Typically involves changing some aspect of the project, i.e. the scope, procurement route, supplier or sequence of activities, so that the threat either can no longer have an impact or can no longer happen.	A critical meeting could be threatened by air travel disruption so the project chooses to hold the meeting by conference call instead.
Reduce (threat)	Proactive actions taken to: ■ Reduce the probability of the event occurring, by performing some form of control ■ Reduce the impact of the event should it occur.	To reduce the likelihood of users not using a product, the number of training events is increased. To reduce the timescale impact should a prototype be damaged in transit, two prototypes are built.
Fallback (threat)	Putting in place a fallback plan for the actions that will be taken to reduce the impact of the threat should the risk occur. This is a reactive form of the 'reduce' response which has no impact on likelihood.	The company's test facility is only available for two weeks in August. To reduce the impact should the product not be available in time, there is a fallback plan to hire an alternate test facility (at a greater expense).
Transfer (threat)	A third party takes on responsibility for some of the financial impact of the threat. (For example, through insurance or by means of appropriate clauses in a contract.) This is a form of the 'reduce' response which only reduces the financial impact of the threat.	To reduce the financial impact should a prototype be damaged in transit, it is insured. To reduce the financial impact if a product is not available to launch in time for a trade show, the contract with the supplier includes liquidated damage clauses for any delays.
Accept (threat)	A conscious and deliberate decision is taken to retain the threat, having discerned that it is more economical to do so than to attempt a threat response action. The threat should continue to be monitored to ensure that it remains tolerable.	There is a threat that a competitor may launch a rival product first, thus affecting the expected market share for the product. The choice is to accelerate the project by increasing the resources, to reduce the product's scope so that it can be finished earlier, or to do nothing. Accelerating the project may lead to product quality issues; reducing the scope may make the product less appealing; so the risk is accepted and the 'do nothing' option is chosen.
Share (threat or opportunity)	Modern procurement methods commonly entail a form of risk sharing through the application of a pain/gain formula: both parties share the gain (within pre-agreed limits) if the cost is less than the cost plan; and share the pain (again within pre-agreed limits) if the cost plan is exceeded. Several industries include risk-sharing principles within their contracts with third parties.	The cost of the project could be adversely affected due to fluctuations in the cost of oil. The customer and supplier agree to share the cost of price increases or the savings from price reductions equally from a midpoint fixed at the time of agreeing the contract.
Exploit (opportunity)	Seizing an opportunity to ensure that the opportunity **will** happen and that the impact **will** be realized.	There is a risk that the project will be delayed. If it is delayed, a later version of software could be implemented instead which would reduce ongoing maintenance. The Project Board agree to change the project timescale and scope, enabling the later version of the software to be bought and implemented.

Enhance (opportunity)	Proactive actions taken to: ▪ Enhance the probability of the event occurring ▪ Enhance the impact of the event should it occur.	It is possible that the product completes user acceptance testing in a single test cycle, rather than the scheduled two, enabling it to be delivered early and prior to a competitor's rival product. The Project Board decide to hold a test rehearsal to increase the likelihood that the product will pass its first user acceptance tests, and prepare for the option of an earlier launch date.
Reject (opportunity)	A conscious and deliberate decision is taken not to exploit or enhance the opportunity, having discerned that it is more economical not to attempt an opportunity response action. The opportunity should continue to be monitored.	It is possible that the product completes user acceptance testing in a single test cycle, rather than the scheduled two, enabling it to be delivered early and prior to a competitor's rival product. The Project Board decide not to take advantage of an early release and to stick with the planned launch date.

8.3.5.5 Communicate

Communication is a step that is carried out continually. The 'Communicate' step should ensure that information related to the threats and opportunities faced by the project is communicated both within the project and externally to stakeholders. Risks are communicated as part of the following management products:

- Checkpoint Reports
- Highlight Reports
- End Stage Reports
- End Project Reports
- Lessons Reports.

Care should be taken in using these reports to communicate risks with external stakeholders and reference should be made to the Communication Management Strategy for the most appropriate method.

There are numerous other communication methods, such as bulletins, notice boards, dashboards, discussion threads, briefings etc., that could be considered alongside the PRINCE2 management products.

A number of aspects of communication should be recognized and addressed if risk management is to be effective:

- A project's exposure to risk is never static: effective communication is key to the identification of new risks or changes in existing risks. This depends on the maintenance of a good communications network, including relevant contacts and sources of information, to facilitate the identification of changes that may affect the project's overall risk exposure
- Effective risk management is dependent on participation and, in turn, participation is dependent on effective communication.

8.3.6 Risk budget

A risk budget, if used, is a sum of money included within the project budget and set aside to fund specific management responses to the project's threats and opportunities (for example, to cover the costs of any fallback plans should they need to be implemented).

In order to arrive at a risk budget for the project, a financial approach to risk management is needed. Each risk must be fully analysed for the impact costs, response costs and likelihood. The aggregation of the costs (for responses and impact) weighted by each risk's probability generates the expected monetary value for the set of risks. The expected monetary value can be used to determine a risk budget. The assumption is that the risk budget is expected to be used over the course of the project. Care needs to be taken that the aggregation of the factored costs is not skewed by a small number of large risks. This is where analytical techniques, such as Monte Carlo analysis and associated software tools, can help.

As the risk budget is part of the project budget, there may be a tendency to treat it as just another sum of money that the Project Manager can spend. This culture should be discouraged in favour of the Risk Management Strategy defining the mechanisms for control of, and access to, this budget. As the project progresses, some of the risks previously identified will occur and others will not. New risks may be identified during the life of the project whose response costs will not have been included within the risk budget. It is always prudent to set the risk budget to cover the known risks (as identified) and to make a provision for unknown risks (yet to be identified).

8.4 RESPONSIBILITIES

Table 8.3 outlines the responsibilities relevant to the Risk theme. Refer to Appendix C for further details of project management team roles and their associated responsibilities.

Table 8.3 Responsibilities relevant to the Risk theme

Role	Responsibilities
Corporate or programme management	Provide the corporate risk management policy and risk management process guide (or similar documents).
Executive	Be accountable for all aspects of risk management and, in particular, ensure a project Risk Management Strategy exists.
	Ensure that risks associated with the Business Case are identified, assessed and controlled.
	Escalate risks to corporate or programme management as necessary.
Senior User	Ensure that risks to the users are identified, assessed and controlled (such as the impact on benefits, operational use and maintenance).
Senior Supplier	Ensure that risks relating to the supplier aspects are identified, assessed and controlled (such as the creation of the project's products).
Project Manager	Create the Risk Management Strategy.
	Create and maintain the Risk Register.
	Ensure that project risks are being identified, assessed and controlled throughout the project lifecycle.
Team Manager	Participate in the identification, assessment and control of risks.
Project Assurance	Review risk management practices to ensure that they are performed in line with the project's Risk Management Strategy.
Project Support	Assist the Project Manager in maintaining the project's Risk Register.

Change

9

9 Change

9.1 PURPOSE

> The purpose of the Change theme is to identify, assess and control any potential and approved changes to the baseline.

Change is inevitable during the life of a project, and every project needs a systematic approach to the identification, assessment and control of issues that may result in change.

As changes may arise from project team members, stakeholder requests, complaints or a wide range of other factors, PRINCE2 provides a common approach to issue and change control.

PRINCE2 provides both a systematic and common approach, which ensures that issues possibly affecting the project's performance targets (time, cost, quality, scope, risk and benefits) are appropriately managed.

Issue and change control is a continual activity, performed throughout the life of the project. Without an ongoing and effective issue and change control procedure, a project will either become totally unresponsive to its stakeholders or quickly drift out of control.

The aim of issue and change control procedures is not to prevent changes; it is to ensure that every change is agreed by the relevant authority before it takes place. Change can only be considered in relation to an established status quo, i.e. a baseline. Therefore, a prerequisite of effective issue and change control is the establishment of an appropriate configuration management system which records baselines for the project's products and ensures that the correct versions are delivered to the customer.

9.2 CHANGE DEFINED

9.2.1 Issue and change control

Issue and change control procedures ensure that all issues and changes which may affect the project's agreed baselines are identified, assessed and either approved, rejected or deferred.

9.2.2 Configuration management

Configuration management is the technical and administrative activity concerned with the creation, maintenance and controlled change of configuration throughout the life of a product (or item).

A configuration item is an entity that is subject to configuration management. The entity may be a component of a product, a product or a set of products that form a release. For example:

- A component of a product: an electronic motor that is part of a piece of machinery
- A product: a piece of machinery
- A release: a piece of machinery, the refitted machine room, training materials, and the necessary health and safety certificates.

A release is a complete and consistent set of products that are managed, tested and deployed as a single entity to be handed over to the user(s).

Issue and change control procedures need to be integrated with the configuration management system used by the project.

9.2.3 Issues

PRINCE2 uses the term 'issue' to cover any relevant event that has happened, was not planned, and requires management action. It can be a concern, query, request for change, suggestion or off-specification raised during a project. Project issues can be about anything to do with the project.

9.2.4 Types of issue

Issues may be raised at any time during the project, by anyone with an interest in the project or its outcome.

Table 9.1 provides a summary of the different types of issue that need to be dealt with during a project.

Table 9.1 Types of issue

Types of issue	Definition	Examples
Request for change	A proposal for a change to a baseline.	The Senior User would like to increase the capacity of a product from 100 to 150 users.
Off-specification	Something that should be provided by the project, but currently is not (or is forecast not to be) provided. This might be a missing product or a product not meeting its specification.	Advice from a supplier that they can no longer deliver one of the products specified by the customer.
Problem/concern	Any other issue that the Project Manager needs to resolve or escalate.	Advice from a Team Manager that a team member has been taken ill and as a result the target end date for a Work Package will slip by a week.
		Notification that one of the suppliers has gone bankrupt, resulting in the need to identify and engage a new supplier.

9.3   THE PRINCE2 APPROACH TO CHANGE

9.3.1 Establish controls

The project's controls for issues, changes and configuration management will be defined and established by the Initiating a Project process and then reviewed and (if necessary) updated towards the end of each management stage by the Managing a Stage Boundary process. The following management products are used to establish and maintain the project's controls for issues, changes and configuration management:

- Configuration Management Strategy
- Configuration Item Records
- Product Status Accounts
- Daily Log
- Issue Register
- Issue Reports.

The importance and use of each of these management products are described in sections 9.3.1.1–9.3.1.6.

9.3.1.1 Configuration Management Strategy

Effective issue and change control is only possible if it is supported by a configuration management system that facilitates impact assessments (relationships between products) and maintains product baselines (the basis from which the entity will change).

The starting point for all projects will be to identify whether there are any corporate or programme policies and processes that need to be applied,

and incorporate them into the project's own Configuration Management Strategy. The project's Configuration Management Strategy should define:

- The configuration management procedure (e.g. planning, identification, control, status accounting, verification and audit)
- The issue and change control procedure (e.g. capturing, examining, proposing, decision making, implementing)
- The tools and techniques that will be used
- The records that will be kept
- How the performances of the procedures will be reported
- Timing of configuration management and issue and change control activities
- The roles and responsibilities for configuration management and issue and change control activities (including whether any corporate or programme management roles are to be involved).

The Configuration Management Strategy should define the way issues are handled. During the initiation stage, the Project Manager and Project Board need to agree:

- The scale for prioritizing issues
- The scale for rating the severity of issues
- What severity of issues can be handled at what management level.

Example of priority and severity

There are numerous ways to prioritize issues, one of which is called MoSCoW where (for requests for change) the issue is rated as either:

- **Must have**   The change is essential for the viability of the project
- **Should have**   The change is important and its absence weakens the Business Case
- **Could have**   The change is useful but its absence does not weaken the Business Case
- **Won't have (for now)**   The change is not essential nor important and can wait.

There are numerous ways to rate the severity of issues, such as numeric (e.g. 1–4) or descriptive (e.g. minor, significant, major, critical). The Project Manager and Project Board might agree that minor issues can be dealt with by the Project Manager, and significant issues by a Change Authority, but that major issues need to be escalated to the Project Board, and critical issues to corporate or programme management.

When deciding what severity of issues can be dealt with by what level of management, the Project Board may consider delegating some decision making for accepting/rejecting requests for change or off-specifications to a Change Authority and whether to provide a budget to pay for changes:

- **Change Authority**   It is the Project Board's responsibility to review and approve requests for change and off-specifications. In a project where few changes are envisaged, it may be reasonable to leave this authority in the hands of the Project Board. But for projects where there are likely to be lots of changes, the Project Board may choose to delegate some decisions to a person or group, called the Change Authority. The Project Manager and/or the people with delegated Project Assurance responsibilities may act as the Change Authority. It may be appropriate, for example, to make the Project Manager the Change Authority for Work Packages so that any changes that are within the delegated authority limits can be made without referral to the Project Board for approval
- **Change budget**   This is a sum of money that the customer and supplier agree will be used to fund the cost of requests for change, and

possibly also their analysis costs. Unless the anticipated level of change on a project is low, it is advisable for a budget to be set up to pay for changes. This arrangement can reduce the number of trivial exceptions arising in projects where the frequency of requests for change is forecast to be high. Including a change budget provides for a more realistic expectation of the overall costs/timeframe of the project. Where a change budget is given to a Change Authority, the Project Board may wish to put a limit on (a) the cost of any single change, and (b) the amount spent on change in any one stage without reference to the Project Board. The change control procedure would then be defined in such a way as to control access to the change budget. If used, the change control budget is documented in the relevant plan.

See Appendix A for a Product Description of a Configuration Management Strategy.

9.3.1.2 Configuration Item Records

The purpose of the Configuration Item Records is to provide a set of records that describe information such as the status, version and variant of each configuration item and any details of important relationships between the items.

See Appendix A for the Product Description of the Configuration Item Records.

9.3.1.3 Product Status Account

The purpose of the Product Status Account is to provide information about the state of the products within defined limits. The limits can vary. For example, the report could cover the entire project, a particular stage, a particular area of the project or even the history of a single product. It is particularly useful if the Project Manager wishes to confirm the version numbers of products.

See Appendix A for the Product Description of a Product Status Account.

9.3.1.4 Daily Log

A Daily Log is used to record problems/concerns that can be handled by the Project Manager informally. Issues initially captured on the Daily Log may later be transferred to the Issue Register if, after examining them, it is decided they need to be treated more formally.

The Daily Log can also be used to record required actions or significant events not caught by other PRINCE2 registers and logs. It acts as the project diary.

See Appendix A for the Product Description of a Daily Log.

9.3.1.5 Issue Register

The purpose of the Issue Register is to capture and maintain information on all of the issues that are being managed formally. The Issue Register should be monitored by the Project Manager on a regular basis.

See Appendix A for the Product Description of an Issue Register.

9.3.1.6 Issue Report

An Issue Report is a report containing the description, impact assessment and recommendations for a request for change, off-specification or a problem/concern. It is only created for those issues that need to be handled formally.

9.3.2 Configuration management

Configuration management procedures can vary, but they typically comprise five core activities:

- **Planning** Deciding what level of configuration management will be required by the project and planning how this level is to be achieved. The level of control required will vary from project to project. The maximum level of control possible is determined by breaking down the project's products until the level is reached at which a component can be independently installed, replaced or modified. However, the level of control exercised will be influenced by the importance of the project and the complexity of the relationship between its products

- **Identification** Specifying and identifying all components of the project's products (known as configuration items) at the required level of control. A coding system should be established, enabling a unique identifier for each configuration item to be allocated and various attributes of the product recorded

- **Control** The ability to approve and baseline products and to make changes only with the agreement of appropriate authorities. Once

a product has been approved, the motto is 'Nothing moves and nothing changes without authorization'. A baseline is a reference level against which an entity is monitored and controlled. In configuration management terms, it is a snapshot of a release, product and any component products, frozen at a point of time for a particular purpose. This purpose may be when a product is ready to be reviewed or when it has been approved. If the product that has been baselined is to be changed, a new version is created to accommodate the change, and the baseline version is kept unchanged. Old baseline versions should be archived where possible, not discarded. Configuration control also includes: the storing and retrieving of all information relevant to the management of the project; ensuring the safety and security of configuration items and controlling who has access to them; distribution of copies of all configuration items; and the archiving of all documentation produced during the project lifecycle. Both management and specialist products are subject to configuration control.

- **Status accounting** The reporting of all current and historical data concerning each product in the form of a Product Status Account. The Project Manager may call for a Product Status Account towards the end of a stage, at the end of the project, or as part of examining issues and risks

- **Verification and audit** A series of reviews and configuration audits to compare the actual status of all products against the authorized state of products as registered in the Configuration Item Records, looking for any discrepancies. These reviews and audits also check that the configuration management procedure is being undertaken in accordance with the Configuration Management Strategy. The reviews are typically undertaken at the end of each stage and at the end of the project.

9.3.3 Issue and change control procedure

PRINCE2 provides a common approach to dealing with requests for change, off-specifications and problems/concerns, as shown in Figure 9.1.

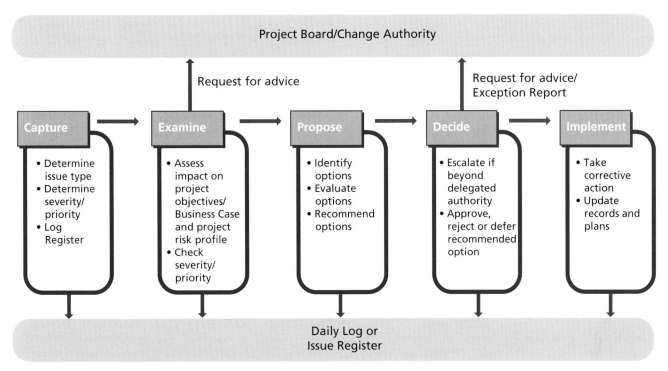

Figure 9.1 Issue and change control procedure

9.3.3.1 Capture

The first step in the procedure is to undertake an initial analysis to determine the type of issue that has been raised and whether it can be managed informally or formally.

The Project Manager is likely to receive many issues that can be handled without having to treat them formally, particularly if the issue can be immediately resolved – for example, a team member raising an issue that their site access pass is about to expire. In such cases, the Project Manager should decide on the best course of corrective action.

The purpose of distinguishing between those issues that can be managed informally and those that need to be managed formally is to:

■ Ensure decisions are made at an appropriate level within the project management team
■ Avoid the Project Board being inundated with too many issues and therefore diluting the time it has available to deal with the key issues affecting the project
■ Reduce the administrative burden on the Project Manager when dealing with the day-to-day issues that may arise.

Issues being managed formally should be entered in the Issue Register and given a unique identifier.

An Issue Report should be created to capture what is already known about the issue. It is often useful to ask the person who raised the issue to create the initial Issue Report.

9.3.3.2 Examine

The next step is to examine the issue by undertaking an impact analysis.

The Project Manager needs to consider whether it is worthwhile doing a detailed impact analysis as the duration and effort required to undertake one may itself cause a deviation from the plan.

The impact analysis should consider the impact the issue has (or will have) on:

■ The project performance targets in terms of time, cost, quality and scope
■ The project Business Case, especially in terms of the impact on benefits
■ The project risk profile, i.e. the impact on the overall risk exposure of the project.

If the project is part of a programme, the impact of the change on the programme as a whole should be considered. There may also be effects on other projects that are not necessarily part of the programme.

Examining the impact of issues can be wrongly taken to mean only the impact on the customer.

Impact analysis must cover the three areas of business, user and supplier – for example, the supplier's cost and effort required to implement a change and what products would have to be changed. Having undertaken the impact analysis, the severity or priority should be re-evaluated.

The Issue Register and Issue Report should be updated to include the above information and the person who raised the issue and the person who created the Issue Report (if different) should be kept informed of its status.

It may be necessary to request advice from the Project Board to check their understanding of the issue's priority or severity before proposing resolutions.

9.3.3.3 Propose

Having gained a full understanding of the impact of the issue, the next step is to consider alternative options for responding to it and proposing a course of action to take.

Consideration should be given as to the effect each of the options will have on the project's time, cost, quality, scope, benefit and risk performance targets. There must be a balance between the advantage to be gained by implementing the option, and the time, cost and risk of implementing it, as illustrated in Figure 9.2.

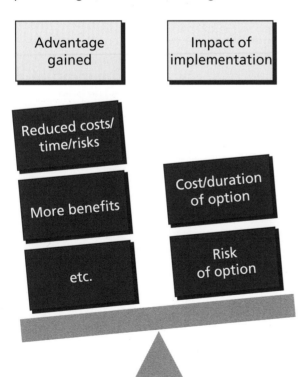

Figure 9.2 Options analysis

The risk considerations should include both project risks (i.e. of not completing within tolerances) and operational risks (e.g. potential performance issues once the project's products are in use).

If any of the proposed options would take the stage or project beyond any tolerances, consider preparing an Exception Report for that option to accompany the Issue Report.

9.3.3.4 Decide

The Project Manager may be able to resolve issues without the need to escalate them to the Project Board. For example, a minor change to an approved detailed design document that does not affect any other products could be handled by the Project Manager (if allowed in the Configuration Management Strategy), as long as it is formally recorded.

Other issues may need to be escalated to the Project Board (or its delegated Change Authority) for a decision. The escalation could be in the form of an Issue Report (as part of a request for advice) or in the form of an Exception Report (if the selected option to address the issue would cause an exception – see Chapter 10).

For escalated issues and exceptions, the likely Project Board responses are shown in Table 9.2.

9.3.3.5 Implement

The Project Manager will either:

- Take the necessary corrective action (such as updating a Work Package or issuing a new one), or
- Create an Exception Plan for approval by the Project Board.

In both cases, the Project Manager will update the Issue Register and Issue Report with the decision and inform all interested parties.

Once the issue is closed, the Project Manager should update the Issue Register and the Issue Report.

9.4 RESPONSIBILITIES

Table 9.3 outlines the responsibilities relevant to the Change theme. Refer to Appendix C for further details of project management team roles and their associated responsibilities.

Table 9.2 Project Board decisions

Request	Project Board (or Change Authority) response	Considerations
Request for change	■ Approve the change ■ Reject the change ■ Defer decision ■ Request more information ■ Ask for an Exception Plan (if the request for change cannot be implemented within the limits delegated to the Change Authority).	If a request for change involves extra cost, there are three principal ways to fund it: ■ Use the change budget (if being used and if of sufficient size) ■ Increase the project budget ■ De-scope other elements of the project. Tolerance should not be used to fund requests for change.
Off-specification	■ Grant a concession ■ Instruct that the off-specification be resolved ■ Defer decision ■ Request more information ■ Ask for an Exception Plan (if the concession cannot be granted within the limits delegated to the Change Authority).	The Project Board may decide to accept the off-specification without immediate corrective action. This is referred to as a **concession**. When a product is granted a concession, the Product Description will need to be revised before the product is handed over to the User.
Problem/concern	■ Provide guidance ■ Ask for an Exception Plan	Could the problem/concern be resolved by relaxing the stage tolerances?

Table 9.3 Responsibilities relevant to the Change theme

Role	Responsibilities
Corporate or programme management	Provide the corporate or programme strategy for change control, issue resolution and configuration management.
Executive	Determine the Change Authority and change budget.
	Set the scale for severity ratings for issues.
	Set the scale for priority ratings for requests for change and off-specifications.
	Respond to requests for advice from the Project Manager.
	Make decisions on escalated issues, with particular focus on continued business justification.
Senior User	Respond to requests for advice from the Project Manager.
	Make decisions on escalated issues with particular focus on safeguarding the expected benefits.
Senior Supplier	Respond to requests for advice from the Project Manager.
	Make decisions on escalated issues, with particular focus on safeguarding the integrity of the complete solution.
Project Manager	Manage the configuration management procedure, assisted by Project Support where possible.
	Manage the issue and change control procedure, assisted by Project Support where possible.
	Create and maintain the Issue Register, assisted by Project Support where possible.
	Implement corrective actions.
Team Manager	Implement corrective actions.
Project Assurance	Advise on examining and resolving issues.
Project Support	Administer the configuration management and issue and change control procedures: ■ Maintain Configuration Item Records ■ Produce Product Status Accounts ■ Assist the Project Manager to maintain the Issue Register.

Progress 10

10 Progress

10.1 PURPOSE

> The purpose of the Progress theme is to establish mechanisms to monitor and compare actual achievements against those planned; provide a forecast for the project objectives and the project's continued viability; and control any unacceptable deviations.

Two of the principles of PRINCE2 are managing by stages and continued business justification. The Progress theme provides the mechanisms for monitoring and control, enabling the critical assessment of ongoing viability.

The Progress theme provides such mechanisms for all management levels (delivering, managing, directing) within the project management team, and for corporate or programme management outside the project.

Another PRINCE2 principle is that projects are managed by exception, setting tolerances for project objectives to establish limits of delegated authority. Tolerances define the amount of discretion that each management level can exercise without the need to refer up to the next level for approval. The Progress theme provides the mechanisms to monitor progress against the allowed tolerances, and the controls to escalate to the next level should any forecast suggest that one or more tolerances will be exceeded.

Control of progress is all about decision making and is central to project management, ensuring that the project remains viable against its approved Business Case.

10.2 PROGRESS DEFINED

10.2.1 What is progress?

Progress is the measure of the achievement of the objectives of a plan. It can be monitored at Work Package, stage and project level.

10.2.2 What are progress controls?

Progress controls ensure that for each level of the project management team the next level of management can:

- Monitor progress
- Compare level of achievement with plan
- Review plans and options against future situations
- Detect problems and identify risks
- Initiate corrective action
- Authorize further work.

10.2.3 Exceptions and tolerances

An exception is a situation where it can be forecast that there will be a deviation beyond the agreed tolerance levels.

Tolerances are the permissible deviation above and below a plan's target for time and cost without escalating the deviation to the next level of management. There may also be tolerance levels for quality, scope, benefit and risk.

If tolerances are not implemented, there is no clear measure of discretion if things do not go to plan. For example, if every minor deviation is escalated to the Project Board, the Project Manager is merely monitoring the work and making no effort to implement corrective action – clearly unsatisfactory from the Project Board members' point of view. In effect, the Project Board is having to do the Project Manager's job. On the other hand, if the Project Manager carries on working to put things right, implementing corrective actions, there is the risk that Project Board members will see this as exceeding the Project Manager's (unwritten) discretion, and will question why the problems were not escalated earlier. In this instance, the Project Manager is seen as taking on the Project Board's role.

Table 10.1 describes where tolerances may be usefully applied and shows in which management product they are documented.

Table 10.1 The six tolerance areas by level

Tolerance areas	Project level tolerances	Stage level tolerances	Work Package level tolerances	Product level tolerances
Time +/- amounts of time on target completion dates	Project Plan	Stage Plan	Work Package	NA
Cost +/- amounts of planned budget	Project Plan	Stage Plan	Work Package	NA
Scope Permitted variation of the scope of a project solution, e.g. MoSCoW prioritization of requirements (Must have, Should have, Could have, Won't have for now).	Project Plan (note 1)	Stage Plan (note 1)	Work Package (note 1)	NA
Risk Limit on the aggregated value of threats (e.g. expected monetary value to remain less than 10% of the plan's budget); and Limit on any individual threat (e.g. any threat to operational service)	Risk Management Strategy	Stage Plan (note 2)	Work Package (note 2)	NA
Quality Defining quality targets in terms of ranges, e.g. a product that weighs 300g +/- 10g	Project Product Description	NA (note 3)	NA (note 3)	Product Description
Benefits Defining target benefits in terms of ranges, e.g. to achieve minimum cost savings of 5% per branch, with an average of 7% across all branches	Business Case	NA	NA	NA

Note 1 – the scope of a plan is defined by the set of products to be delivered. Scope tolerance (if used) should be in the form of a note on or reference to the product breakdown structure for the plan. Scope tolerance at the stage or Work Package level is of particular use if applying a time-bound iterative development method such as Agile.

Note 2 – more specific stage level risk tolerances may be set by the Project Board when authorizing a stage or by the Project Manager when commissioning Work Packages, especially from external suppliers.

Note 3 – quality tolerances are not summarily defined at the stage or Work Package level but are defined per Product Description within the scope of the plan.

10.3 THE PRINCE2 APPROACH TO PROGRESS

Progress control involves measuring actual progress against the performance targets of time, cost, quality, scope, benefits and risk, and then using this information to make decisions (such as whether to approve a stage or Work Package, whether to escalate deviations, whether to prematurely close the project etc.) and to take actions as required. PRINCE2 provides progress control through:

■ Delegating authority from one level of management to the level below it

■ Dividing the project into management stages and authorizing the project one stage at a time
■ Time-driven and event-driven progress-reporting and reviews
■ Raising exceptions.

The project's controls should be documented in the Project Initiation Documentation.

10.3.1 Delegating authority

10.3.1.1 The four levels of management

The principle of management by exception uses six types of tolerance against which a project can be controlled. The allocation of tolerances follows the four levels of the project management team as outlined in Figure 10.1 and described below:

- **Corporate or programme management** sits outside the project but sets the overall requirements and tolerance levels for the project. The three levels of management within the project (responsible for directing, managing and delivering) will manage and implement within these tolerances and escalate any forecast breaches of project tolerance

- **The Project Board** has overall control at a project level, as long as forecasts remain within project tolerance, and will allocate tolerances for each management stage to the Project Manager. The Project Board has the ability to review progress and decide whether to continue, change or stop the project. During execution of the Project Plan, if any forecasts indicate that the project is likely to exceed the agreed project tolerances, then the deviation should be referred to corporate or programme management by the Project Board in order to get a decision on corrective action

- **The Project Manager** has day-to-day control for a management stage within the tolerance limits laid down by the Project Board. During execution of a Stage Plan, if any forecasts indicate that the stage is likely to exceed the agreed stage tolerances, then the deviation should be referred to the Project Board by the Project Manager in order to get a decision on corrective action

- **The Team Manager** has control for a Work Package, but only within the Work Package tolerances agreed with the Project Manager. During execution of the Work Package, if any forecasts indicate that it is likely that the agreed tolerances will be exceeded, then the deviation should be referred to the Project Manager by the Team Manager in order to get a decision on corrective action.

10.3.1.2 Project Board controls

The main controls available to the Project Board include:

- **Authorizations** The Project Board uses the Directing a Project process to authorize initiation, authorize the project, authorize each stage and, finally, authorize project closure:

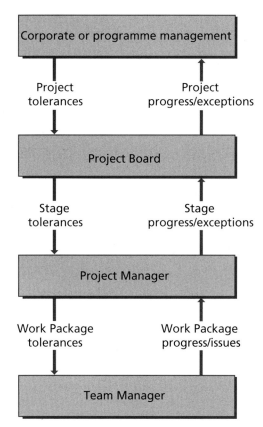

Figure 10.1 Delegating tolerance and reporting actual and forecast progress

- After the pre-project process Starting up a Project, the Project Board authorizes progress to the initiation stage, which is the official 'start' of the project
- After the Initiating a Project process, the Project Board reviews the information from the Project Initiation Documentation and, if satisfied that there is sufficient reason to go ahead with the project, can approve the Project Initiation Documentation and authorize the project itself
- After the Managing a Stage Boundary process, the Project Board reviews a Stage Plan or Exception Plan, and can either approve the plan, with its relevant tolerances for the next management stage, or, if there is insufficient justification to continue with the project, trigger premature closure of the project
- After the Closing a Project process, the Project Board reviews the End Project Report and, if satisfied that the project is complete or has nothing more to offer, can authorize its closure

- **Progress updates** Including Highlight Reports and End Stage Reports
- **Exceptions and changes** Including Exception Reports and Issue Reports.

When the Project Board has agreed stage tolerances with the Project Manager, it is kept informed of progress by means of Highlight Reports. There is no need for regular progress meetings during this stage, although personnel with Project Assurance responsibilities will require regular contact with the Project Manager and team members.

10.3.1.3 Project Manager controls

The main controls available to the Project Manager include:

- **Authorizations** Project Manager authorizations occur during the process Controlling a Stage (see Chapter 15). The Project Manager will be responsible for agreeing and authorizing Work Packages and Work Package tolerances
- **Progress updates** Including Checkpoint Reports produced by Team Managers or team members
- **Exceptions and changes** Use of project registers and logs to review progress and identify issues and risks that may need to be resolved. These are discussed further in section 10.3.3.2.

10.3.2 Use of management stages for control

Management stages are partitions of the project with management decision points. A management stage is a collection of activities and products whose delivery is managed as a unit. As such, this stage is a subset of the project and, in PRINCE2 terms, is the element of work that the Project Manager is managing on behalf of the Project Board at any one time.

Management stages:

- Provide review and decision points, giving the Project Board the opportunity to assess the project viability at defined intervals, rather than let it run on in an uncontrolled manner
- Give the ability to ensure that key decisions are made prior to the detailed work needed to implement them
- Allow clarification of what the impact will be of an identified external influence, such as the corporate budget round or the finalization of legislation

- Facilitate the management by exception principle by delegating authority to the Project Manager on a stage-by-stage basis.

The Project Board authorizes one management stage of the project at a time. Towards the end of each stage, during the Managing a Stage Boundary process, the Project Manager will review the Business Case and Project Plan, update the project documentation with the results of the stage, and create an End Stage Report and Stage Plan to request authorization to commence the next management stage. The End Stage Report, together with the Stage Plan for the next stage, should contain all the information necessary to enable the Project Board to conduct an end stage assessment and make a decision as to whether to proceed. The Project Board only authorizes the next management stage if there is sufficient business justification to continue. If the project no longer has a valid Business Case, the Project Board has the authority to prematurely close it.

The Project Board delegates the authority for day-to-day control of a stage, within agreed tolerances, to the Project Manager. As long as the stage is forecast to remain within tolerance, the Project Manager has discretion to make adjustments as required. This allows the Project Board to manage by exception, retaining the level of control it requires while reducing the administrative overhead of being involved.

10.3.2.1 Number of stages

The use of management stages in a PRINCE2 project is mandatory, but the number of stages is flexible and depends on the scale and risk of the project. Every PRINCE2 project consists of at least two management stages. The initiation stage is mandatory as it ensures that there is a firm basis for the project, which is understood by all parties. There should also be at least one other management stage to cover the remainder of the project. For larger projects, additional management stages may be needed to enable the project management team to have an optimal level of planning and control.

Defining management stages is fundamentally a process of balancing:

- How far ahead in the project it is sensible to plan
- Where the key decision points need to be on the project

- The amount of risk within a project
- Too many short management stages (increasing the project management overhead) versus too few lengthy ones (reducing the level of control)
- How confident the Project Board and Project Manager are in proceeding.

The number of management stages required will be dictated by the nature of the project and its duration. For short-duration projects (where the project can be completed within the planning horizon, for example), the introduction of multiple management stages could result in unnecessary 'overheads' and additional costs.

10.3.2.2 Length of stages

PRINCE2 does not define how long a management stage should be. Stages should be shorter when there is greater risk, uncertainty or complexity, for example at the beginning and end of projects. They can be longer when risk is lower, typically in the middle of projects. Further, the length of those management stages may vary depending on the point within the project lifecycle. Factors that will influence this decision include:

- **The planning horizon at any point in time** The planning horizon may vary depending on the nature of the work being undertaken. For example, the work involved in installing a computer system during an application migration project may be better understood and less risky than the work involved with migrating the application itself
- **The technical stages within the project** The end of management stages do not necessarily need to occur at the same time as the end of technical stages, but there are often benefits if they do. For example, the Project Board may wish to be able to understand any effects on the Business Case of the results of a 'proof of concept' before committing to a full-scale deployment
- **Alignment with programme activities** It may be a requirement to align the end of a management stage with the end-of-tranche review within the programme. This will allow the project to contribute fully to the assessment of the ongoing viability of the programme itself

- **The level of risk** Management stages can be very useful as a means of bringing Project Board control to risky projects. Stage breaks can be inserted at key points when risks to the project can be reviewed before major commitments of money or resources.

10.3.2.3 Technical stages

Another method of grouping work is by the set of techniques used or the products created. This results in stages covering elements such as design, build and implementation. Such stages are **technical** stages and are a separate concept from the management stages already introduced.

Technical stages often overlap (as in Figures 10.2 and 10.3) but management stages do not. Technical stages are typified by the use of a particular set of specialist skills. Management stages equate to commitment of resources and authority to spend.

Often the boundary of the two types of stage will coincide – for instance, where the management decision is based on the output from the technical stage. However, on other occasions the stage boundaries will not coincide – for example, there might be more than one technical stage per management stage.

Where a technical stage spans a management stage boundary, the extent to which the product(s) of the technical stage should be complete at the stage boundary should be clear in the Product Description(s) concerned.

Figures 10.2, 10.3 and 10.4 give examples of the distinction between technical and management stages. Figure 10.2 shows a project with five technical stages.

Figure 10.3 shows the same project from Figure 10.2, but broken down into four management stages. Two of the technical stages span more than one management stage.

Figure 10.4 shows that the technical stage of 'designing' has been broken into three product groups. The overall design now falls within management stage 1; detailed design and training syllabus form the second management stage; and periphery design is scheduled for management stage 3, together with the creation of the built facility and trained staff.

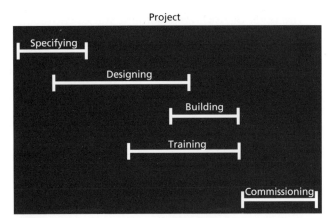

Figure 10.2 Specialist work defined in technical stages

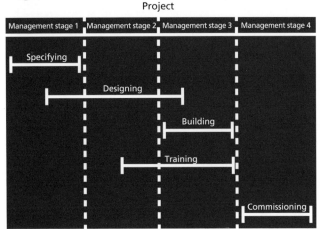

Figure 10.3 Specialist work crossing management stage boundaries

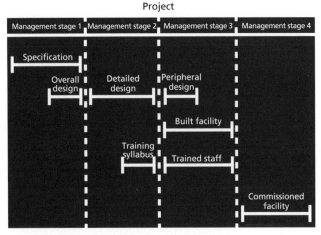

Figure 10.4 Specialist work aligned to management stages

The PRINCE2 approach is to concentrate the management of the project on the management stages since these will form the basis of the planning and control processes described throughout the method. To do otherwise runs the risk of the project being driven by the specialist teams instead of the customer's management.

10.3.3 Event-driven and time-driven controls

PRINCE2 provides two types of progress control throughout the life of a project:

- **Event-driven controls** Take place when a specific event occurs. This could be, for example, the end of a stage, the completion of the Project Initiation Documentation or the creation of an Exception Report. It could also include organizational events that might affect the project, such as the end of the financial year

- **Time-driven controls** Take place at predefined periodic intervals. This could be, for example, producing monthly Highlight Reports for the Project Board or weekly Checkpoint Reports showing the progress of a Work Package.

Monitoring and reporting requires a time-based approach, whereas control (decision making) is an event-based activity.

The following sections describe the management products that are used to establish and execute event-driven and time-driven controls.

10.3.3.1 Baselines for progress control

It is only possible to control at the level of resolution in the plans, i.e. if you want to have Checkpoint Reports weekly, you need to know (in the Stage Plan) what you expect to achieve week by week.

The following management products assist the Project Manager in establishing baselines for progress control:

- **Project Plan** This will include the project-level performance targets and tolerances. Any threat to the project-level tolerances needs to be escalated to the Project Board, which will seek advice from corporate or programme management for corrective action

- **Stage Plans** These form the basis of the day-to-day control of the stage. They should contain details of the activities to be conducted during a management stage, their timescales, and the resources needed to carry them out

- **Exception Plan** The Project Board may request an Exception Plan after having considered an Exception Report during the process Directing a Project. The Exception Plan should be produced at the same level as the plan that it replaces

- **Work Packages** The Project Manager authorizes a Work Package in order to trigger an individual team member or a Team Manager to undertake a piece of work during a stage. This means that work cannot be undertaken unless the Project Manager has specifically authorized it. Details of the work to be completed within what tolerances must be agreed between the Project Manager and Team Manager or team member, and documented in the Work Package. Work Package authorization is a particularly useful control when dealing with contractors or subcontractors. The individuals or teams monitor progress against the Work Package and report back to the Project Manager via Checkpoint Reports. A project may be a mix of internal and external teams. It may therefore be valid to use a mixture of formal and informal Work Packages of varying sizes, with tight or loose tolerances, depending on the needs of the project.

10.3.3.2 Reviewing progress

As part of Controlling a Stage, the Project Manager will regularly review the progress of work through Checkpoint Reports and maintain a set of project registers and logs. The Project Manager will use this information to update the Stage Plan with actual progress achieved. The frequency of checkpoint reporting required may change according to the needs of individual Work Packages.

It is also useful to look at trends to get a view of the overall 'health' of the stage. For example, the stage may seem to be progressing well in terms of the products being completed against the schedule. However, the Issue Register may reveal an increasing number of issues which are not being resolved and which may be a cause for concern. Similarly, a high number of outstanding items against a product in the Quality Register may show design issues with that product.

The following management products assist the Project Manager in reviewing progress:

- **Daily Log** This is a useful tool for recording actions. Project actions may arise from many sources, including checkpoints, quality reviews, end stage assessments or ad hoc conversations. There is a danger that actions may get 'lost' if they are only recorded in minutes or progress reports. Small actions may simply be recorded on the Daily Log and marked off when completed. Actions involving significant effort may need to be incorporated into the Stage Plan. If such actions cannot be incorporated into the plan within tolerances, then an issue should be raised to examine their impact on the stage and project. The Daily Log can also be used to record informal issues and any other notes or observations that are not captured by any other registers or logs. The Daily Log is a useful way of recording individual observations that on their own may seem insignificant, but when collated may alert the Project Manager to a new issue or risk

- **Issue Register** This will contain details of all formal issues raised during the project, which could take the form of requests for change, off-specifications or problems/concerns. Reviewing the Issue Register may uncover progress issues – for example, a sudden increase in the number of requests for change, or an increasing number of overdue corrective actions

- **Product Status Account** This provides a snapshot of the status of products within the project, management stage or a particular area of the project. It can reveal progress issues as it shows the planned and actual dates for key points in the production, review and approval of the products to be delivered by the plan. The Product Status Account is derived from the Configuration Items Records

- **Quality Register** This is a record of all planned and implemented quality activities. The Quality Register can reveal progress issues as the Project Manager can assess whether any quality activities are outstanding or whether there are any useful trends in the quality results – for example, an increasing number of products failing quality review or an increase in the average number of quality review actions

- **Risk Register** This is a record of all identified risks. The Project Manager should review the Risk Register as part of reviewing stage status. As risks are driven by uncertainty, the number of risks should generally decrease as the project progresses and the level of certainty increases. The Risk Register should be reviewed to determine whether the aggregated risks may impact on progress for the remainder of the stage and project, e.g. there may be a large number of risks with similar proximity in time, indicating a period where progress may be affected.

Progress evaluation techniques

Measuring the progress of a management stage involves looking backwards, at the progress made against plans, and forwards, at what still needs to be completed with what time and resources. There are many techniques available to measure project progress, including:

- **Milestone chart** This is a graphical chart showing key planned and actual milestones in a stage
- **S-curve** This is a graph showing cumulative actual figures (for example, costs or hours) plotted against time. The curve is usually shaped like the letter 'S', reflecting the fact that a project typically consumes fewer resources and costs at the start and end of the project, and more in the middle. The steeper the curve, the more resources required. When planned and actual figures are shown on the same chart, this can be used to identify potential overspend or forecast areas where tolerances may be exceeded
- **Earned value management** This is a technique to measure the scope, schedule and cost performance compared with plans, by comparing the completed products and the actual cost and time taken against their schedule and cost estimates. PRINCE2's product-based approach to planning provides the prerequisites needed for earned value management.

10.3.3.3 Capturing and reporting lessons

The following management products are used for capturing and reporting lessons when reviewing progress:

- **Lessons Log** One of the principles of a PRINCE2 project is that the project management team learns from experience, which means that lessons are sought, recorded and actioned throughout. It is often in the reviewing of progress that lessons are identified. Lessons could include information about management or specialist processes, products, techniques or procedures that either made a contribution to the project's achievements or caused a problem – for example, the performance of the project management team, the success of tailoring

PRINCE2 to the project, or the analysis of quality statistics and measurements

- **Lessons Report** Although lessons may be identified and recorded during a project, learning lessons involves taking action to implement improvements. These actions may apply to the current project, in which case they should be incorporated into the appropriate plans and Work Packages, or they may be relevant to different projects. If a lesson is significant and has relevance for future projects, it should be included in the Lessons Report. It is important to note that actions to learn lessons can be taken, and the Lessons Report created, at any appropriate time during a project. As a minimum, however, a Lessons Report should be produced during the Closing a Project process.

10.3.3.4 Reporting progress

The frequency of reporting should reflect the level of control required, and this is likely to vary during the project. For example:

- During the design stage, less frequent control may be required than during later management stages
- If the team is highly experienced then less frequent reporting may be appropriate, whereas for an inexperienced team the Project Manager may wish to increase the frequency of reporting until sufficient confidence has been gained on the capability of the team.

The following management products are used for progress reporting:

- **Checkpoint Report** The Team Manager will produce this to provide the Project Manager with details of progress against the Work Package. The Work Package will include the frequency of Checkpoint Reports required. The Project Manager will collate Checkpoint Reports and use these as part of the progress assessment when reviewing stage status
- **Highlight Report** The Project Manager produces this report on management stage progress for the Project Board. The Project Board will determine the frequency of Highlight Reports required, either for the whole project or stage by stage, and document this in the Communication Management Strategy. The Highlight Report allows members of the Project Board to manage by exception between end stage assessments as they are aware of the

tolerances agreed with the Project Manager in the Stage Plan. The Highlight Report should confirm that progress is being made within these tolerances and provide early warning of possible problems which may need actions. As part of the Communication Management Strategy, the Project Board can request that copies of the Highlight Report be sent to other interested parties outside the project. The Project Board may also issue the Highlight Report (or a summary of it) to corporate or programme management

■ **End Stage Report** This is produced by the Project Manager towards the end of each management stage, providing the Project Board with the information on the progress to date, the overall project situation and (in tandem with the next Stage Plan) sufficient information to ask for a Project Board decision on what to do next with the project

■ **End Project Report** This is produced by the Project Manager towards the end of the project, during the Closing a Project process, and is used by the Project Board to evaluate the project and authorize closure.

10.3.4 Raising exceptions

The output from reviewing progress is a decision as to whether the Work Package, Stage Plan or Project Plan remain, or are forecast to remain, within agreed tolerances:

■ **Work-Package-level exceptions** Having agreed Work Package tolerances with the Team Manager, the Project Manager should be kept informed of progress through regular Checkpoint Reports. If a Work Package is forecast to exceed its tolerances, the Team Manager should inform the Project Manager by raising an issue. The Project Manager will advise of any corrective actions required

■ **Stage-level exceptions** If the stage is forecast to exceed its tolerances, the Project Manager should produce an Issue Report to capture and analyse the details of the deviation and then provide an Exception Report for the Project Board. Based on information in this report, the Project Board may request that the Project Manager produces an Exception Plan to replace the plan that was forecast to exceed tolerance. The Project Board may also remove the cause, accept and adjust tolerance, or request more

time to consider or reject the recommendations in the Issue Report. If an Exception Plan is requested, the Project Board will conduct an exception assessment, similar to the end stage assessment, to review and approve the Exception Plan

■ **Project-level exceptions** If the forecast is for project tolerances to be exceeded, the Project Board no longer has the authority to manage the project and must refer the matter to corporate or programme management for a decision. The Project Board may request the Project Manager to produce an Exception Plan for the project.

Refer to Chapter 9 for more information on issue and change control procedures.

10.4 RESPONSIBILITIES

Table 10.2 outlines the responsibilities relevant to the Progress theme. Refer to Appendix C for further details of project management team roles and their associated responsibilities.

Table 10.2 Responsibilities relevant to the Progress theme

Role	Responsibilities
Corporate or programme management	Provide project tolerances and document them in the project mandate.
	Make decisions on Exception Plans when project-level tolerances are forecast to be exceeded.
Executive	Provide stage tolerances.
	Ensure that progress towards the outcome remains consistent from the business perspective.
	Make decisions on Exception Plans when stage-level tolerances are forecast to be exceeded.
	Recommend future action on the project to corporate or programme management if the project tolerance is forecast to be exceeded.
Senior User	Ensure that progress towards the outcome remains consistent from the user perspective.
Senior Supplier	Ensure that progress towards the outcome remains consistent from the supplier perspective.
Project Manager	Authorize Work Packages.
	Monitor progress against Stage Plans.
	Produce Highlight Reports, End Stage Reports , Lessons Reports and End Project Report.
	Produce Exception Reports for the Project Board when stage- or project-level tolerances are forecast to be exceeded.
	Maintain the project's registers and logs.
Team Manager	Agree Work Packages with the Project Manager.
	Inform Project Support of completed quality activities.
	Produce Checkpoint Reports.
	Notify the Project Manager of any forecast deviation from Work Package tolerances.
Project Assurance	Verify the Business Case against external events and project progress.
	Verify changes to the Project Plan to see whether there is any impact on the needs of the business or the Business Case.
	Confirm stage and project progress against agreed tolerances.
Project Support	Assist with the compilation of reports.
	Contribute specialist tool expertise (for example, planning and control tools).
	Number, record, store and distribute Issue Reports and Exception Reports.
	Assist the Project Manager in maintaining the Issue Register and Risk Register.
	Maintain the Quality Register on behalf of the Project Manager.

Introduction to processes

11

11 Introduction to processes

11.1 THE PRINCE2 PROCESSES

PRINCE2 is a process-based approach for project management. A process is a structured set of activities designed to accomplish a specific objective. It takes one or more defined inputs and turns them into defined outputs.

There are seven processes in PRINCE2, which provide the set of activities required to direct, manage and deliver a project successfully.

Figure 11.1 shows how each process is used throughout a project's life.

11.2 THE PRINCE2 JOURNEY

The Project Board sets direction and makes key decisions throughout the life of the project. The Project Board's activities are covered by the Directing a Project process (see Chapter 13), which runs from pre-project through to, and including, the final stage.

11.2.1 Pre-project

In the beginning, someone has an idea or a need. This may result from new business objectives, responding to competitive pressures, changes in legislation, or a recommendation in a report or an audit. The trigger for the project could be almost anything. In PRINCE2, this trigger is called a project mandate. The project mandate is provided by the commissioning organization (corporate or programme management) and can vary in form from a verbal instruction to a well-defined and justified project definition.

Prior to the activity to scope the project fully, it is important to verify that the project is worthwhile and viable. Such activities are covered by the process Starting up a Project (see Chapter 12), which culminates in the production of a Project Brief and a Stage Plan for project initiation.

The Project Board reviews the Project Brief and decides whether to initiate the project, and states

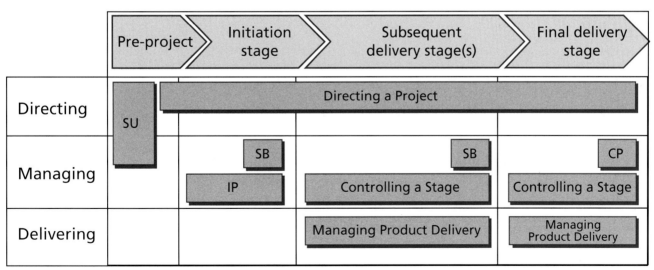

Key
SU = Starting up a Project
IP = Initiating a Project
SB = Managing a Stage Boundary
CP = Closing a Project

Note
- Starting up a Project is used by both the directing and managing levels.
- There should be at least two management stages, the first of which is the initiation stage.
- Managing a Stage Boundary is first used at the end of the initiation stage and repeated at the end of each subsequent stage except the final stage. It is also used to prepare Exception Plans, which can be done at any time including in the final stage.
- For complex or lengthy initiations, Controlling a Stage and Managing Product Delivery can optionally be used to manage the initiation stage.

Figure 11.1 The PRINCE2 processes

the levels of authority to be delegated to the Project Manager for the initiation stage.

11.2.2 Initiation stage

Once there is a decision to go ahead with the project, it needs to be planned in detail. Funding needs to be obtained and controls should be defined to ensure that the project proceeds in accordance with the wishes of those people paying for the project and those who will make use of what the project delivers. The detailed planning, establishment of the project management strategies and controls, development of a robust Business Case, and a means of reviewing benefits are covered by the Initiating a Project process (see Chapter 14). Also, during the initiation stage, the Managing a Stage Boundary process (Chapter 17) is used to plan the next stage in detail.

The initiation stage culminates in the production of the Project Initiation Documentation, which is reviewed by the Project Board to decide whether to authorize the project. As the contents of the Project Initiation Documentation are likely to change throughout the project (under change control), this version of the Project Initiation Documentation is preserved as input for later performance reviews.

11.2.3 Subsequent delivery stages

The Project Board delegates day-to-day control to the Project Manager on a stage-by-stage basis. The Project Manager needs to assign work to be done, ensure that the outputs of such work (products) meet relevant specifications, and gain suitable approval where appropriate. The Project Manager also needs to ensure that progress is in line with the approved plan and that the forecasts for the project's performance targets are within agreed tolerances. The Project Manager ensures that a set of project records (Daily Log, Lessons Log, Issue Register, Risk Register, Quality Register and Configuration Item Records) are maintained to assist with progress control. The Project Manager informs the Project Board of progress through regular Highlight Reports. The activities to control each stage are covered by the Controlling a Stage process (see Chapter 15).

In the Managing Product Delivery process (see Chapter 16), the Team Manager(s) or team members execute assigned Work Packages (that will deliver one or more products) and keep the Project Manager appraised of progress via Checkpoint Reports.

Towards the end of each management stage, the Project Manager requests permission to proceed to the next stage by reporting how the stage performed, providing an update to the Business Case and planning the next management stage in detail. The Project Manager provides the information needed by the Project Board in order for it to assess the continuing viability of the project and to make a decision to authorize the next management stage. The activities to manage each stage boundary are covered in the Managing a Stage Boundary process (see Chapter 17).

11.2.4 Final delivery stage

As a project is a temporary undertaking, during the final stage (once the Project Manager has gained approval for all of the project's products) it is time to decommission the project. The Project Board needs to be satisfied that the recipients of the project's products are in a position to own and use them on an ongoing basis. Should this be the case, the products can be transitioned into operational use and the project can close. The project documentation should be tidied up and archived, the project should be assessed for performance against its original plan and the resources assigned to the project need to be released. The closure activities include planning post-project benefits reviews to take place for those benefits that can only be assessed after the products have been in use (and therefore after the project has closed). The activities to decommission a project are covered by the Closing a Project process (see Chapter 18).

11.3 THE PRINCE2 PROCESS MODEL

The PRINCE2 process model is shown in Figure 11.2.

The processes are aligned to the management levels of corporate or programme, directing, managing and delivering. The triggers between each process are shown.

11.4 STRUCTURE OF THE PROCESS CHAPTERS

Each process within PRINCE2 is described using the following structure and format.

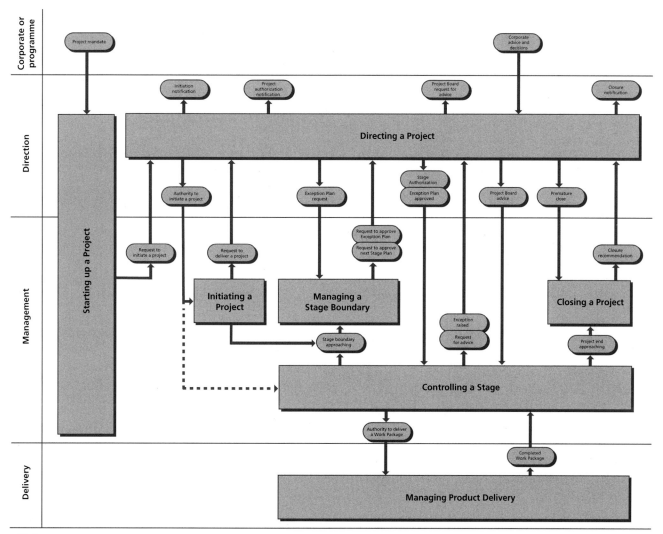

Figure 11.2 PRINCE2 process model

Notes:

Note 1: at the end of the initiation stage, the Initiating a Project process is used to request Project Board approval to initiate the project (with the submission of the Project Initiation Documentation) and in parallel the Managing a Stage Boundary process is used to request Project Board approval of the Stage Plan for the second management stage.

Note 2: the closure activities are planned and approved as part of the stage approval for the final stage; therefore the Closing a Project process takes place in the final stage.

11.4.1 Purpose
This section describes the reason for the process.

11.4.2 Objective
This section describes the specific objectives to be achieved by the process.

11.4.3 Context
This section puts each process in context with the other processes and activities going on within the project and from corporate or programme management.

11.4.4 Activities
PRINCE2 **processes** comprise a set of **activities**, which may be run in series or in parallel. PRINCE2 activities comprise a set of **recommended actions** designed to achieve a particular result.

The relationship between processes, activities and actions is shown in Figure 11.3.

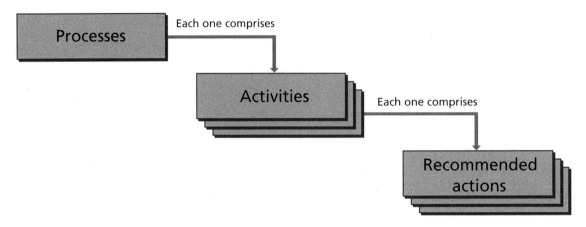

Figure 11.3 Relationship between processes, activities and actions

A diagram is provided for each **activity** showing the inputs and outputs, including those products that are created or updated by that activity. The recommended actions to be taken to achieve the objectives of the activity are described.

Each activity is concluded by a table showing the responsibilities for each product created or updated during the activity, as illustrated in Table 11.1.

Note that management products created during one process may be approved in another (e.g. a Stage Plan is created in the Managing a Stage Boundary process but is approved in the Directing a Project process). However, the complete set of responsibilities is shown, and those covered by another process are indicated by being shown in parentheses, e.g. (A).

Table 11.1 An example of a table of responsibilities

Producer – responsible for product's production
Reviewer – ideally independent of production
Approver – confirms approval

Product	Action	Corporate/Programme	Executive	Senior User	Senior Supplier	Project Manager	Team Manager	Project Assurance	Project Support	Product Description available
Stage Plan	Create		(A)	(A)	(A)	P		R		A16

Table 11.2 Key to process diagrams

Symbol	Key
Starting up a Project	This is a PRINCE2 process.
Authorize initiation	This is an activity. Each process comprises a number of activities.
Exception Plan request Corrective action	This is an event or decision that triggers another process or is used to notify corporate or programme management. The arrow shows which process is triggered by the event. Double triggers indicate where there are alternative triggers from one process to another (e.g. a request to approve the next Stage Plan or a request to approve an Exception Plan). Those with dotted lines are triggers internal to a process (e.g. corrective action is a trigger from one activity in the Controlling a Stage process to another).
Business Case Follow-on action recommendations	These are management products that are created or updated by a process's activities. Those with hard lines are defined management products with Product Description outlines in Appendix A. Those with dotted lines are components of a management product or are non-defined management products where PRINCE2 does not require specific composition or quality criteria.

Starting up a Project

12

12 Starting up a Project

12.1 PURPOSE

The purpose of the Starting up a Project process is to ensure that the prerequisites for Initiating a Project are in place by answering the question: do we have a viable and worthwhile project?

Nothing should be done until certain base information needed to make rational decisions about the commissioning of the project is defined, key roles and responsibilities are resourced and allocated, and a foundation for detailed planning is available.

The purpose of the Starting up a Project process is as much about preventing poorly conceived projects from ever being initiated as it is about approving the initiation of viable projects. As such, Starting up a Project is a lighter process compared to the more detailed and thorough Initiating a Project process. The aim is to do the minimum necessary in order to decide whether it is worthwhile to even initiate the project.

12.2 OBJECTIVE

The objective of the Starting up a Project process is to ensure that:

■ There is a business justification for initiating the project (documented in an outline Business Case)
■ All the necessary authorities exist for initiating the project
■ Sufficient information is available to define and confirm the scope of the project (in the form of a Project Brief)
■ The various ways the project can be delivered are evaluated and a project approach selected
■ Individuals are appointed who will undertake the work required in project initiation and/or will take significant project management roles in the project
■ The work required for project initiation is planned (documented in a Stage Plan)
■ Time is not wasted initiating a project based on unsound assumptions regarding the project's scope, timescales, acceptance criteria and constraints.

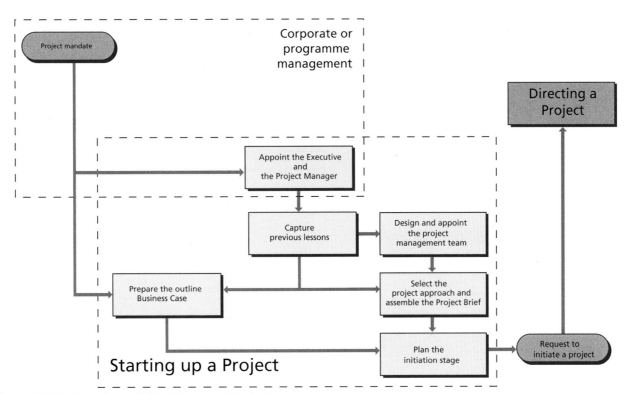

Figure 12.1 Overview of Starting up a Project

12.3 CONTEXT

Projects can be identified in a variety of ways and thus have a wide variation in the information available at the time of start-up. PRINCE2 calls the trigger for the project the project mandate, which is provided by the responsible authority which is commissioning the project – typically the corporate or programme management organization. The term project mandate applies to whatever information is used to trigger the project, be it a feasibility study or the receipt of a 'request for proposal' in a supplier environment. The project mandate should provide the terms of reference for the project and should contain sufficient information to identify at least the prospective Executive of the Project Board. The mandate is refined to develop the Project Brief.

The Project Board must be provided with sufficient information to make the decision to initiate the project. The Project Brief is prepared for this purpose.

The effort involved in Starting up a Project will vary enormously from project to project. If the project is part of a programme, the programme itself should provide the Project Brief and will appoint some, if not all, members of the Project Board, thus eliminating much of the work required in this process. In such cases, the Project Manager should validate what is provided by the programme and, if necessary, recommend modifications.

The preparation of the outline Business Case and the assembling of the Project Brief (which are parallel and iterative activities) require regular and frequent interaction and consultations between the Project Manager, the Project Board members and other stakeholders. The more time spent on getting the requirements clearly captured during the Starting up a Project process, the more time will be saved during project delivery by avoiding issues, exceptions and replanning.

The contents of the Project Brief are later extended and refined into the Project Initiation Documentation via the Initiating a Project process.

12.4 ACTIVITIES

The activities within the Starting up a Project process are likely to be shared between corporate or programme management, the Executive and the Project Manager. The activities are to:

- Appoint the Executive and the Project Manager
- Capture previous lessons
- Design and appoint the project management team
- Prepare the outline Business Case
- Select the project approach and assemble the Project Brief
- Plan the initiation stage.

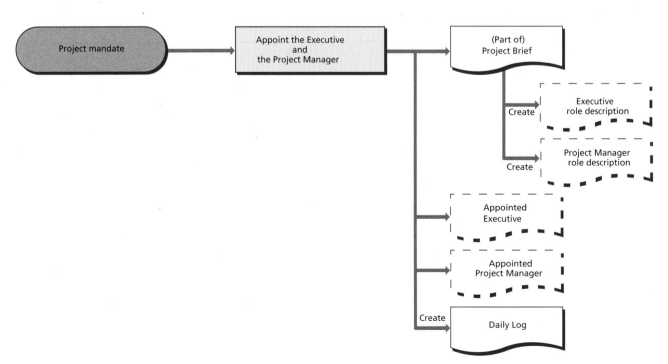

Figure 12.2 Appoint the Executive and the Project Manager: activity summary

12.4.1 Appoint the Executive and the Project Manager

To get anything done in the project, a decision maker with appropriate authority is needed – the Executive – who represents the interests of the business stakeholder(s). The appointment of the Executive is a prerequisite to ensuring that the project is justified.

The appointment of a Project Manager allows for the project to be managed on a day-to-day basis on behalf of the Executive. The Executive may need to consult with, and gain agreement from, corporate or programme management when appointing a Project Manager.

Figure 12.2 shows the inputs to, and outputs from, this activity. For more details on project organization, see Chapter 5.

PRINCE2 recommends the following actions:

■ Review the project mandate and check understanding

■ Appoint the Executive (the appointment is made by the commissioning organization – typically corporate or programme management):

● Establish the responsibilities for the Executive

● Prepare the role description for the Executive based on the role description in Appendix C

● Estimate the time and effort required for the Executive role (this will be refined later)

● Identify candidates for the Executive from the project's stakeholders and select the most appropriate person for the role

● Confirm the selected person's availability, their acceptance of the role, and their commitment to carry it out

● Assign the selected person to the role of Executive

■ The Executive to appoint the Project Manager:

● Establish the responsibilities for the Project Manager

● Prepare a role description for the Project Manager, based on the role description in Appendix C, and gain agreement from corporate or programme management

● Identify candidates for the Project Manager and select the most appropriate person for the role

Table 12.1 Appoint the Executive and the Project Manager: responsibilities

Producer – responsible for product's production
Reviewer – ideally independent of production
Approver – confirms approval

Product	Action	Corporate/Programme	Executive	Senior User	Senior Supplier	Project Manager	Team Manager	Project Assurance	Project Support	Product Description available
Project mandate	Provide	P								
Executive role description	Create	P								
Appointed Executive	Confirm	P								
Project Manager role description	Create	A	P							
Appointed Project Manager	Confirm	A	P							
Daily Log	Create					P				A7

- Estimate the time and effort required for the Project Manager role (this will be refined later)
- Confirm the selected person's availability, their acceptance of the role, and their commitment to carry it out
- Assign the selected person to the role of Project Manager
- Confirm the appointment with corporate or programme management
■ Create the Daily Log as a repository for project information that is not yet being captured elsewhere.

Table 12.1 shows the responsibilities for this activity.

12.4.2 Capture previous lessons

A number of lessons may have been learned by other projects, corporate or programme management, and external organizations about weaknesses or strengths of the processes, procedures, techniques and tools used, when they were used, how they were used, and by whom.

The design of the project management team, outline Business Case, the contents of the Project Brief, and the Stage Plan for the initiation stage can be influenced by lessons learned from previous projects.

It may be useful to hold a workshop as a means to capture relevant lessons. Attendees could include any interested parties and people who have worked on previous similar projects. If the organization has not done this type of project before, it may be helpful to include people external to the organization who have the relevant experience.

When moving from the general view in Starting up a Project to the detailed view in Initiating a Project and updated view in Managing a Stage Boundary, it may be necessary to look beyond the Lessons Log, by repeating this activity, to capture any further relevant external lessons.

Figure 12.3 shows the inputs to, and outputs from, this activity.

PRINCE2 recommends the following actions:

■ Create the Lessons Log
■ Review related Lessons Reports from similar previous projects to identify lessons that can be applied to this project. This may include, for example, the results of audits and project reviews
■ Review any lessons from corporate management, programme management and external organizations
■ Consult with individuals or teams with previous experience of similar projects
■ If appropriate, record any lessons identified in the Lessons Log.

Table 12.2 shows the responsibilities for this activity.

12.4.3 Design and appoint the project management team

The project needs the right people in place, with the authority, responsibility and knowledge to make decisions in a timely manner. The project management team needs to reflect the interests of all parties who will be involved, including business, user and supplier interests.

It is essential for a well-run project that every individual involved in the management of the project understands and agrees who is accountable to whom for what, who is responsible for what, and what the reporting and communication lines are.

Figure 12.4 shows the inputs to, and outputs from, this activity. For more details on project organization, see Chapter 5.

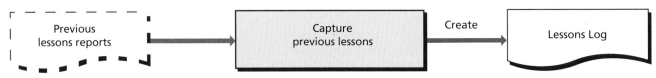

Figure 12.3 Capture previous lessons: activity summary

Table 12.2 Capture previous lessons: responsibilities

Producer – responsible for product's production

Reviewer – ideally independent of production

Approver – confirms approval

Product	Action	Corporate/Programme	Executive	Senior User	Senior Supplier	Project Manager	Team Manager	Project Assurance	Project Support	Product Description available
Lessons Log	Create		R			P				A14

PRINCE2 recommends the following actions:

- Review the Lessons Log for lessons related to the project management team structure
- Design the project management team:
  - Prepare the project management team structure
  - Create role descriptions for the remaining Project Board roles based on the role descriptions in Appendix C
  - Assess whether any members of the Project Board are likely to delegate any of their assurance responsibilities, and create the role description(s) for Project Assurance (where appropriate) based on the role description in Appendix C

- Consider whether separate individuals are likely to be needed as Team Manager(s) or whether the Project Manager will be filling this role. If appropriate, create role descriptions for the Team Manager(s) based on the role description in Appendix C
- Consider whether the Project Manager will be performing the Project Support role or whether a separate individual(s) will be required. If this role is to be delegated, create the role description for the Project Support role based on the role description in Appendix C
- Confirm the reporting and communication lines within the role descriptions

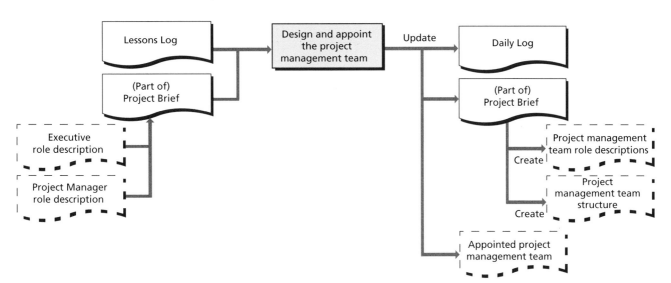

Figure 12.4 Design and appoint the project management team: activity summary

■ Appoint the project management team:
  ● Estimate the time and effort required by each of the roles identified (this will be refined later)
  ● Identify candidates for each of the roles, and propose the most appropriate people for them:
    ● It may be appropriate to undertake an analysis of the stakeholders (see section 5.3.5) in order to identify suitable candidates for the roles
    ● It is possible that candidates may not be known at this time, in which case they will need to be selected later (see sections 14.4.5 and 17.4.1). This is particularly true if Team Managers are to be sourced from subcontractors
    ● Consider whether identified candidates match the competencies required of the role and, if not, whether any training or support (e.g. coaching) is required
  ● Confirm the selected people's availability (if they are known), their understanding and acceptance of the roles, and their commitment to carry them out
  ● Assign the selected people to each of the roles identified and confirm the appointment with corporate or programme management

■ If any risks are identified, add them to the Daily Log.

Table 12.3 shows the responsibilities for this activity.

12.4.4 Prepare the outline Business Case

When setting up, and particularly while running the project, it is all too easy to concentrate on **what** is being done and **how** it is to be done, while ignoring **why** it needs to be done. The Business Case states **why** the work is worth doing and, as such, is a crucial element of the project.

If the project is part of a programme, then the Business Case may already have been defined at the programme level.

Given the information available, the outline Business Case is likely to be only a high-level view at this time. It provides an agreed foundation for a more extensive Business Case developed in the Initiating a Project process.

Figure 12.5 shows the inputs to, and outputs from, this activity. For more details on the Business Case, see Chapter 4.

Table 12.3 Design and appoint the project management team: responsibilities

Producer – responsible for product's production

Reviewer – ideally independent of production

Approver – confirms approval

Product	Action	Corporate/Programme	Executive	Senior User	Senior Supplier	Project Manager	Team Manager	Project Assurance	Project Support	Product Description available
Daily Log	Update					P				A7
Project management team role descriptions	Create		A			P				
Project management team structure	Create		A			P				
Appointed project management team	Confirm	A	P							

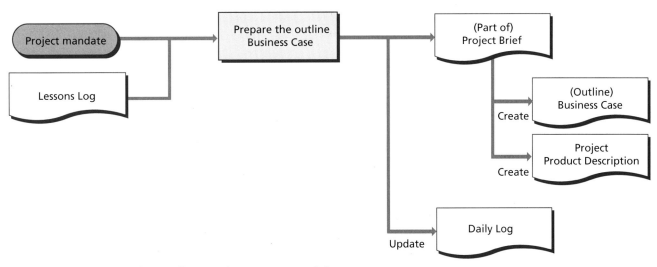

Figure 12.5 Prepare the outline Business Case: activity summary

PRINCE2 recommends the following actions:

- Executive to draft the outline Business Case based on what is currently known about the project:
  - Understand the objectives of, and the reasons for, the project as defined in the project mandate
  - Understand how the project will contribute toward corporate and/or programme objectives
  - Understand how the project will be funded
  - Review the Lessons Log for lessons related to business justification

- Check for any standards mandated for the format and presentation of the Business Case (templates, cost metrics etc.)
- Assemble any relevant background information, e.g. contracts, feasibility reports, service level agreements etc.
- If necessary, seek approval of the outline Business Case from corporate or programme management

- Project Manager to consult with the Senior User and Executive to define what the project is to deliver, and create the Project Product Description (see Chapter 6):

Table 12.4 Prepare the outline Business Case: responsibilities

Producer – responsible for product's production

Reviewer – ideally independent of production

Approver – confirms approval

Product	Action	Corporate/Programme	Executive	Senior User	Senior Supplier	Project Manager	Team Manager	Project Assurance	Project Support	Product Description available
Outline Business Case	Create	A	P	R	R	R		R		A2
Project Product Description	Create		(A)	(A)	(A)	P		R		A21
Daily Log	Update					P				A7

- Capture the customer's quality expectations
- Capture and agree the project's acceptance criteria
- Check feasibility of the timescale requirements from the project mandate or as required by the outline Business Case
- Determine any key milestones
- Capture any new risks in the Daily Log
- ■ Review the risks captured in the Daily Log and summarize the key risks affecting viability of the project in the outline Business Case.

Table 12.4 shows the responsibilities for this activity.

12.4.5 Select the project approach and assemble the Project Brief

Before any planning of the project can be done, decisions must be made regarding how the work of the project is going to be approached. For example, will the solution be developed in-house or contracted to third parties? Will the solution be a modification to an existing product or built from scratch? Will the solution be based on a commercial off-the-shelf product (often referred to as COTS) or something that is custom-designed?

The way in which the work is to be conducted will depend on any customer or supplier standards, practices and guidelines – for example, any specific development lifecycles that may apply. These should be captured in the Project Brief as part of the project approach, as they will influence the project strategies to be created in the Initiating a Project process. It also ensures that the project approach is clearly understood between customer and supplier, and does not jeopardize the project in any way.

An agreed Project Brief ensures that the project has a commonly understood and well-defined start point.

Figure 12.6 shows the inputs to, and outputs from, this activity.

PRINCE2 recommends the following actions:

- ■ Evaluate the possible delivery solutions and decide upon the project approach appropriate to delivering the project product and achieving the outline Business Case:
  - Review the Lessons Log for lessons related to the project approach

- Consider any corporate or programme strategies that are relevant, and put the project in context with any other work or corporate initiatives by establishing external dependencies and prerequisites
- Consider any corporate or programme standards or practices that should apply (in a commercial customer/supplier context there are likely to be different standards and practices which need to be accommodated)
- Consider the current thinking about the provision of solutions within the industry sectors and specialist skill areas involved (including any technical options for the development lifecycle for the project product)
- Define the operational environment into which the solution must fit (including operational or maintenance implications and constraints) and how the project product can be brought into that environment
- Consider any security constraints that apply to the project or the operation of its products
- Consider any training needs for user personnel
- ■ Assemble the Project Brief:
  - Define the project:
    - Confirm current status of the project (e.g. project background and any preparation work carried out to date)
    - Confirm the objectives and desired outcomes
    - Confirm the project scope and exclusions
    - Identify any constraints and assumptions
    - Identify the project tolerances
    - Identify the user(s) and any other known interested parties
    - Identify the interfaces that the project must maintain
  - Incorporate the outline Business Case
  - Incorporate the Project Product Description
  - Incorporate the project approach
  - Review the project management team structure and role descriptions to identify any additional roles or skills required to conduct the work. Prepare additional role descriptions as necessary
  - Incorporate the project management team structure and role descriptions

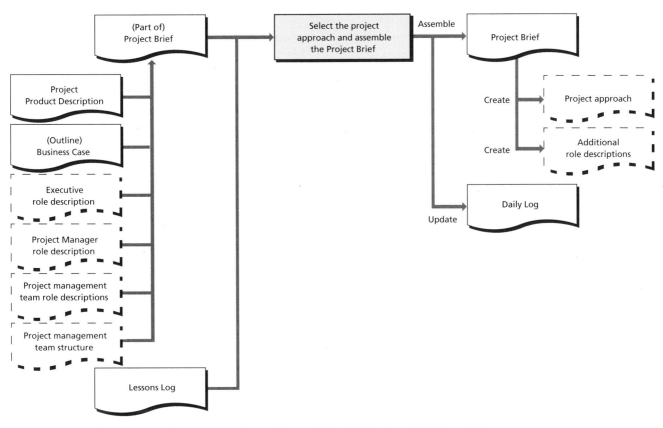

Figure 12.6 Select the project approach and assemble the Project Brief: activity summary

Table 12.5 Select the project approach and assemble the Project Brief: responsibilities

Producer – responsible for product's production

Reviewer – ideally independent of production

Approver – confirms approval

Product	Action	Corporate/Programme	Executive	Senior User	Senior Supplier	Project Manager	Team Manager	Project Assurance	Project Support	Product Description available
Project approach	Create/select		(A)	(R)	(R)	P		R		
Additional role descriptions	Create		(A)	(R)	(R)	P		R		
Project Brief	Assemble		(A)	(R)	(R)	P		R		A19
Daily Log	Update					P				A7

■ Use the Daily Log to record any new issues or risks.

Table 12.5 shows the responsibilities for this activity.

12.4.6 Plan the initiation stage

Initiating a Project takes time and consumes resources. The work should be planned and approved like any other project work. This also ensures that initiation is not aimless and unstructured.

If the project is part of a programme, the end date for the initiation stage should be checked against that held in the programme's plans. The Stage Plan for the initiation stage will also give the programme management team warning of any requirements from the programme.

The application of PRINCE2 processes during Initiating a Project needs to be considered as part of the Starting up a Project process. For example, the project may choose to apply the Controlling a Stage and Managing Product Delivery processes during the Initiating a Project process.

Figure 12.7 shows the inputs to, and outputs from, this activity. For more details on planning, see Chapter 7.

PRINCE2 recommends the following actions:

■ Based on the project approach, decide upon suitable management controls for the project sufficient for it to be initiated:
- Review the Lessons Log for lessons related to project controls
- Define the reporting and control arrangements for the initiation stage

■ Identify any constraints on time and costs for the initiation stage and produce the Stage Plan for this stage according to the principles and techniques in Chapter 7

■ Review any risks in the Daily Log and assess their impact on the Stage Plan for the initiation stage

■ If any new risks are identified (or existing ones have changed), update the Daily Log

■ Request authorization to initiate the project.

Table 12.6 shows the responsibilities for this activity.

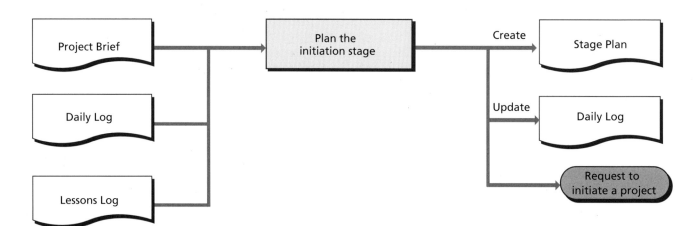

Figure 12.7 Plan the initiation stage: activity summary

Table 12.6 Plan the initiation stage: responsibilities

Producer – responsible for product's production
Reviewer – ideally independent of production
Approver – confirms approval

Product	Action	Corporate/Programme	Executive	Senior User	Senior Supplier	Project Manager	Team Manager	Project Assurance	Project Support	Product Description available
Stage Plan	Create		(A)	(A)	(A)	P		R		A16
Daily Log	Update					P				A7

Directing a Project

13

13 Directing a Project

13.1 PURPOSE

The purpose of the Directing a Project process is to enable the Project Board to be accountable for the project's success by making key decisions and exercising overall control while delegating day-to-day management of the project to the Project Manager.

13.2 OBJECTIVE

The objective of the Directing a Project process is to ensure that:

- There is authority to initiate the project
- There is authority to deliver the project's products
- Management direction and control are provided throughout the project's life, and that the project remains viable
- Corporate or programme management has an interface to the project
- There is authority to close the project
- Plans for realizing the post-project benefits are managed and reviewed.

13.3 CONTEXT

The Directing a Project process starts on completion of the Starting up a Project process and is triggered by the request to initiate a project.

The Directing a Project process does not cover the day-to-day activities of the Project Manager, but the activities of those at the level of management above the Project Manager: that is, the Project Board. The Project Board manages by exception. It monitors via reports and controls through a small number of decision points. There should be no need for other 'progress meetings' for the Project Board. The Project Manager will inform the board of any exception situation. It is also important that levels of authority and decision-making processes are clearly identified.

There needs to be a two-way flow of information between the Project Board and corporate or programme management during the project. It is a key role of the Project Board to engage with corporate or programme management and to act as a communication channel. This need, and how it is to be satisfied, should be documented in the Communication Management Strategy.

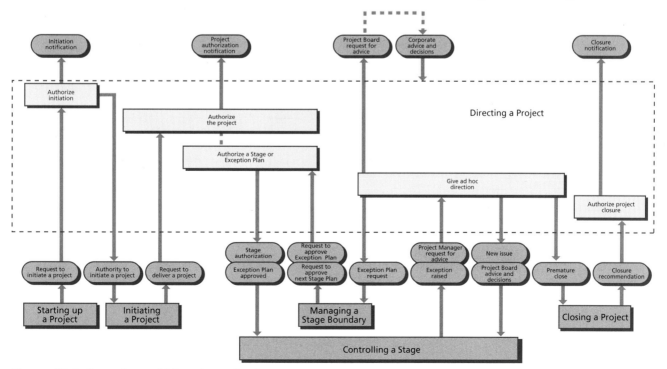

Figure 13.1 Overview of Directing a Project

The Project Board should provide unified direction and guidance to the Project Manager. If the Project Board is unable to provide a single view or if independent, possibly contradictory, advice is given, then the risk of project failure significantly increases. In such cases, the Project Manager should defer to the Executive.

The Project Board is responsible for assuring that there is continued business justification. The Directing a Project process provides a mechanism for the Project Board to achieve such assurance without being overburdened by project activity.

One of the functions of the Project Board is to provide informal advice and guidance to the Project Manager as well as formal direction. The Project Manager should seek advice whenever necessary during the course of the project.

13.4 ACTIVITIES

The activities within the Directing a Project process are Project-Board-oriented and are to:

- Authorize initiation
- Authorize the project
- Authorize a Stage or Exception Plan
- Give ad hoc direction
- Authorize project closure.

13.4.1 Authorize initiation

Projects take time and cost money to initiate, so the activities for initiation should be planned, monitored and controlled. The Project Board activity to authorize initiation ensures that such investment is worthwhile.

Once a request to initiate a project is received from Starting up a Project, the Project Board must decide whether to allow the project to proceed to the initiation stage. This may be done at a formal Project Board meeting. The Project Board can, however, choose to make the decision without the need for a formal meeting, as long as all members are in agreement, and the Project Manager is given documented instruction from the Executive to proceed with initiation.

The Project Board may appoint Project Assurance to undertake some of the reviewing and assessing actions (e.g. inspecting the Initiation Stage Plan to confirm it is viable).

In a commercial customer/supplier relationship, the Senior Supplier may not be appointed at this point, and/or their approval of the Project Brief and its components may not be necessary in order to authorize initiation.

Figure 13.2 shows the inputs to, and outputs from, this activity.

PRINCE2 recommends the following actions:

- Review and approve the Project Brief:
  - Confirm the project definition (including key milestones)
  - Confirm the project approach
  - Formally confirm the appointments to the project management team, and confirm that all members have agreed their roles

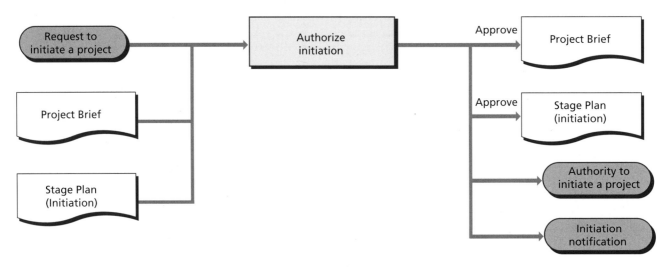

Figure 13.2 Authorize initiation: activity summary

- Review and approve the Project Product Description:
  - Confirm the customer's quality expectations
  - Confirm the acceptance criteria
- Verify that the outline Business Case demonstrates a viable project. At this point, the outline Business Case may only contain sufficient information that reasonably justifies the project as worthwhile. The detailed Business Case will be developed during the initiation stage
- Review and approve the Stage Plan for the initiation stage:
  - Understand any risks that affect the decision to authorize the initiation stage
  - Obtain or commit the resources needed by the Stage Plan for the initiation stage
  - Ensure that adequate reporting and control mechanisms are in place for the initiation stage and set tolerances for it
- Inform all stakeholders and the host sites that the project is being initiated and request any necessary logistical support (e.g. communication facilities, equipment and any project support) sufficient for the initiation stage
- Authorize the Project Manager to proceed with the initiation stage.

Table 13.1 shows the responsibilities for this activity.

13.4.2 Authorize the project

This activity will be triggered by a request from the Project Manager for authorization to deliver the project, and should be performed in parallel with authorizing a Stage or Exception Plan (see section 13.4.3).

The objective of authorizing the project is to decide whether to proceed with the rest of the project. The Project Board has to confirm that:

- An adequate and suitable Business Case exists and that it shows a viable project
- The Project Plan is adequate to deliver the Business Case
- The project's strategies and controls support delivery of the Project Plan
- The mechanisms for measuring and reviewing the projected benefits are established and planned.

If the project is not authorized by the Project Board, then it should be prematurely closed (see Chapter 18).

The Project Board may appoint Project Assurance to undertake some of the reviewing and assessing actions (e.g. inspecting the Communication Management Strategy to confirm all stakeholders are covered).

Figure 13.3 shows the inputs to, and outputs from, this activity.

Table 13.1 Authorize initiation: responsibilities

Producer – responsible for product's production

Reviewer – ideally independent of production

Approver – confirms approval

Product	Action	Corporate/Programme	Executive	Senior User	Senior Supplier	Project Manager	Team Manager	Project Assurance	Project Support	Product Description available
Project Brief	Approve	(R)	A	A	A	(P)		R		A19
Initiation Stage Plan	Approve		A	A	A	(P)		R		A16

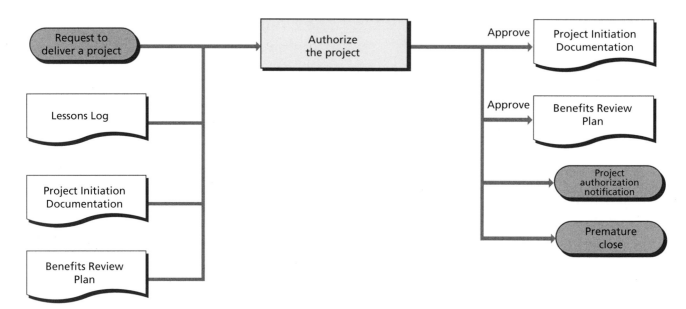

Figure 13.3 Authorize the project: activity summary

PRINCE2 recommends the following actions:

■ Review and approve the Project Initiation Documentation:

- Confirm that the project definition is accurate and complete and that the project approach is achievable
- Confirm that lessons from previous similar projects have been reviewed and incorporated
- Confirm that the Quality Management Strategy is sufficient to ensure that the quality expectations will be met, and approve it
- Confirm that the procedures defined in the Risk Management Strategy are sufficient to keep the risks under control, and approve it. Confirm that there has been a review of the risks, and that risk responses for both threats and opportunities are appropriate and planned
- Confirm that the Configuration Management Strategy will adequately control the status (versions and variants) of the project's products, and approve it
- Ensure that the stakeholder information needs and timing of communications, as defined in the Communication Management Strategy, are adequate, and approve it
- Confirm that all members of the project management team have agreed their roles and agree any delegations of, and limits to,

Project Board authority (for example, to a Change Authority)
- Ensure that the project controls are adequate for the nature of the project
- Confirm the validity and achievability of the Project Plan (including any key milestones and proposed stage structure), and approve it
- Review and approve the Product Description(s)
- Review the tolerances for the project provided by corporate or programme management to ensure they are appropriate and realistic
- Obtain or commit the resources needed by the project (these will be released to the Project Manager on a stage-by-stage basis)
- Confirm the proposals to tailor the corporate (or programme) project management method and any tailoring of PRINCE2
- Verify that the Business Case demonstrates a viable project, and approve it

■ Review and approve the Benefits Review Plan. Confirm it addresses all the expected benefits and meets the needs of corporate or programme management

■ Notify corporate or programme management and other interested parties that the project has been authorized

■ Authorize the Project Manager to deliver the project or instruct the Project Manager to close the project prematurely if it is decided not to proceed.

Table 13.2 Authorize the project: responsibilities

Producer – responsible for product's production

Reviewer – ideally independent of production

Approver – confirms approval

Product	Action	Corporate/Programme	Executive	Senior User	Senior Supplier	Project Manager	Team Manager	Project Assurance	Project Support	Product Description available
Lessons Log	Review		R	R	R	(P)		R		A14
Project Initiation Documentation	Approve	R	A	A	A	(P)		R		A20
Benefits Review Plan	Approve	A	A	A	A	(P)		R		A1

Table 13.2 shows the responsibilities for this activity.

13.4.3 Authorize a Stage or Exception Plan

It is important that a stage starts only when the Project Board says it should. The Project Board authorizes a management stage by reviewing the performance of the current stage and approving the Stage Plan for the next stage. Approval of Stage Plans occurs at the end of every management stage except the last one.

If an exception has occurred during the stage, the Project Board may request that the Project Manager produces an Exception Plan for Project Board approval. Only exceptions to Stage Plans or Project Plans need to be escalated for approval. Deviations from the Project Plan may need corporate or programme management approval. Work Package exceptions are managed by the Project Manager using the Controlling a Stage process (see Chapter 15). If approved, the Exception Plan will replace the plan that is in exception and will become the new baselined plan.

The Project Board may appoint Project Assurance to undertake some of the reviewing and assessing actions (e.g. inspecting the Stage Plan to confirm it is viable).

Figure 13.4 shows the inputs to, and outputs from, this activity.

PRINCE2 recommends the following actions:

■ Review and approve the End Stage Report:
  ● Ascertain the performance of the project to date, asking the Project Manager to explain any deviations from the approved plans and to provide a forecast of project performance for the remainder of the project
  ● If required, review the Lessons Report and agree who should receive it. Ensure that the appropriate groups (for example, corporate or programme management, or a centre of excellence) have been made aware of their responsibility for taking any recommendations forward
  ● Check the risk summary to ensure the exposure is still acceptable and that risk responses for both opportunities and threats are appropriate and planned
  ● If there has been a phased handover of products during the stage:
    ● Verify that the product handover was in accordance with the Configuration Management Strategy and, in particular, that user acceptance, and operational and maintenance acceptance, exist for each product
    ● Ensure that, where appropriate, the resulting changes in the business are supported and sustainable

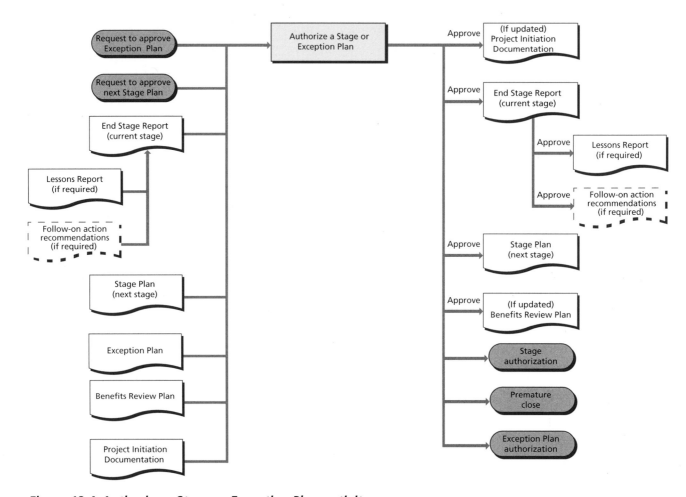

Figure 13.4 Authorize a Stage or Exception Plan: activity summary

- Confirm who should receive which follow-on action recommendation, if any, as summarized in the End Stage Report (in some instances it may be necessary to review the detailed recommendation for some of the follow-on action recommendations). Ensure that the appropriate groups (for example, operations or maintenance) have been made aware of their responsibility for taking any recommendations forward

■ Review the Stage Plan or Exception Plan for which the Project Manager is seeking approval:
  - Confirm the validity and achievability of the Stage Plan/Exception Plan
  - Review and approve any new Product Description(s)
  - Confirm the validity and achievability of the Project Plan. If necessary, secure appropriate approvals from corporate or programme management

- Confirm the strategies and project controls in the (updated) Project Initiation Documentation are adequate for the remainder of the project
- Verify that the (updated) Business Case continues to demonstrate a viable project
- Review and approve the (updated) Benefits Review Plan to ensure that any benefits planned to be achieved within the next stage will be measured and reviewed

■ Make a decision:
  - Approve the plan(s) and authorize the Project Manager to proceed with the submitted plan(s):
    - Obtain or commit the resources needed by the plan(s)
    - Set tolerances for the plan being approved (for the final stage, the Project Board should consider whether any residual tolerances from the previous stages could be assigned to the plan or whether they are better held back in reserve)

- Or ask the Project Manager to revise the rejected plan, giving guidance about the changes required to make it acceptable
- Or instruct the Project Manager to initiate premature closure of the project

■ Communicate the status of the project to corporate or programme management and keep other interested parties informed about project progress (in accordance with the Communication Management Strategy).

Table 13.3 shows the responsibilities for this activity.

13.4.4 Give ad hoc direction

Project Board members may offer informal guidance or respond to requests for advice at any time during a project. The need for consultation between the Project Manager and Project Board is likely to be particularly frequent during the initiation stage and when approaching stage boundaries.

Ad hoc direction may be given collectively or by individual Project Board members. There are a variety of circumstances that might prompt ad hoc direction, including:

■ Responding to requests (e.g. when options need clarifying or where areas of conflict need resolving)
■ Responding to reports (e.g. Highlight Report, Exception Report, Issue Report)
■ Responding to external influences (e.g. changes in corporate priorities)
■ Project Board members' individual concerns
■ Responding to changes in Project Board composition (which may also require corporate or programme approval).

It is also possible that corporate or programme management revises the project mandate in response to events external to the project, or instructs the Project Board to close the project. The Project Board has two primary options should corporate or programme management decide to change the project mandate:

■ Treat it as a request for change (see Chapter 9) – asking the Project Manager to replan the stage and/or project

Table 13.3 Authorize a Stage or Exception Plan: responsibilities

Producer – responsible for product's production

Reviewer – ideally independent of production

Approver – confirms approval

Product	Action	Corporate/Programme	Executive	Senior User	Senior Supplier	Project Manager	Team Manager	Project Assurance	Project Support	Product Description available
Specialist products	Confirm approval		A	A	A	(R)	(P)	(R)		
End Stage Report	Approve		A	A	A	(P)		R		A9
Lessons Report	Distribute		A	R	R	(P)		R		A15
Follow-on action recommendations	Distribute		A	A	A	(P)		R		
Stage Plan for the next stage	Approve		A	A	A	(P)		R		A16
Exception Plan	Approve		A	A	A	(P)		R		A16
(Updated) Project Initiation Documentation	Approve	(R)	A	A	A	(P)		R		A20
(Updated) Benefits Review Plan	Approve	A	A	R	R	(P)		R		A1

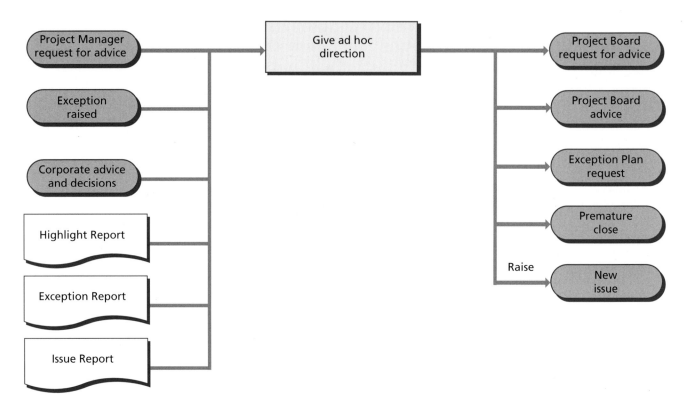

Figure 13.5 Give ad hoc direction: activity summary

■ Stop, and restart the project by triggering premature closure (see Chapter 18). This may result in additional costs compared to the request-for-change option.

The Project Board may appoint Project Assurance to undertake some of the reviewing and assessing actions (e.g. inspecting a request for change to confirm that adequate impact assessment has been undertaken). When making decisions, it is important to consider the impact on all stakeholders (as identified in the Communication Management Strategy).

Figure 13.5 shows the inputs to, and outputs from, this activity.

PRINCE2 recommends the following actions:

■ In response to informal requests for advice and guidance:
  ● Seek advice from corporate or programme management if necessary
  ● Assist the Project Manager as required (this may include asking the Project Manager to produce an Issue Report and/or an Exception Report)

■ In response to an escalated Issue Report (see Chapter 9):
  ● Seek advice from corporate or programme management if necessary
  ● Make a decision within the Project Board's delegated limits of authority. This decision could be regarding:
    ● **A problem/concern** Ask for an Exception Plan or provide guidance
    ● **A request for change** Approve, defer, reject or ask for more information. Consider whether an Exception Plan is required
    ● **An off-specification** Grant a concession, defer, reject or ask for more information. Consider whether an Exception Report is required

■ In response to an Exception Report (see Chapter 10):
  ● Seek advice from corporate or programme management if necessary
  ● Make a decision, within the Project Board's delegated limits of authority, to:
    ● Increase the tolerances that are forecast to be breached

- Instruct the Project Manager to produce an Exception Plan (stating what will be acceptable)
- Instruct the Project Manager to close the project prematurely
- Defer the exception for a fixed period of time. This is a useful response if there is low confidence in the forecast (that tolerances will be exceeded) or if the exception is contingent on a risk occurring

■ In response to the receipt of a Highlight Report (see Chapter 10):
- Review the Highlight Report to understand the status of the project
- Ensure that the project remains focused on the corporate or programme objectives set, and remains justified in accordance with its Business Case
- Ensure that the stage is progressing according to plan
- Keep corporate or programme management and other interested parties informed about project progress, as defined by the Communication Management Strategy
- Take actions as necessary. For example, ask the Project Manager to produce an Issue Report and/or an Exception Report

■ In response to advice and decisions from corporate or programme management:

- Ensure that the project management team is kept informed of external events that may affect it (for example, advising the Project Manager of a change of Project Board personnel)
- Notify the Project Manager of any changes in the corporate or programme environment that may impact on the project, and ensure appropriate action is taken. This may involve:
  - Raising an issue to the Project Manager
  - Instructing the Project Manager to produce an Exception Plan
  - Instructing the Project Manager to close the project prematurely.

Table 13.4 shows the responsibilities for this activity.

13.4.5 Authorize project closure

The controlled close of a project is as important as the controlled start. There must be a point when the objectives set out in the original and current versions of the Project Initiation Documentation and Project Plan are assessed in order to understand:

■ Whether the objectives have been achieved

■ How the project has deviated from its initial basis

■ That the project has nothing more to contribute.

Table 13.4 Give ad hoc direction: responsibilities

Producer – responsible for product's production

Reviewer – ideally independent of production

Approver – confirms approval

Product	Action	Corporate/Programme	Executive	Senior User	Senior Supplier	Project Manager	Team Manager	Project Assurance	Project Support	Product Description available
Highlight Report	Review		R	R	R	(P)		R		A11
Exception Report	Respond		R	R	R	(P)		R		A10
New issue	Raise	P	P	P	P					

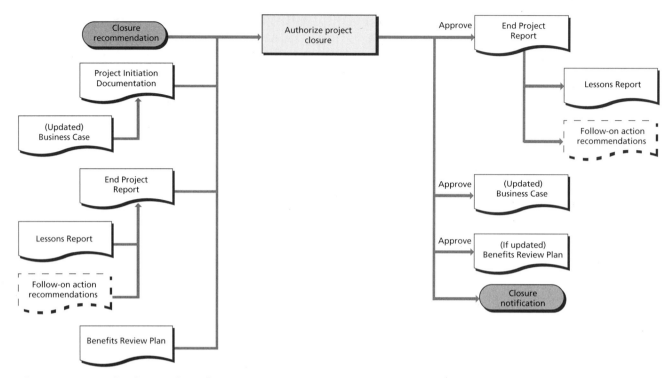

Figure 13.6 Authorize project closure: activity summary

Without this approach, the project may never end; a project can become business as usual and the original focus on benefits will be lost.

Authorizing closure of the project is the last activity undertaken by the Project Board, prior to its own disbandment, and may require endorsement from corporate or programme management.

The Project Board may appoint Project Assurance to undertake some of the reviewing and assessing actions (e.g. inspecting the End Project Report to confirm it is accurate).

Figure 13.6 shows the inputs to, and outputs from, this activity.

PRINCE2 recommends the following actions:

- Review the original and current versions of the Project Initiation Documentation to understand the project's initial baseline, and current strategies and controls
- Review and approve the End Project Report to:
  - Understand the project's actual performance against its initial basis, including a summary of any deviations from the approved plans
  - Confirm who should receive which follow-on action recommendation as summarized in the End Project Report (in some instances it may be necessary to review the detailed recommendation for some of the follow-on actions). Ensure that the appropriate groups (for example, operations or maintenance) have been made aware of their responsibility for taking any recommended actions forward
- Review the Lessons Report and agree who should receive it. Ensure that the appropriate groups (for example, corporate or programme management, or a centre of excellence) have been made aware of their responsibility for taking any recommendations forward
- Verify that the handover of the project's products was in accordance with the Configuration Management Strategy and, in particular, that user acceptance, and operational and maintenance acceptance, exist for each product. Ensure that, where appropriate, the resulting changes in the business are supported and sustainable

- Ensure that the post-project benefits review covers the performance of the project's products in operational use in order to identify whether there have been any side-effects (beneficial or adverse)

- Review and gain approval for the updated Benefits Review Plan, ensuring that it addresses the expected benefits that cannot yet be confirmed. As the Benefits Review Plan includes resources beyond the life of the project, responsibility for this plan needs to transfer to corporate or programme management
- Confirm the updated Business Case by comparing actual and forecast benefits, costs and risks against the original Business Case that was used to justify the project (it may not be possible to confirm all the benefits as some will not be realized until after the project is closed)

- Review and issue a project closure notification in accordance with the Communication Management Strategy. The Project Board advises those who have provided the support infrastructure and resources for the project that these can now be withdrawn. This should indicate a closing date for costs being charged to the project.

Table 13.5 shows the responsibilities for this activity.

Table 13.5 Authorize project closure: responsibilities

Producer – responsible for product's production

Reviewer – ideally independent of production

Approver – confirms approval

Product	Action	Corporate/Programme	Executive	Senior User	Senior Supplier	Project Manager	Team Manager	Project Assurance	Project Support	Product Description available
End Project Report	Approve		A	A	A	(P)		R		A8
Lessons Report	Distribute		A	A	A	(P)		R		A15
Follow-on action recommendations	Distribute		A	A	A	(P)		R		
(Updated) Business Case	Confirm	R	A	R	R	(P)		R		A2
(Updated) Benefits Review Plan	Approve	A	A	R	R	(P)		R		A1

Initiating a Project

14

14 Initiating a Project

14.1 PURPOSE

The purpose of the Initiating a Project process is to establish solid foundations for the project, enabling the organization to understand the work that needs to be done to deliver the project's products before committing to a significant spend.

14.2 OBJECTIVE

The objective of the Initiating a Project process is to ensure that there is a common understanding of:

- The reasons for doing the project, the benefits expected and the associated risks

- The scope of what is to be done and the products to be delivered
- How and when the project's products will be delivered and at what cost
- Who is to be involved in the project decision making
- How the quality required will be achieved
- How baselines will be established and controlled
- How risks, issues and changes will be identified, assessed and controlled
- How progress will be monitored and controlled
- Who needs information, in what format, and at what time

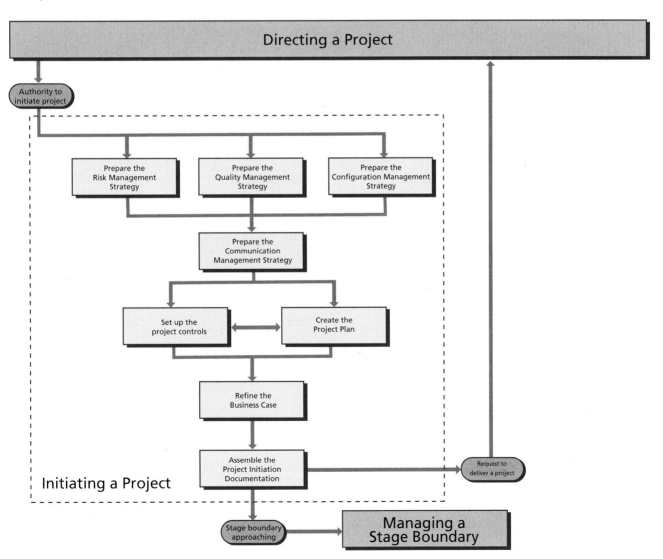

Figure 14.1 Overview of Initiating a Project

- How the corporate (or programme's) project management method will be tailored to suit the project.

14.3 CONTEXT

Initiating a Project is aimed at laying down the foundations in order to achieve a successful project. Specifically, all parties must be clear on what the project is intended to achieve, why it is needed, how the outcome is to be achieved and what their responsibilities are, so that there can be genuine commitment to it.

The Initiating a Project process allows the Project Board, via Directing a Project (see Chapter 13), to decide whether or not the project is sufficiently aligned with corporate or programme objectives to authorize its continuation.

If, instead, the organization proceeds directly from Starting up a Project (see Chapter 12) to Controlling a Stage (see Chapter 15), then it may be forced to commit significant financial resources to a project without fully understanding how its objectives will be achieved. Without a firm definition, the Project Board will be taking a leap of faith.

All activities within the Initiating a Project process need further consideration if the relationship between the customer and the supplier is a commercial one (for example, the reasons for undertaking the project as defined in the supplier's Business Case may be different from those defined in the customer's Business Case) – see Chapter 19 for more details.

During the Initiating a Project process the Project Manager will be creating the suite of management products required for the level of control specified by the Project Board. The Project Manager should have agreed (as part of the Initiation Stage Plan) the means by which the Project Board will review and approve the management products – the two extremes are one at a time or all at once.

14.4 ACTIVITIES

The activities within the Initiating a Project process are Project-Manager-oriented and are to:

- Prepare the Risk Management Strategy
- Prepare the Configuration Management Strategy
- Prepare the Quality Management Strategy
- Prepare the Communication Management Strategy
- Set up the project controls
- Create the Project Plan
- Refine the Business Case
- Assemble the Project Initiation Documentation.

The activities to establish the strategies for the project may be executed in parallel, but it is recommended that the Communications Management Strategy is completed last as it will need to include any communications required by the other strategies.

The strategies are derived from the corporate or programme management strategies, standards or practices that the project needs to comply with, and the customer's quality expectations captured in the Project Product Description. Once the strategies have been defined, it is possible to set up the project controls and create the Project Plan. These are parallel and iterative activities as:

- Each control will need time and resources to operate, which will need to be documented in the Project Plan
- There may be additional controls required as products and activities are identified in the Project Plan.

Once the controls have been established and a Project Plan created, it is then possible to complete the Business Case because forecast time and costs of developing the project's products, and managing the project, are now fully understood.

The final activity in the Initiating a Project process is to assemble the Project Initiation Documentation. This is a compilation of all the documentation developed during initiation that will be used to gain Project Board approval to proceed.

14.4.1 Prepare the Risk Management Strategy

The Risk Management Strategy describes the goals of applying risk management, the procedure that will be adopted, the roles and responsibilities, the risk tolerances, the timing of risk management activities, the tools and techniques that will be used, and the reporting requirements.

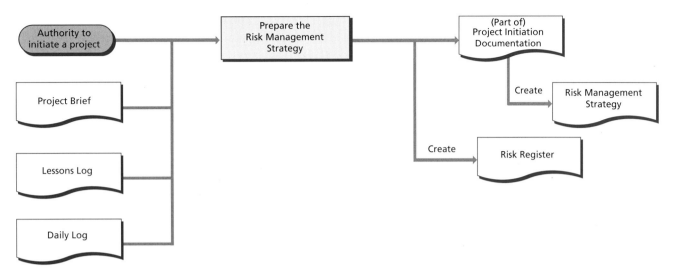

Figure 14.2 Prepare the Risk Management Strategy: activity summary

For more details on risk management, see Chapter 8.

Figure 14.2 shows the inputs to, and outputs from, this activity.

PRINCE2 recommends the following actions:

■ Review the Project Brief to understand whether any corporate or programme management strategies, standards or practices relating to risk management need to be applied by the project

■ Seek lessons from similar previous projects, corporate or programme management, and external organizations related to risk management. Some of these may already have been captured in the Lessons Log

■ Review the Daily Log for any issues and risks related to risk management

■ Define the Risk Management Strategy, including:
  ● The risk management procedure (e.g. Identify, Assess, Plan, Implement, Communicate)
  ● Tools and techniques that will be used
  ● Records that will be kept
  ● How the performance of the risk management procedure will be reported
  ● Timing of risk management activities
  ● The roles and responsibilities for risk management activities
  ● The scales to be used for estimating probability and impact
  ● Guidance on how proximity for risks will be assessed

Table 14.1 Prepare the Risk Management Strategy: responsibilities

Producer – responsible for product's production

Reviewer – ideally independent of production

Approver – confirms approval

Product	Action	Corporate/Programme	Executive	Senior User	Senior Supplier	Project Manager	Team Manager	Project Assurance	Project Support	Product Description available
Risk Management Strategy	Create		(A)	(A)	(A)	P		R		A24
Risk Register	Create and populate					A		R	P	A25

- Definition of risk categories to be used
- Any early-warning indicators to be used
- Tolerances relating to risk
- Whether a risk budget will be established and, if so, how it will be controlled.

■ Consult with Project Assurance to check that the proposed Risk Management Strategy meets the needs of the Project Board and/or corporate or programme management

■ Create the Risk Register in accordance with the Risk Management Strategy, and populate it with any risks from the Daily Log

■ Seek Project Board approval for the Risk Management Strategy (although the Project Board may prefer to review it later as part of the Project Initiation Documentation).

Table 14.1 shows the responsibilities for this activity.

14.4.2 Prepare the Configuration Management Strategy

Configuration management is essential for the project to maintain control over its management and specialist products.

The level of control required will vary from project to project. The maximum level of control possible is determined by breaking down the project's products until the level is reached at which a component can be independently installed,

replaced or modified. However, the level of control exercised will be influenced by the importance of the project and the complexity of the relationship between its products.

The initial set of Configuration Item Records will be created during this activity. The Configuration Management Strategy will define the format and composition of the records that need to be maintained (see Appendix A).

For more details on configuration management, see Chapter 9.

Figure 14.3 shows the inputs to, and outputs from, this activity.

PRINCE2 recommends the following actions:

■ Review the Project Brief to understand whether any corporate or programme management strategies, standards or practices relating to configuration management need to be applied (in particular whether the customer and/or supplier has an existing configuration management system that should be applied)

■ Seek lessons from similar previous projects, corporate or programme management, and external organizations related to configuration management. Some of these may already have been captured in the Lessons Log.

■ Review the Risk Register and Daily Log for risks and issues associated with configuration management

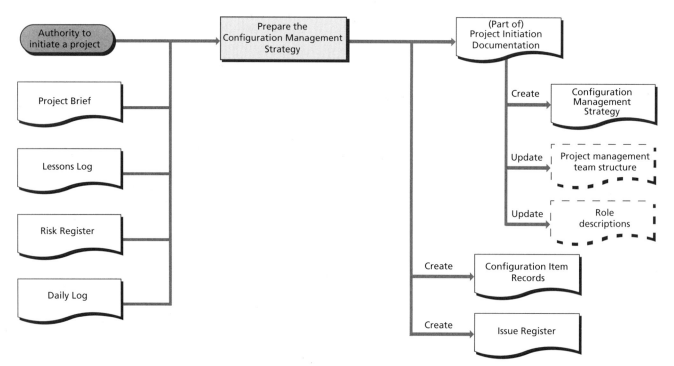

Figure 14.3 Prepare the Configuration Management Strategy: activity summary

- Define the Configuration Management Strategy, including:
  - The configuration management procedure (e.g. planning, identification, control, status accounting, verification and audit)
  - The issue and change control procedure (e.g. capturing, examining, proposing, deciding, implementing)
  - Tools and techniques that will be used
  - Records that will be kept
  - How the performance of the procedures will be reported
  - Timing of configuration management activities and issue and change control activities
  - The roles and responsibilities for the procedures. Consider whether a Change Authority and/or change budget should be established
  - The scales for priority and severity of issues

- Consult with Project Assurance to check that the proposed Configuration Management Strategy meets the needs of the Project Board and/or corporate or programme management
- Create the initial Configuration Item Records (at this point there will only be Configuration Item Records for the management products that have already been created and any pre-existing project documentation that needs to be controlled, e.g. feasibility study, request for proposal etc.)

- Create the Issue Register and consider whether any issues already captured in the Daily Log need to be managed formally and therefore transferred
- If any new risks or issues are identified (or existing ones have changed), then update the Risk Register, Issue Register and/or Daily Log
- Seek Project Board approval for the Configuration Management Strategy (the Project Board may prefer to review it later as part of the Project Initiation Documentation).

Table 14.2 shows the responsibilities for this activity.

14.4.3 Prepare the Quality Management Strategy

A key success factor of any project is that it delivers what the user expects and finds acceptable. This will only happen if these expectations are both stated and agreed at the beginning of the project, together with the standards to be used and the means of assessing their achievement. The purpose of the Quality Management Strategy is to ensure such agreements are captured and maintained.

For more details on quality management, see Chapter 6.

Figure 14.4 shows the inputs to, and outputs from, this activity.

Table 14.2 Prepare the Configuration Management Strategy: responsibilities

Producer – responsible for product's production

Reviewer – ideally independent of production

Approver – confirms approval

Product	Action	Corporate/Programme	Executive	Senior User	Senior Supplier	Project Manager	Team Manager	Project Assurance	Project Support	Product Description available
Configuration Management Strategy	Create		(A)	(A)	(A)	P		R		A6
(Initial) Configuration Item Records	Create					A		R	P	A5
Issue Register	Create and populate					A		R	P	A12

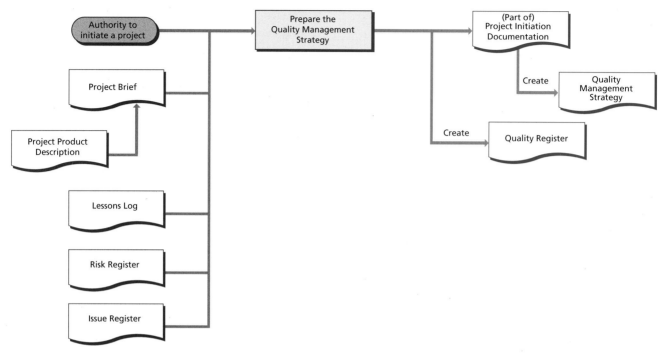

Figure 14.4 Prepare the Quality Management Strategy: activity summary

PRINCE2 recommends the following actions:

- Review the Project Product Description to understand the customer's quality expectations and to check that the project's acceptance criteria are sufficiently defined
- Review the Project Brief to understand whether any corporate or programme management strategies, standards or practices relating to quality management need to be applied by the project (in particular whether the customer and/ or supplier has an existing quality management

system that should be applied to aspects of the project)

- Seek lessons from similar previous projects, corporate or programme management, and external organizations related to quality management. Some of these may already have been captured in the Lessons Log
- Review the Risk Register and Issue Register for issues and risks associated with quality management

Table 14.3 Prepare the Quality Management Strategy: responsibilities

Producer – responsible for product's production

Reviewer – ideally independent of production

Approver – confirms approval

Product	Action	Corporate/Programme	Executive	Senior User	Senior Supplier	Project Manager	Team Manager	Project Assurance	Project Support	Product Description available
Quality Management Strategy	Create		(A)	(A)	(A)	P		R		A22
Quality Register	Create					A		R	P	A23

- Define the Quality Management Strategy, including:
  - The quality management procedure (e.g. quality planning, quality control, quality assurance)
  - Tools and techniques that will be used
  - Records that will be kept
  - How the performance of the quality management procedure will be reported
  - Timing of quality management activities
  - The roles and responsibilities for quality management activities (check links to any corporate or programme quality assurance function and ensure that all project quality activities support, and are supported by, this function)
- Consult with Project Assurance to check that the proposed Quality Management Strategy meets the needs of the Project Board and/or corporate or programme management
- Create a Quality Register in readiness to record details of all quality activities

- If any new risks or issues are identified (or existing ones have changed), then update the Risk Register, Issue Register and/or Daily Log
- Seek Project Board approval for the Quality Management Strategy (although the Project Board may prefer to review it later as part of the Project Initiation Documentation).

Table 14.3 shows the responsibilities for this activity.

14.4.4 Prepare the Communication Management Strategy

The Communication Management Strategy addresses both internal and external communications. It should contain details of how the project management team will send information to, and receive information from, the wider organization(s) involved with, or affected by, the project. In particular, where the project is part of a programme, details should be given on how information is to be fed to the programme.

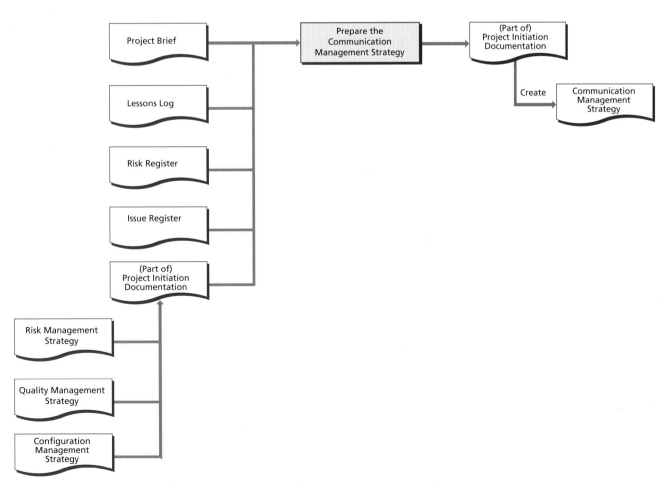

Figure 14.5 Prepare the Communication Management Strategy: activity summary

If a formal stakeholder engagement procedure is needed (such as that described in Chapter 5), this should also be documented as part of the Communication Management Strategy and should record the types of stakeholder, desired relationships and key messages, strategies for communication, and methods for evaluating the success of communications.

Figure 14.5 shows the inputs to, and outputs from, this activity.

PRINCE2 recommends the following actions:

- Review the Project Brief to understand whether any corporate or programme management strategies, standards or practices relating to communication management need to be applied by the project
- Seek lessons from similar previous projects, corporate or programme management, and external organizations related to communication management. Some may already have been captured in the Lessons Log
- Review the Risk Register and Issue Register for risks and issues associated with communication management
- Identify and/or review stakeholders, and consult them for their information needs:
  - Identify desired relationships
  - Clarify key communication messages
  - Determine desired outcomes from successful communications

- Establish the information needs associated with the Quality Management Strategy, the Risk Management Strategy and the Configuration Management Strategy
- Define the Communication Management Strategy, including:
  - The communication management procedure
  - Tools and techniques that will be used
  - Records that will be kept
  - How the performance of the communication management procedure will be reported
  - Timing of communication activities
  - The roles and responsibilities for communication activities
  - Stakeholder analysis
- Consult with Project Assurance to check that the proposed Communication Management Strategy meets the needs of the Project Board and/or corporate or programme management
- If any new risks or issues are identified (or existing ones have changed), then update the Risk Register, Issue Register and/or Daily Log
- Seek Project Board approval for the Communication Management Strategy (although the Project Board may prefer to review it later as part of the Project Initiation Documentation).

Table 14.4 shows the responsibilities for this activity.

14.4.5 Set up the project controls

The level of control required by the Project Board after initiation needs to be agreed and

Table 14.4 Prepare the Communication Management Strategy: responsibilities

Producer – responsible for product's production

Reviewer – ideally independent of production

Approver – confirms approval

Product	Action	Corporate/Programme	Executive	Senior User	Senior Supplier	Project Manager	Team Manager	Project Assurance	Project Support	Product Description available
Communication Management Strategy	Create		(A)	(A)	(A)	P		R		A4

the mechanism for such controls needs to be established – as does the level of control required by the Project Manager of the work to be undertaken by Team Managers.

Project controls enable the project to be managed in an effective and efficient manner that is consistent with the scale, risks, complexity and importance of the project. Effective project controls are a prerequisite for managing by exception.

Project controls can include:

■ The frequency and format of communication between the project management levels (see Chapter 5)

■ The number of stages and hence end stage assessments (see Chapter 7)

■ Mechanisms to capture and analyse issues and changes (see Chapter 9)

■ Mechanisms to escalate exceptions (see Chapter 10)

■ Tolerances for delegated authority (see Chapter 10)

■ How delegated authority from one level of management to another will be monitored (see Chapter 10).

Many of these controls will have been defined in the project's strategies but not necessarily set up. The focus of this activity is to establish such controls and to make sure that they make sense as a coherent set.

Figure 14.6 shows the inputs to, and outputs from, this activity.

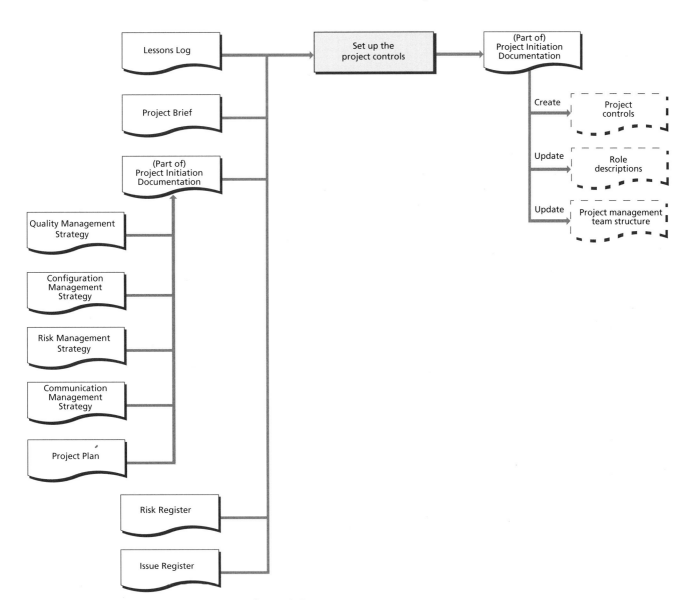

Figure 14.6 Set up the project controls: activity summary

PRINCE2 recommends the following actions:

■ Review the Project Brief to understand whether any corporate or programme management strategies, standards or practices relating to controls need to be applied by the project. Identify whether any of these require PRINCE2 to be tailored

■ Review the Quality Management Strategy, Configuration Management Strategy, Risk Management Strategy and Communication Management Strategy to identify which controls need to be established

■ Seek lessons from similar previous projects, corporate or programme management, and external organizations related to project controls. Some of these may already have been captured in the Lessons Log

■ Review the Risk Register and Issue Register for risks and issues associated with project controls. The aggregated set of risks will have an impact on the scale and rigour of control activities

■ Confirm and document the management stage boundaries required to provide the appropriate level of control

■ Allocate the various levels of decision making required within the project to the most appropriate project management level. Establish any decision-making procedures that may be appropriate, possibly by tailoring procedures within an existing quality management system or other standard procedures

■ Incorporate the agreed decision-making authority and responsibility into the project management team structure and role descriptions where appropriate; this may include finalizing any roles not previously allocated, re-allocating roles previously filled and, if necessary, re-designing the project management team

■ Confirm the tolerances for the project and the escalation procedures (from Team Managers to Project Manager, Project Manager to Project Board, and Project Board to corporate or programme management)

■ Summarize the project controls in the Project Initiation Documentation

■ Consult with Project Assurance to check that the proposed project controls are consistent with the nature of the project and meet the needs of the Project Board and/or corporate or programme management

■ If any new risks or issues are identified (or existing ones have changed), then update the Risk Register, Issue Register and/or Daily Log

■ Seek Project Board approval for the project controls (the Project Board may prefer to review them later as part of the Project Initiation Documentation).

Table 14.5 shows the responsibilities for this activity.

Table 14.5 Set up the project controls: responsibilities

Producer – responsible for product's production

Reviewer – ideally independent of production

Approver – confirms approval

Product	Action	Corporate/Programme	Executive	Senior User	Senior Supplier	Project Manager	Team Manager	Project Assurance	Project Support	Product Description available
Project controls	Create		(A)	(A)	(A)	P		R		
Role descriptions	Update		(A)	(A)	(A)	P		R		
Project management team structure	Update		(A)	(A)	(A)	P				

14.4.6 Create the Project Plan

Before committing to major expenditure on the project, the timescale and resource requirements must be established. This information is held in the Project Plan and is needed so that the Business Case can be refined and the Project Board can control the project.

Planning is not an activity that the Project Manager performs in isolation but, rather, something that should be done with close involvement of the user(s) and supplier(s). It is often useful to hold planning workshops to help identify all the products required, their details, and the dependencies between them.

For more details on planning, see Chapter 7.

Figure 14.7 shows the inputs to, and outputs from, this activity.

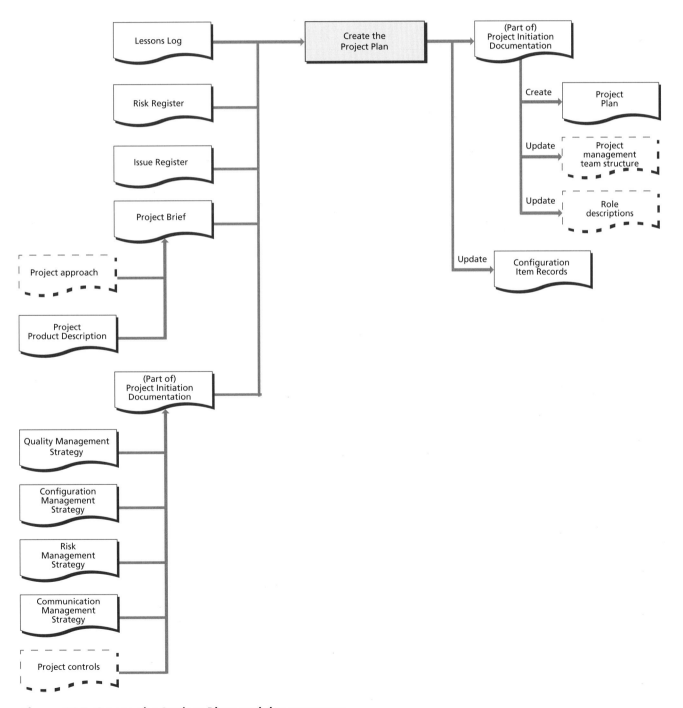

Figure 14.7 Create the Project Plan: activity summary

PRINCE2 recommends the following actions:

- Review the Project Brief to:
  - Understand what the project is to deliver and check for any predetermined milestones as defined in the Project Brief
  - Check whether there are any corporate or programme management strategies, standards or practices relating to planning that the project needs to follow
  - Check understanding of any prerequisites, external dependencies, constraints and assumptions documented in the Project Brief
  - Check understanding of the selected solution as described by the project approach

- Seek lessons from similar previous projects, corporate or programme management, and external organizations related to planning. Some of these may already have been captured in the Lessons Log
- Review the Risk Register and Issue Register for risks and issues associated with planning
- Decide on the format and presentation of the Project Plan, given the audience for the plan and how it will be used (for example, is it sufficient to use a product checklist for presenting the plan to the Project Board?). See the Product Description for a Plan in Appendix A for more information
- Identify any planning and control tools to be used by the project
- Choose the method(s) of estimating for the project's plans
- Review the Quality Management Strategy, Risk Management Strategy, Configuration Management Strategy and Communication Management Strategy to understand the resources, standards, methods and costs for the work to be carried out
- Create a product breakdown structure, product flow diagram and Product Descriptions for the major products in the Project Plan. Identify the arrangements for the transition of the project's products into operational use. Where the project's products are likely to require potentially expensive maintenance once operational, plan for a suitable service agreement or contract to be drawn up between the support group and the user. In such instances, it will be necessary to include any agreement as a product in the Project Plan
- Consider whether the Project Product Description needs to be updated (for example, if the understanding of the acceptance criteria

Table 14.6 Create the Project Plan: responsibilities

Producer – responsible for product's production

Reviewer – ideally independent of production

Approver – confirms approval

Product	Action	Corporate/Programme	Executive	Senior User	Senior Supplier	Project Manager	Team Manager	Project Assurance	Project Support	Product Description available
Project Plan	Create		(A)	(A)	(A)	P		R		A16
Product Descriptions	Create		(A)	(A)	(A)	P		R		A17
Configuration Item Records	Create/update					A		R	P	A5
Project management team structure	Update		(A)	(A)	(A)	P		R		
Role descriptions	Update		(A)	(A)	(A)	P		R		

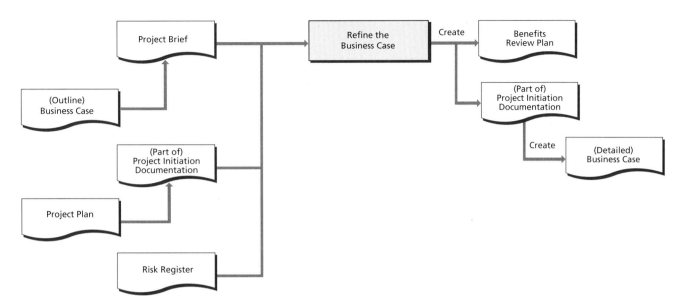

Figure 14.8 Refine the Business Case: activity summary

has changed or been refined in the course of initiating the project)

■ Create or update the Configuration Item Records for each product to be delivered by the plan

■ Identify and confirm resources required. Confirm the selected people's availability, their acceptance of these roles and their commitment to carry them out. See Chapter 5 for more details

■ Identify the activities, resources and timings for the project controls and include them in the plan

■ Document the Project Plan

■ Consult with Project Assurance to check that the proposed Project Plan meets the needs of the Project Board and/or corporate or programme management

■ If any new risks or issues are identified (or existing ones have changed), then update the Risk Register, Issue Register and/or Daily Log

■ Seek Project Board approval for the Project Plan (although the Project Board may prefer to review it later as part of the Project Initiation Documentation).

Table 14.6 shows the responsibilities for this activity.

14.4.7 Refine the Business Case

The outline Business Case produced during Starting up a Project needs to be updated to reflect the estimated time and costs, as determined by the

Project Plan, and the aggregated risks from the updated Risk Register.

The detailed Business Case will be used by the Project Board to authorize the project and provides the basis of the ongoing check that the project remains viable.

For more details on business justification, see Chapter 4.

Figure 14.8 shows the inputs to, and outputs from, this activity.

PRINCE2 recommends the following actions:

■ Review the Project Brief to check whether there are any corporate or programme management requirements for the format and content of the Business Case

■ Seek lessons from similar previous projects, corporate or programme management, and external organizations related to Business Case development. Some of these may already have been captured in the Lessons Log

■ Create the detailed Business Case with the additional detail gained, namely:
  ● The costs and timescale as calculated in the Project Plan
  ● The major risks that affect the viability and achievability of the project (from the Risk Register)
  ● The benefits to be gained
  ● The tolerances allowed for each of the benefits

Table 14.7 Refine the Business Case: responsibilities

Producer – responsible for product's production

Reviewer – ideally independent of production

Approver – confirms approval

Product	Action	Corporate/Programme	Executive	Senior User	Senior Supplier	Project Manager	Team Manager	Project Assurance	Project Support	Product Description available
Benefits Review Plan	Create	(A)	(A)	(A)	(A)	P		R		A1
Detailed Business Case	Create	(R)	(A)	(A)	(A)	P		R		A2

- Create the Benefits Review Plan:
  - Review the Business Case and check understanding of the benefits expected of the project
  - Identify how the achievement of each benefit is to be measured and capture the current baseline measures
  - Identify the timing of benefits reviews (most likely to align to stage boundaries)
  - If the project is part of a programme, the Benefits Review Plan may be created, maintained and executed at the programme level
- If any new risks or issues are identified (or existing ones have changed), then update the Risk Register, Issue Register and/or Daily Log
- Consult with Project Assurance to check that the proposed Business Case and Benefits Review Plan meet the needs of the Project Board and/ or corporate or programme management
- Seek Project Board approval for the Business Case and Benefits Review Plan (although the Project Board may prefer to review them later as part of the Project Initiation Documentation).

Table 14.7 shows the responsibilities for this activity.

14.4.8 Assemble the Project Initiation Documentation

There needs to be a focal point at which all information relating to the 'what, why, who, how, where, when, and how much' of the project is:

- Gathered for agreement by the key stakeholders
- Available for guidance and information for those involved in the project.

This information is collated into the Project Initiation Documentation. The Project Initiation Documentation is an aggregation of many of the management products created during initiation and used to gain authorization for the project to proceed. It is not necessarily (and rarely) a single document, but a collection of documents.

The version of the Project Initiation Documentation created during the Initiating a Project process, and used to gain authorization for the project to proceed, should be preserved. It will be used later as a means to compare the project's actual performance against the original forecasts that formed the basis of approval.

Figure 14.9 shows the inputs to, and outputs from, this activity.

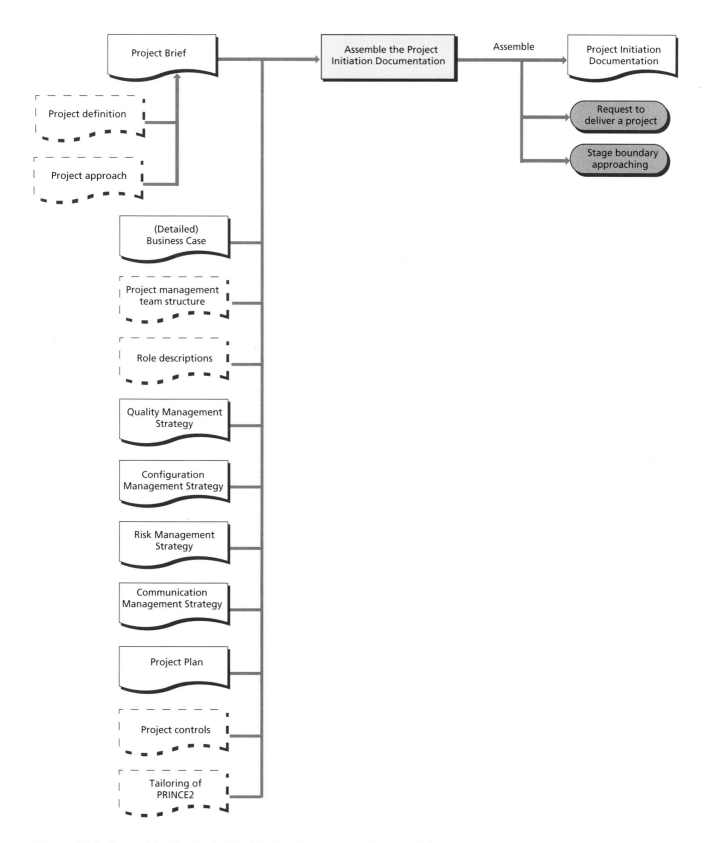

Figure 14.9 Assemble the Project Initiation Documentation: activity summary

Table 14.8 Assemble the Project Initiation Documentation: responsibilities

Producer – responsible for product's production

Reviewer – ideally independent of production

Approver – confirms approval

Product	Action	Corporate/Programme	Executive	Senior User	Senior Supplier	Project Manager	Team Manager	Project Assurance	Project Support	Product Description available
Project Initiation Documentation	Assemble		(A)	(A)	(A)	P		R		A20

PRINCE2 recommends the following actions:

- Extract and, if necessary, revise information from the Project Brief (project definition and project approach)
- Include or reference information in the:
  - Project's management team structure and role descriptions
  - Business Case
  - Quality Management Strategy
  - Configuration Management Strategy
  - Risk Management Strategy
  - Communication Management Strategy
  - Project Plan
- Include or reference the project controls and summarize how the project has tailored PRINCE2
- Assemble the Project Initiation Documentation
- Carry out a cross-check of the information in the various elements to ensure that they are compatible
- Consult with Project Assurance to check that the assembled Project Initiation Documentation meets the needs of the Project Board and/or corporate or programme management
- Prepare for the next stage (which triggers the Managing a Stage Boundary process)
- Request authority from the Project Board to deliver the project.

Table 14.8 shows the responsibilities for this activity.

Controlling a Stage

15

15 Controlling a Stage

15.1 PURPOSE

The purpose of the Controlling a Stage process is to assign work to be done, monitor such work, deal with issues, report progress to the Project Board, and take corrective actions to ensure that the stage remains within tolerance.

15.2 OBJECTIVE

The objective of the Controlling a Stage process is to ensure that:

■ Attention is focused on delivery of the stage's products. Any movement away from the direction and products agreed at the start of the stage is monitored to avoid uncontrolled change ('scope creep') and loss of focus

■ Risks and issues are kept under control

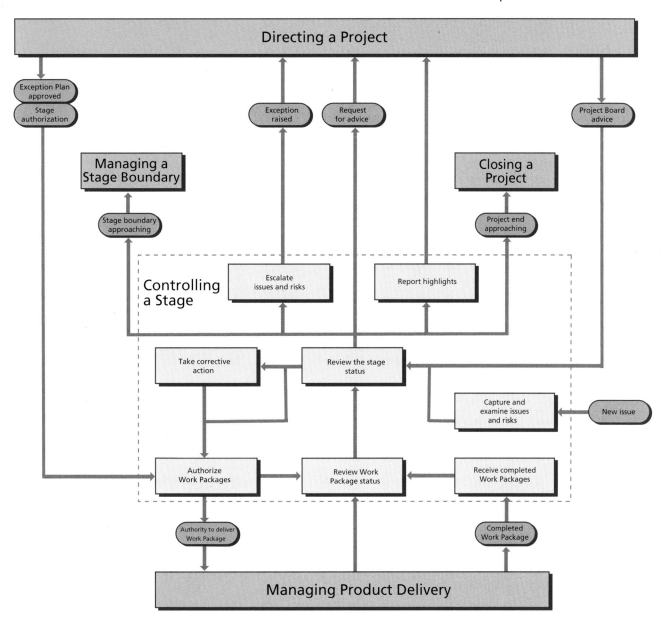

Figure 15.1 Overview of Controlling a Stage

- The Business Case is kept under review
- The agreed products for the stage are delivered to stated quality standards, within cost, effort and time agreed, and ultimately in support of the achievement of the defined benefits
- The project management team is focused on delivery within the tolerances laid down.

15.3 CONTEXT

The Controlling a Stage process describes the work of the Project Manager in handling the day-to-day management of the stage. This process will be used for each delivery stage of a project. Towards the end of each stage, except the final one, the activities within the Managing a Stage Boundary process (see Chapter 17) will occur.

The Controlling a Stage process is normally first used after the Project Board authorizes the project, but it may optionally be used during the initiation stage for large or complex projects with a lengthy initiation.

Work Packages are used to define and control the work to be done, and also to set tolerances for the Team Manager(s). In the case where the Project Manager is fulfilling the Team Manager role, Work Packages should still be used to define and control the work of the individual team members being assigned work. Where this is the case, references to Team Manager throughout the Controlling a Stage process should be regarded as references to the individual team member being assigned work.

Central to the ultimate success of the project is the day-to-day control of the work that is being conducted. Throughout a stage, this will consist of a cycle of:

- Authorizing work to be done
- Monitoring progress information about that work, including signing off completed Work Packages
- Reviewing the situation (including that for product quality) and triggering new Work Packages
- Reporting highlights
- Watching for, assessing and dealing with issues and risks
- Taking any necessary corrective action.

Towards the end of the last stage, the Closing a Project process (see Chapter 18) will be invoked.

15.4 ACTIVITIES

Controlling a Stage activities are Project-Manager-oriented and comprise:

- Work Packages:
  - Authorize a Work Package
  - Review Work Package status
  - Receive completed Work Packages

- Monitoring and reporting:
  - Review the stage status
  - Report highlights

- Issues:
  - Capture and examine issues and risks
  - Escalate issues and risks
  - Take corrective action.

15.4.1 Authorize a Work Package

It would be chaotic to have the people who are working on the project starting activities whenever they think fit. There must be a level of autonomy within the project team(s), but there will be wider issues involved of which they cannot be expected to be aware. It is therefore important that work only commences and continues with the consent of the Project Manager. The vehicle for this is the production, execution and delivery of a Work Package.

A Work Package may include extracts from, or simply cross-reference elements of, the Project Plan, Stage Plan or Project Initiation Documentation.

A Work Package should cover the work to create one or more products. If a product requires more than one Work Package to create it, then it should be broken down into further products with their supporting Product Descriptions.

The triggers for the Project Manager to authorize a Work Package include:

- Stage authorization – the Project Board gives authority to execute a Stage Plan
- Exception Plan approved – the Project Board gives authority to execute an Exception Plan
- New Work Package required – an output from reviewing the stage status (see section 15.4.4)
- Corrective action – in response to an issue or risk.

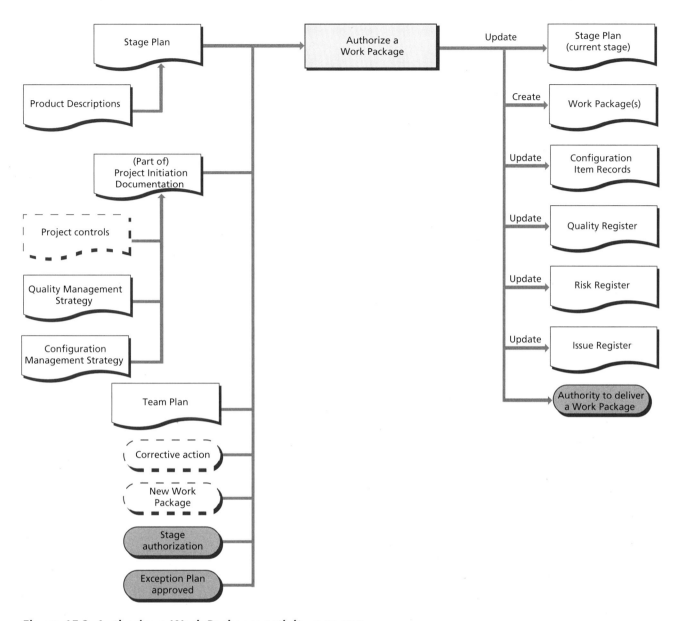

Figure 15.2 Authorize a Work Package: activity summary

This activity is used to authorize new Work Packages or to authorize amendments to existing ones.

Figure 15.2 shows the inputs to, and outputs from, this activity.

PRINCE2 recommends the following actions:

- Examine the Stage Plan for the current management stage in order to understand the:
  - Products to be produced
  - Cost and effort that the work is expected to consume
  - Tolerances available
- Examine the Project Initiation Documentation in order to understand:

- The project controls required (for example, progress reporting arrangements)
- The quality standards required, as defined in the Quality Management Strategy
- If any products are to be handed over, how this will be done (as defined in the Configuration Management Strategy)

- Define each Work Package to be authorized (or amended):
  - Obtain the relevant Product Descriptions for inclusion in the Work Package
  - Define the techniques, processes and procedures to be used
  - Define the development interfaces to be maintained

- Define the operational and maintenance interfaces to be maintained
- Define the configuration management requirements
- Define the joint agreements on effort, cost, start and end dates, key milestones and tolerances
- Define any constraints that may apply
- Define the reporting, problem handling and escalation arrangements
- Define the approval method
- Provide relevant references (e.g. Stage Plan, Product Descriptions)

■ Review the Work Package with the Team Manager, ensure that they have accepted it, and authorize them to begin work (see Chapter 16)

■ Review the Team Manager's Team Plan (or the milestone extract from it if the commercial environment means it is inappropriate for the Project Manager to see its contents) and update the Stage Plan to reflect the timing of the Work Package(s) authorized

■ Update the Configuration Item Records to reflect the content of the Work Package(s) authorized

■ Update the Quality Register for planned quality management activities. Consult with Project Assurance that the identified and selected quality reviewers are acceptable

■ If necessary, update the Risk Register in accordance with the Risk Management Strategy

■ If necessary, update the Issue Register.

Table 15.1 shows the responsibilities for this activity.

15.4.2 Review Work Package status

This activity provides the means for a regular assessment of the status of the Work Package(s). The frequency and formality of this activity will usually be aligned with the frequency of reporting defined in the Work Package(s) and supported by the Stage Plan for the current stage.

Table 15.1 Authorize a Work Package: responsibilities

Producer – responsible for product's production

Reviewer – ideally independent of production

Approver – confirms approval

Product	Action	Corporate/Programme	Executive	Senior User	Senior Supplier	Project Manager	Team Manager	Project Assurance	Project Support	Product Description available
Work Package	Create					P	(A)	R		A26
Configuration Item Record(s)	Create/update					A	(R)	R	P	A5
Quality Register	Update					R	(R)	R	P	A23
Risk Register	Update					P				A25
Issue Register	Update					P				A12
Team Plan	Review					R	(P)			
Stage Plan	Update					P	(R)	R		A16

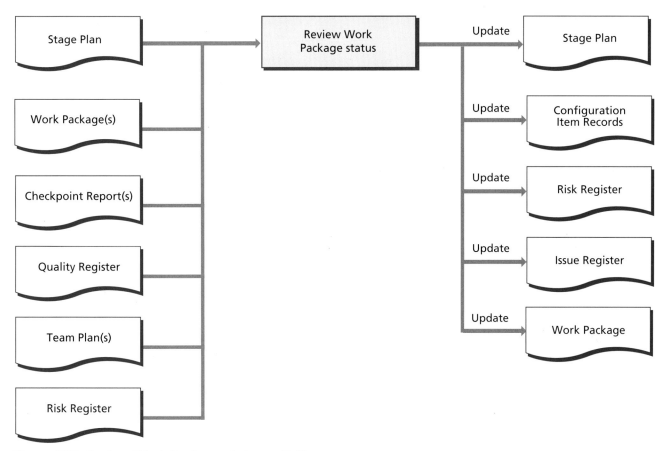

Figure 15.3 Review Work Package status: activity summary

Table 15.2 Review Work Package status: responsibilities

Producer – responsible for product's production

Reviewer – ideally independent of production

Approver – confirms approval

Product	Action	Corporate/Programme	Executive	Senior User	Senior Supplier	Project Manager	Team Manager	Project Assurance	Project Support	Product Description available
Checkpoint Report	Review					R	(P)			A3
Team Plan	Review					R	(P)			
Stage Plan	Update					P		R		A16
Configuration Item Record(s)	Update					A	(R)	R	P	A5
Risk Register	Update					P				A25
Issue Register	Update					P				A12

Figure 15.3 shows the inputs to, and outputs from, this activity.

PRINCE2 recommends the following actions for each Work Package in progress:

- Collect and review progress information from the Checkpoint Report for the Work Package being executed:
  - Assess the estimated time and effort to complete any unfinished work (including that not yet started)
  - Review the Team Plan with the Team Manager (or the milestone extract from it if the commercial environment means it is inappropriate for the Project Manager to see its contents) to ascertain whether work will be completed on time and to budget
  - Review entries in the Quality Register to understand the current status of quality management activities
  - Confirm that the Configuration Item Record for each product in the Work Package matches its status
- If necessary, update the Risk Register and Issue Register
- Update the Stage Plan for the current stage with actuals to date, forecasts and adjustments.

Table 15.2 shows the responsibilities for this activity.

15.4.3 Receive completed Work Package

Where work has been allocated to individuals or teams, there should be a matching confirmation that the work has been completed and approved.

Once approved, any subsequent changes to the product(s) must pass through change control (see Chapter 9). This should be an automatic part of any configuration management method being used.

Figure 15.4 shows the inputs to, and outputs from, this activity.

PRINCE2 recommends the following actions:

- Ensure that the Team Manager has completed the work defined by the Work Package
- Check that the Quality Register entries relating to the product(s) are complete
- Ensure that each product in the Work Package has gained its requisite approval (as defined in the quality responsibilities in its Product Description)
- Confirm that the Configuration Item Record for each approved product has been updated
- Update the Stage Plan to show the Work Package as completed.

Table 15.3 shows the responsibilities for this activity.

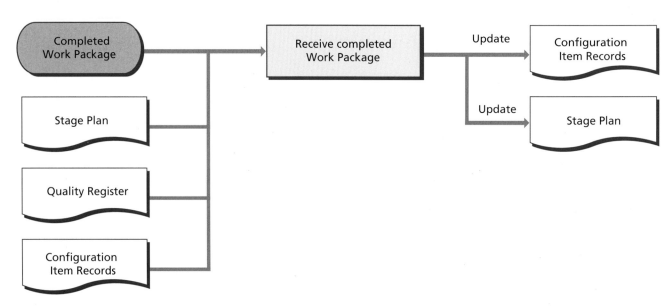

Figure 15.4 Receive completed Work Package: activity summary

Table 15.3 Receive completed Work Package: responsibilities

Producer – responsible for product's production

Reviewer – ideally independent of production

Approver – confirms approval

Product	Action	Corporate/Programme	Executive	Senior User	Senior Supplier	Project Manager	Team Manager	Project Assurance	Project Support	Product Description available
Configuration Item Record(s)	Confirm					A	(R)	R	P	A5
Stage Plan	Update					P		R		A16

15.4.4 Review the stage status

If the project is not checked on a timely basis, there is a danger that it will get out of control. There needs to be a balance between planning ahead and reacting to events.

In order to make informed decisions and exercise rational control, it is necessary to compare what has actually happened with what was expected to happen and what might happen next (including any issues and risks). It is therefore essential to have a steady flow of information that provides an overall view of progress and simple, robust monitoring systems to supply that information.

The objective of this activity, therefore, is to maintain an accurate and current picture of progress on the work being carried out and the status of resources.

This activity occurs at a frequency defined in the Stage Plan, may be triggered by Project Board advice, or forms part of the analysis of new issues and risks.

Figure 15.5 shows the inputs to, and outputs from, this activity.

PRINCE2 recommends the following actions:

■ Review progress for the stage:
  ● Review Checkpoint Reports for the period
  ● Review the current Stage Plan forecast and actuals

  ● Request a Product Status Account from Project Support to identify any variation between planned progress, reported progress and actual progress
  ● Check for any quality issues shown in the Quality Register
  ● Check the Risk Register for any new or revised risks and assess their impact on the Business Case, Stage Plan or the Project Plan
  ● Check the Issue Register to see whether anything has happened within the project or externally that will impact on the Business Case, Stage Plan or the Project Plan
  ● Check the status of any corrective actions
  ● Assess the utilization of resources in the period under review and their availability for the remainder of the stage (or project). Check for any variation in the expected future resource availability
  ● Check the Benefits Review Plan to see whether any benefits reviews are due, and execute them as necessary

■ Based on the above analysis, decide whether any actions are required. For example, whether to:
  ● Authorize a Work Package (section 15.4.1)
  ● Report highlights (section 15.4.5) in accordance with the Communication Management Strategy

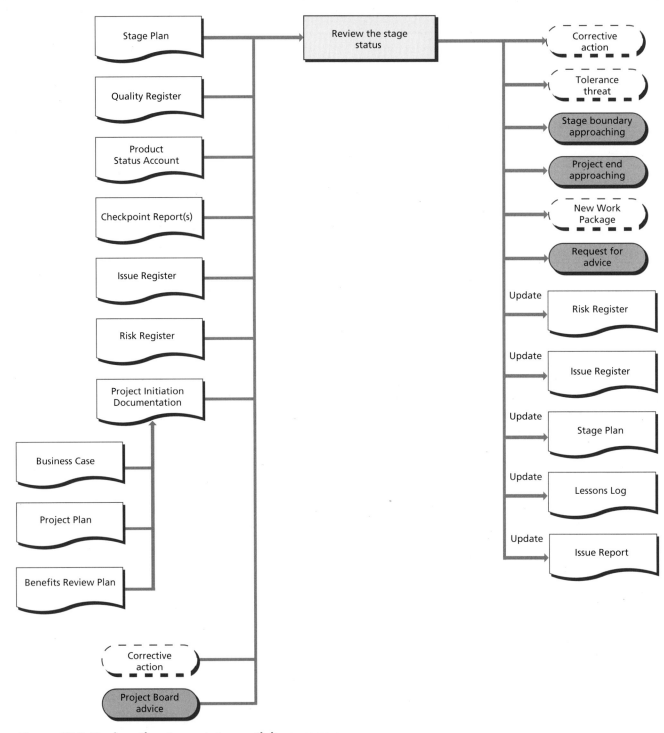

Figure 15.5 Review the stage status: activity summary

- Capture and examine issues and risks (section 15.4.6)
- Escalate issues and risks (section 15.4.7) if tolerances are threatened
- Take corrective action (section 15.4.8)
- Seek Project Board advice (and if necessary provide them with the Issue Report)
- Log any lessons that have been identified

- Continue as planned
- Revise the Risk Register and Issue Register as necessary
- Update the Stage Plan if the aggregated assessment changes any forecasts
- If ownership of any of the products is to be transferred to the customer as part of a phased handover:

Table 15.4 Review the stage status: responsibilities

Producer – responsible for product's production

Reviewer – ideally independent of production

Approver – confirms approval

Product	Action	Corporate/Programme	Executive	Senior User	Senior Supplier	Project Manager	Team Manager	Project Assurance	Project Support	Product Description available
Risk Register	Update					P				A25
Issue Register	Update					P				A12
Stage Plan	Update					P		R		A16
Lessons Log	Update					P				A14
Issue Report	Update					P				A13

- Request a Product Status Account for the release being handed over
- Ensure that the:
  - Products have been approved by those specified in its Product Description
  - Products meet all the quality criteria, or are covered by approved concessions
  - Operation and maintenance organizations are ready to take responsibility for the products
  - Hand over the products (see Chapter 18)
- Consider whether to review lessons now or wait until a later review of stage status or when approaching a stage end
- If the end of the current stage is approaching (as indicated by, for example, the Stage Plan, the contents of the Quality Register, a milestone etc.), prepare for the next stage (see Chapter 17)
- If the end of the final stage is approaching, prepare to close the project (see Chapter 18).

Table 15.4 shows the responsibilities for this activity.

15.4.5 Report highlights

The Project Manager must provide the Project Board with summary information about the status of the stage and project and distribute other information to stakeholders at a frequency documented in the Communication Management Strategy (as defined by the Project Board). For more details on progress controls, see Chapter 10.

Figure 15.6 shows the inputs to, and outputs from, this activity.

PRINCE2 recommends the following actions:

- Assemble the information from the Checkpoint Reports, Risk Register, Issue Register, Quality Register, Lessons Log, Product Status Account and any significant revisions to the Stage Plan for the current reporting period (the information is gained from the review of the stage status – see section 15.4.4)
- Assemble a list of corrective actions (as noted in the Daily Log and/or recorded in the Issue Register) undertaken during the reporting period. This will, for example, assure the Project Board that the Project Manager is acting within the agreed tolerances (the information is gained from taking corrective action – see section 15.4.8)

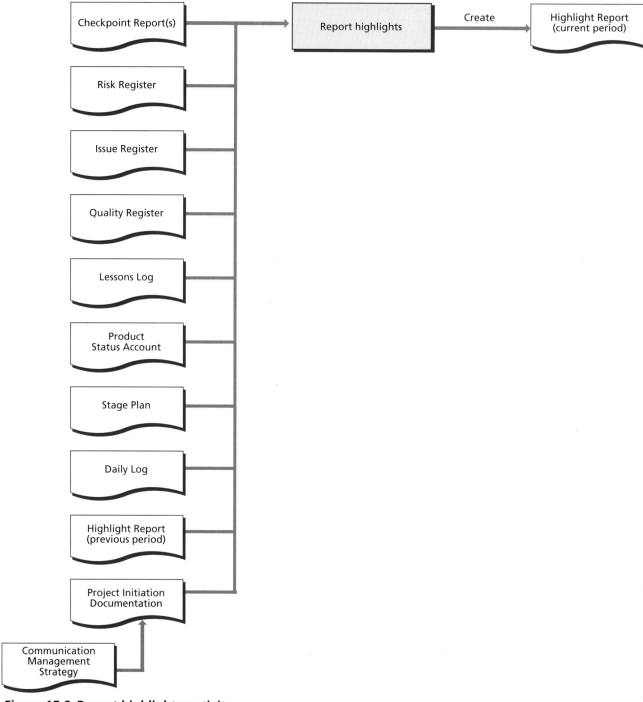

Figure 15.6 Report highlights: activity summary

- Review the Highlight Report for the previous reporting period
- Produce the Highlight Report for the current reporting period
- Distribute the Highlight Report to the Project Board and any other recipients identified in the Communication Management Strategy.

Table 15.5 shows the responsibilities for this activity.

15.4.6 Capture and examine issues and risks

In the course of managing the project, various issues will occur and risks may be identified. They will arrive in an ad hoc manner and will need to be captured in a consistent and reliable way. Any member of the project, corporate or programme management, or other stakeholders may raise an issue or risk.

Table 15.5 Report highlights: responsibilities

		Corporate/Programme	Executive	Senior User	Senior Supplier	Project Manager	Team Manager	Project Assurance	Project Support	Product Description available
Producer – responsible for product's production **R**eviewer – ideally independent of production **A**pprover – confirms approval										
Product	**Action**									
Highlight Report	Create					P		R		A11

Before making a decision on a course of action, each issue or risk should be registered and then assessed for its impact.

For more details on risk management, see Chapter 8.

For more details on issue and change control procedures, see Chapter 9.

Figure 15.7 shows the inputs to, and outputs from, this activity.

PRINCE2 recommends the following actions:

- If an issue can be dealt with by the Project Manager informally, then this should be done, and a note made in the Daily Log (see Chapter 9 for more information)
- For issues that need to be managed formally (see Chapter 9 for more information):
  - Check the requirements of the issue and change control procedure in the Configuration Management Strategy
  - Enter the issue in the Issue Register as soon as it is captured
  - Categorize the issue (is it a request for change, an off-specification or a problem/concern?)
  - Assess the severity of the issue
  - Assess the priority of the issue (for requests for change and off-specifications)
  - Assess the impact of the issue on the Stage Plan, Project Plan and Business Case

  - Document the issue by creating an Issue Report
  - Report the status of the issue in accordance with the Configuration Management Strategy and check the Communication Management Strategy to see whether there are any external parties that need to be informed of the issue
- For risks (see Chapter 8 for more information):
  - Check the requirements of the risk management procedure in the Risk Management Strategy
  - Enter the risk in the Risk Register as soon as it is captured
  - Identify the risk event and describe its cause and effect
  - Assess the risk against the Stage Plan, Project Plan and Business Case and plan the selected risk response
  - Report the status of the risk in accordance with the Risk Management Strategy and check the Communication Management Strategy to see whether there are any external parties that need to be informed of the risk
- If it is necessary either to take corrective action, seek advice from the Project Board, or to escalate an issue or risk, then review the stage status first so that a full picture can be considered (see section 15.4.4).

Table 15.6 shows the responsibilities for this activity.

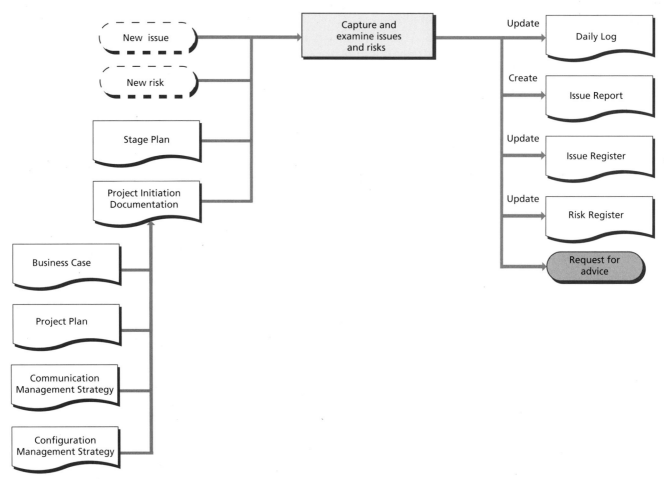

Figure 15.7 Capture and examine issues and risks: activity summary

Table 15.6 Capture and examine issues and risks: responsibilities

Producer – responsible for product's production

Reviewer – ideally independent of production

Approver – confirms approval

Product	Action	Corporate/Programme	Executive	Senior User	Senior Supplier	Project Manager	Team Manager	Project Assurance	Project Support	Product Description available
Daily Log	Update					P				A7
Issue Report	Create					P				A13
Issue Register	Update					P				A12
Risk Register	Update					P				A25

15.4.7 Escalate issues and risks

A stage should not exceed the tolerances agreed with the Project Board. The Project Manager can only take corrective action or maintain the status quo as long as the stage (or project) is forecast to be completed within the tolerances set by the Project Board. This activity applies where any corrective action within the Project Manager's control would not save the stage (or project) from going beyond the tolerances agreed. This applies to all types of issue and risk (or aggregation of them) that cannot be resolved within the tolerances set by the Project Board.

As it may take some time to gather the information to create an Exception Report, it is recommended that the Project Board be alerted as early as possible. Therefore, the Project Manager may wish to execute this activity in two steps: an early notification to the Project Board of the forecast exception situation in order to prepare

them, followed by supporting information in the form of an Exception Report.

The Project Manager should execute any decision by the Project Board in response to the escalation.

Escalating issues and risks is good practice and should not be seen as failure. The earlier that issues are escalated, the more time is available to implement any corrective actions.

For more details on management of risk, see Chapter 8.

For more details on issue and change control, see Chapter 9.

For more details on exception management, see Chapter 10.

Figure 15.8 shows the inputs to, and outputs from, this activity.

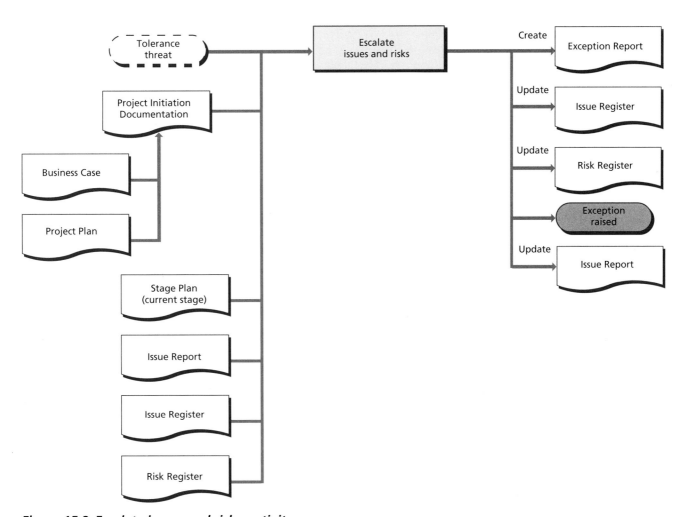

Figure 15.8 Escalate issues and risks: activity summary

PRINCE2 recommends the following actions:

- Examine the Stage Plan to define the extent of the deviation and the unfinished products, and to extrapolate what would happen if the deviation were allowed to continue
- Examine the Project Plan for the project status and overall effect of any deviation (using the current baseline of the Project Initiation Documentation)
- Determine the options for recovery and assess them against the Business Case
- Assess the impact of the options for recovery against the Stage Plan for the current stage. Consideration should be given to the availability of individuals or groups with the skills or experience to assess the impact
- Put the situation, options and the recommendation for a course of action to the Project Board in an Exception Report. The Project Board will then decide on an appropriate course of action (which may support or otherwise the Project Manager's recommendation). This may include:
  - Requesting more information or more time to consider their response
  - Approving, deferring or rejecting a request for change

- Granting a concession for an off-specification, or deferring or rejecting it
- Increasing the tolerances that are forecast to be breached
- Instructing the Project Manager to produce an Exception Plan, stating what will be acceptable (see Chapter 17)
- Instructing the Project Manager to close the project prematurely (see Chapter 18).

Table 15.7 shows the responsibilities for this activity.

15.4.8 Take corrective action

Changes and adjustments to the project need to be made in a considered and rational way, even when they appear to be easily manageable and within tolerances.

In taking corrective action, the objective is to select and, within the limits of the stage and project tolerances, implement actions that will resolve deviations from the plan. Corrective action is triggered during the review of the stage status (section 15.4.4) and typically involves dealing with advice and guidance received from the Project Board, and with issues raised by Team Managers.

Table 15.7 Escalate issues and risks: responsibilities

Producer – responsible for product's production

Reviewer – ideally independent of production

Approver – confirms approval

Product	Action	Corporate/Programme	Executive	Senior User	Senior Supplier	Project Manager	Team Manager	Project Assurance	Project Support	Product Description available
Exception Report	Create		(A)	(R)	(R)	P		R		A10
Issue Register	Update					P				A12
Risk Register	Update					P				A25
Issue Report	Update					P				A13

For more details on planning, see Chapter 7. For more details on issue and change control, see Chapter 9.

Figure 15.9 shows the inputs to, and outputs from, this activity.

PRINCE2 recommends the following actions:

■ Collect any relevant information about the deviation (from the Configuration Item Records, Issue Register, Risk Register, Issue Report, Exception Report, Project Board advice, Daily Log)

■ Identify the potential ways of dealing with the deviation and select the most appropriate option

■ Trigger corrective action via authorizing a Work Package (see section 15.4.1)

■ Update the Configuration Item Records of the affected products

■ Update the Issue Report (if necessary) to show the status of the corrective action

■ Update the Issue Register with any changes resulting from the corrective action (or if being handled informally, update the Daily Log with the details and status of the corrective action)

■ Update the Risk Register with any changes resulting from the corrective action

■ Update the Stage Plan for the current stage.

Table 15.8 shows the responsibilities for this activity.

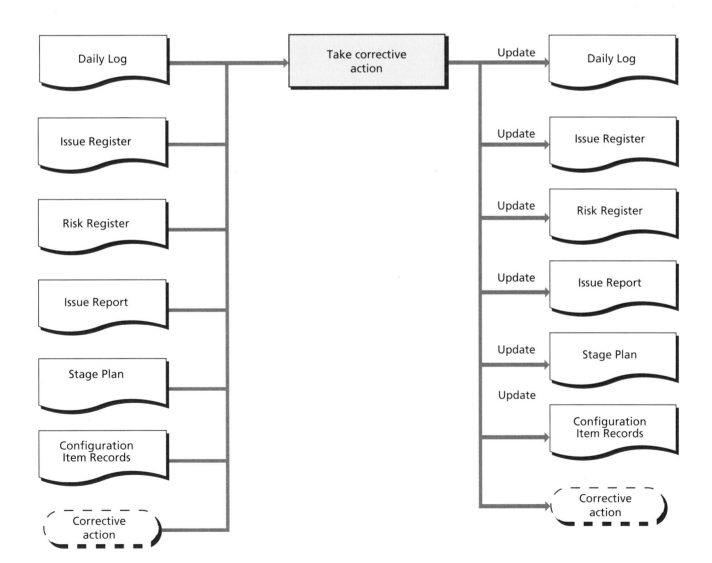

Figure 15.9 Take corrective action: activity summary

Table 15.8 Take corrective action: responsibilities

Producer – responsible for product's production

Reviewer – ideally independent of production

Approver – confirms approval

Product	Action	Corporate/Programme	Executive	Senior User	Senior Supplier	Project Manager	Team Manager	Project Assurance	Project Support	Product Description available
Issue Register	Update					P				A12
Risk Register	Update					P				A25
Issue Report	Update					P		R		A13
Stage Plan	Update					P		R		A16
Configuration Item Records	Update					P	(R)		R	A5
Daily Log	Update					P				A7

Managing Product
Delivery

16

16 Managing Product Delivery

16.1 PURPOSE

The purpose of the Managing Product Delivery process is to control the link between the Project Manager and the Team Manager(s), by placing formal requirements on accepting, executing and delivering project work.

The role of the Team Manager(s) is to coordinate an area of work that will deliver one or more of the project's products. They can be internal or external to the customer's organization.

16.2 OBJECTIVE

The objective of the Managing Product Delivery process is to ensure that:

- Work on products allocated to the team is authorized and agreed
- Team Managers, team members and suppliers are clear as to what is to be produced and what is the expected effort, cost or timescales
- The planned products are delivered to expectations and within tolerance
- Accurate progress information is provided to the Project Manager at an agreed frequency to ensure that expectations are managed.

16.3 CONTEXT

Managing Product Delivery views the project from the Team Manager's perspective, while the Controlling a Stage process views it from the Project Manager's perspective.

The Team Manager ensures that products are created and delivered by the team to the project by:

- Accepting and checking authorized Work Packages from the Project Manager
- Ensuring that interfaces identified in the Work Package are maintained
- Creating a Team Plan for the Work Packages being assigned (this may be done in parallel with the Project Manager creating the Stage Plan for the management stage)
- Ensuring that the products are developed in accordance with any development method(s) specified in the Work Package
- Demonstrating that each product meets its quality criteria through the quality method(s) specified in the Product Description – this may include using the PRINCE2 quality review technique (see Chapter 6)
- Obtaining approval for completed products from the authorities identified in the Product Description

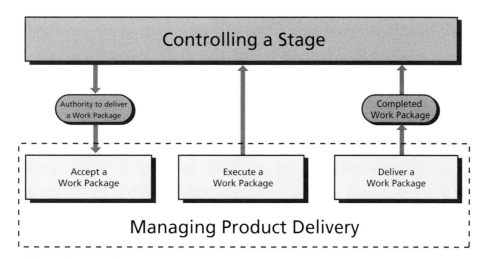

Figure 16.1 *Overview of Managing Product Delivery*

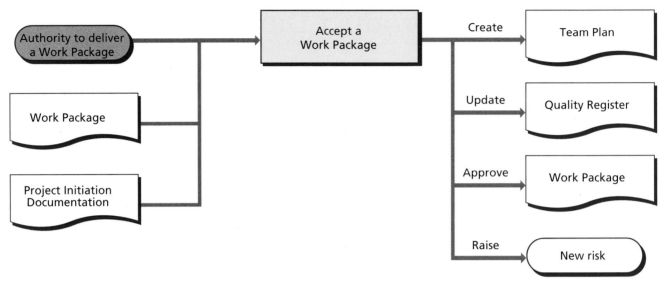

Figure 16.2 Accept a Work Package: activity summary

Table 16.1 Accept a Work Package: responsibilities

Producer – responsible for product's production

Reviewer – ideally independent of production

Approver – confirms approval

Product	Action	Corporate/Programme	Executive	Senior User	Senior Supplier	Project Manager	Team Manager	Project Assurance	Project Support	Product Description available
Team Plan	Create				(A)	(A)	P	R		
Risk	Raise					(R)	P			
Quality Register	Update					(R)	R		(P)	A23
Work Package	Approve					(P)	A	R		A26

- Delivering the products to the Project Manager in accordance with any procedures specified in the Work Package.

If the project uses external suppliers that are not using PRINCE2, Managing Product Delivery provides a statement of the required interface between the Team Manager and the PRINCE2 method being used in the project by the Project Manager. The Work Package may be part of a contractual agreement. Therefore, the formality of a Team Plan could vary from simply appending a schedule to the Work Package, to creating a fully formed plan that is presented in a similar style to a Stage Plan.

16.4 ACTIVITIES

The activities within the Managing Product Delivery process are Team-Manager-oriented and are to:

- Accept a Work Package
- Execute a Work Package
- Deliver a Work Package.

16.4.1 Accept a Work Package

The fundamental principle is that before a Work Package is allocated to a team, there should be agreement between the Project Manager and the Team Manager as to what is to be delivered, the reporting requirements, what constraints apply, any procedures to be applied, and whether the requirements of the Work Package are reasonable and can be achieved.

Figure 16.2 shows the inputs to, and outputs from, this activity.

PRINCE2 recommends the following actions:

- Review the Work Package:
  - Obtain any referenced documentation
  - Clarify with the Project Manager what is to be delivered
  - Negotiate with the Project Manager, on behalf of the team, the constraints within which the work is to be done
  - Agree tolerances for the Work Package
  - Understand the reporting requirements
  - Understand how, and from whom, approval for the product(s) is to be obtained
  - Understand how the approved product(s) is to be formally handed over
  - Confirm how the Project Manager is to be informed about the completion of the Work Package

- Produce a Team Plan to show that the product(s) can be completed within the given constraints. Consult with Project Assurance (supplier) that the Team Plan is viable and in accordance with relevant supplier standards. Seek necessary approval for the Team Plan (although in a commercial customer/supplier relationship, it may be inappropriate for the Project Manager to review and approve the Team Plan, in which case the key milestones will be summarized in the Work Package. In a commercial context, the Senior Supplier may review and approve the Team Plans)

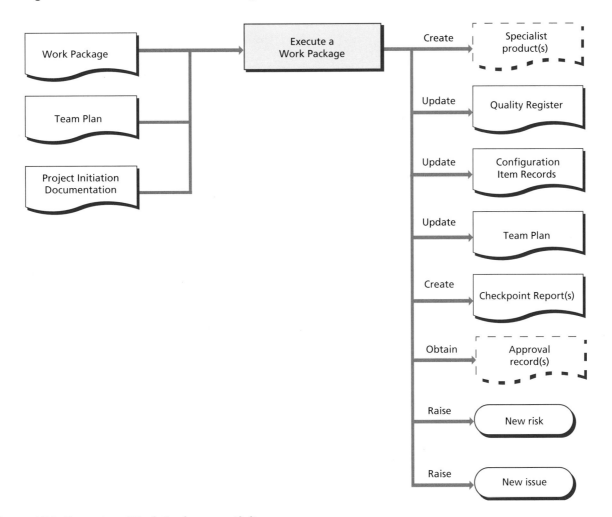

Figure 16.3 Execute a Work Package: activity summary

- Undertake a review of the risks against the Team Plan, and advise the Project Manager of any additional or modified risks (and if the Work Package allows the Team Manager to directly log the risks, then the Team Manager should update the Risk Register)
- Consult with Project Assurance as to whether any extra reviewers are required and ensure that the Quality Register is updated accordingly (check the Work Package for the procedure to update the Quality Register)
- Agree to deliver the Work Package.

Table 16.1 shows the responsibilities for this activity.

16.4.2 Execute a Work Package

The work has to be executed and monitored to the requirements defined in the authorized Work Package.

While developing the products, the Team Manager should not exceed the Work Package tolerances agreed with the Project Manager. The Team Manager can only proceed with the Work Package or take corrective action while the Work Package

is forecast to complete within the tolerances set by the Project Manager. As soon as Work Package tolerances are forecast to be exceeded, the Team Manager should raise an issue to the Project Manager who will decide upon a course of action.

Figure 16.3 shows the inputs to, and outputs from, this activity.

PRINCE2 recommends the following actions:

- Manage the development of the required products:
  - Develop the product(s) required by the Work Package to the quality criteria defined in the Product Description(s)
  - Ensure that the work is conducted in accordance with the required techniques, processes and procedures specified in the Work Package
  - Maintain the development and operational and support interfaces as detailed in the Work Package
  - Check the Work Package for the procedure to update the Quality Register (for example, to record completed quality management activities)

Table 16.2 Execute a Work Package: responsibilities

Producer – responsible for product's production

Reviewer – ideally independent of production

Approver – confirms approval

Product	Action	Corporate/Programme	Executive	Senior User	Senior Supplier	Project Manager	Team Manager	Project Assurance	Project Support	Product Description available
Specialist products	Create		(A)	(A)	(A)	(R)	P	R		
Quality Register	Update					(R)	R		(P)	A23
Configuration Item Records	Update						P		P	A5
Team Plan	Update						P	R		
Checkpoint Report	Create					(R)	P			A3
Issue	Raise					(R)	P			
Risk	Raise					(R)	P			
Approval records	Obtain					(R)	P	R	R	

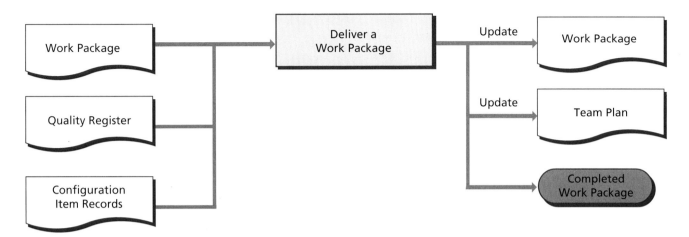

Figure 16.4 Deliver a Work Package: activity summary

Table 16.3 Deliver a Work Package: responsibilities

Producer – responsible for product's production

Reviewer – ideally independent of production

Approver – confirms approval

Product	Action	Corporate/Programme	Executive	Senior User	Senior Supplier	Project Manager	Team Manager	Project Assurance	Project Support	Product Description available
Work Package	Update					(A)	P	R		A26
Team Plan	Update					(R)	P	R		

- Capture and record the effort expended
- Monitor and control any issues and risks associated with the Work Package and advise the Project Manager of their status

■ Notify the Project Manager of any new issues, risks or lessons. The Project Manager can then decide on an appropriate course of action

■ Take the action required by the Project Manager

■ Obtain approvals for completed products:
- Check the Work Package and follow the method of obtaining and issuing approval records
- Check the Work Package and follow the procedure to update the Configuration Item Records (to change the status of the products that have been completed)

■ Review and report the status of the Work Package to the Project Manager:
- Determine the status of each product in the Work Package
- Update the Team Plan and, if necessary, consult with Project Assurance (supplier) regarding its viability

190 I Managing Product Delivery

- Feed the progress information back to the Project Manager in Checkpoint Reports, in the manner and at the frequency defined in the Work Package
- If the agreed tolerances for the Work Package are forecast to be exceeded, notify the Project Manager by raising an issue.

Table 16.2 shows the responsibilities for this activity.

16.4.3 Deliver a Work Package

Just as the Work Package was accepted from the Project Manager, notification of its completion must be returned to the Project Manager.

Figure 16.4 shows the inputs to, and outputs from, this activity.

PRINCE2 recommends the following actions:

- Review the Quality Register to verify that all the quality activities associated with the Work Package are complete
- Review the approval records to verify that all the products to be delivered by the Work Package are approved
- Update the Team Plan to show that the Work Package is complete
- Check the Work Package and follow the procedure to deliver completed products. Notify the Project Manager that the Work Package is complete.

Table 16.3 shows the responsibilities for this activity.

Managing a
Stage Boundary

17

17 Managing a Stage Boundary

17.1 PURPOSE

The purpose of the Managing a Stage Boundary process is to enable the Project Board to be provided with sufficient information by the Project Manager so that it can review the success of the current stage, approve the next Stage Plan, review the updated Project Plan, and confirm continued business justification and acceptability of the risks.

Therefore, the process should be executed at, or close to the end of, each management stage.

Projects do not always go to plan and in response to an Exception Report (if the stage or project is forecast to exceed its tolerances) the Project Board may request that the current stage (and possibly the project) is replanned. The output from replanning is an Exception Plan which is submitted

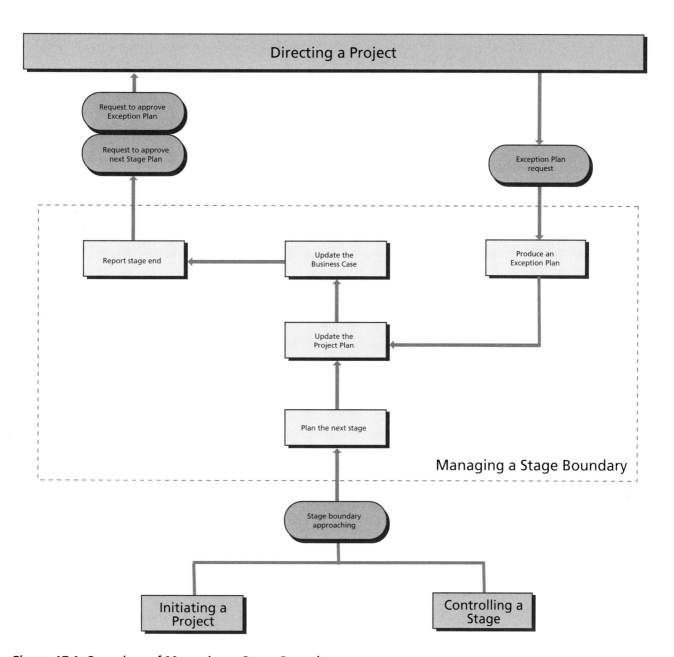

Figure 17.1 Overview of Managing a Stage Boundary

for Project Board approval in the same way that a Stage Plan is submitted for approval.

17.2 OBJECTIVE

The objective of the Managing a Stage Boundary process is to:

■ Assure the Project Board that all products in the Stage Plan for the current stage have been completed and approved

■ Prepare the Stage Plan for the next stage

■ Review and, if necessary, update the Project Initiation Documentation (in particular the Business Case, Project Plan, project approach, strategies, project management team structure and role descriptions)

■ Provide the information needed for the Project Board to assess the continuing viability of the project – including the aggregated risk exposure

■ Record any information or lessons that can help later stages of this project and/or other projects

■ Request authorization to start the next stage.

For exceptions, the objectives of the Managing a Stage Boundary process are to:

■ Prepare an Exception Plan as directed by the Project Board

■ Seek approval to replace the Project Plan or Stage Plan for the current stage with the Exception Plan.

Managing a Stage Boundary is not used towards the end of the final stage (unless there is a need to create an Exception Plan) because the activities to review the performance of the final stage are included in the activities to review the performance of the whole project as part of the Closing a Project process.

17.3 CONTEXT

The Managing a Stage Boundary process is predicated on dividing the project into management stages (see Chapter 10).

A project, whether large or small, needs to ensure that the products it creates will deliver the benefits being sought, either in their own right or as part of a larger programme. The continuing correct focus of the project should be confirmed at the end of each stage. If necessary, the project can be redirected or stopped to avoid wasting time and money.

It is also important to recognize that projects can go wrong or can be affected by external factors that invalidate the business justification. An early identifier of potential failure is the Project Manager's forecast that any of the project or stage tolerances are likely to be exceeded. In such cases it is important to have a mechanism for corrective action in order to bring the project back into the right direction.

A positive decision not to proceed is not failure. However, providing insufficient information that prevents the Project Board from making an informed decision is itself a failure as it may lead to a wrong decision.

The Managing a Stage Boundary process provides a means by which an exception process can be implemented.

17.4 ACTIVITIES

The activities within the Managing a Stage Boundary process are Project-Manager-oriented and are to:

■ Plan the next stage

■ Update the Project Plan

■ Update the Business Case

■ Report stage end

■ Produce an Exception Plan.

17.4.1 Plan the next stage

The Stage Plan for the next management stage is produced near the end of the current stage. Closure activities should be planned as part of the Stage Plan for the final stage.

Planning is not an activity undertaken in isolation. The Project Manager will need to consult with the Project Board, Project Assurance, Team Managers and possibly other stakeholders in order to create a viable plan. The more people involved in planning, the more robust the plan will be (so long as the right people are involved). See Chapter 7 for more details on planning.

Figure 17.2 shows the inputs to, and outputs from, this activity.

PRINCE2 recommends the following actions:

■ Review the components of the Project Initiation Documentation. It may be necessary to consult with the Project Board regarding any required changes. The following should be reviewed and, if necessary, updated:

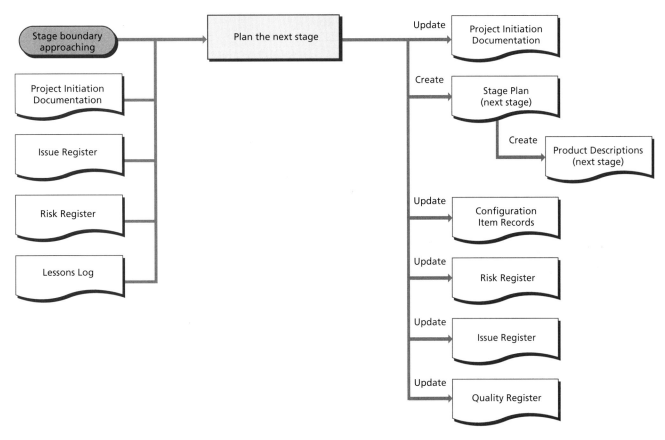

Figure 17.2 Plan the next stage: activity summary

Table 17.1 Plan the next stage: responsibilities

Producer – responsible for product's production

Reviewer – ideally independent of production

Approver – confirms approval

Product	Action	Corporate/Programme	Executive	Senior User	Senior Supplier	Project Manager	Team Manager	Project Assurance	Project Support	Product Description available
Project Initiation Documentation	Update	(R)	(A)	(A)	(A)	P		R		A20
Stage Plan	Create		(A)	(A)	(A)	P		R		A16
Configuration Item Records	Create/update					P		R	R	A5
Risk Register	Update					P		R		A25
Issue Register	Update					P		R		A12
Quality Register	Update					R		R	P	A23

- Any change to the customer's quality expectations, acceptance criteria or project approach
- The relevance and suitability of the strategies and controls
- Any change in the project management team or their role descriptions (in particular the situation with regard to external resources or suppliers as these may affect the Stage Plan)

■ Produce the Stage Plan for the next stage:
  - Decide how the plan can best be presented given its audience, and how it will be used
  - Review the Project Plan to understand the products required for the next stage
  - Examine the Quality Management Strategy for the quality standards and procedures required
  - Create (or update) the product breakdown structure, Product Descriptions and product flow diagram for the products to be delivered by the next stage
  - Review the Issue Register as it may contain issues marked for assessment at the stage end or information that affects the next stage
  - Review the Risk Register for any risks that may affect the Stage Plan for the next stage, and check the status of risk responses by consulting with the risk owners

■ Create (or update) Configuration Item Records for products to be produced in the next stage

■ Update the Issue Register and Risk Register if any new issues or risks have been identified (or if existing ones need to be modified)

■ Update the Quality Register for planned quality management activities. This should include target review and approval dates for the products.

Table 17.1 shows the responsibilities for this activity.

17.4.2 Update the Project Plan

The Project Board uses the Project Plan throughout the project to measure progress.

The Project Plan is updated to incorporate actual progress from the stage that is finishing, and to include forecast duration and costs from the Exception Plan or Stage Plan for the stage about to begin.

Details of any revised costs or end dates are used when updating the Business Case.

See Chapter 7 for more details on planning.

Figure 17.3 shows the inputs to, and outputs from, this activity.

PRINCE2 recommends the following actions:

■ Check that the current Stage Plan is up to date with actual progress and update if necessary

■ Revise the Project Plan to reflect:
  - Actuals from the current Stage Plan
  - Forecasts from the next Stage Plan, or the impact of the Exception Plan

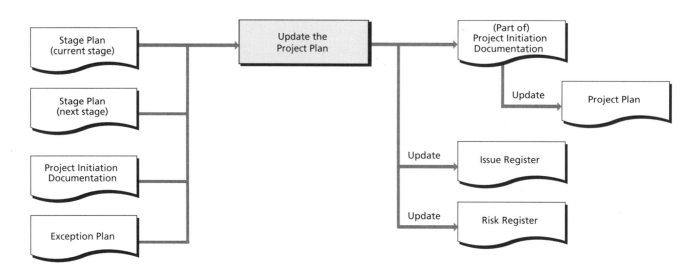

Figure 17.3 Update the Project Plan: activity summary

Table 17.2 Update the Project Plan: responsibilities

Producer – responsible for product's production

Reviewer – ideally independent of production

Approver – confirms approval

Product	Action	Corporate/Programme	Executive	Senior User	Senior Supplier	Project Manager	Team Manager	Project Assurance	Project Support	Product Description available
Project Plan	Update		(A)	(A)	(A)	P		R		A16
Issue Register	Update					P		R		A12
Risk Register	Update					P		R		A25

- Any changes to the Project Product Description
- The implications of any issues or risks
- Any new or changed PRINCE2 process-tailoring requirements for the project
- Any changed or extra products sanctioned by the Project Board
- Any changes within the Project Initiation Documentation (e.g. revised project approach, strategies, project controls, project management team structure or role descriptions)

■ Update the Issue Register and Risk Register if any new issues or risks have been identified (or if existing ones need to be modified).

Table 17.2 shows the responsibilities for this activity.

17.4.3 Update the Business Case

It is a PRINCE2 principle that projects have continued business justification.

The Project Board is ordinarily only authorized to continue while the project remains viable (that is, the benefits will be realized within the cost, time, quality, scope and risk parameters set out in the currently agreed Business Case).

Projects, however, do not take place in a static environment. The environment external to the project changes, as do the nature and timing of the project's products. The Business Case needs to reflect these changes and must be reviewed and amended to keep it relevant to the project.

As the Executive is responsible for the Business Case, the Project Manager should consult with the Executive when reviewing and updating the Business Case in preparation for Project Board approval.

For further details on business justification, see Chapter 4.

Figure 17.4 shows the inputs to, and outputs from, this activity.

PRINCE2 recommends the following actions:

■ Check whether there have been any changes to the risk appetite and risk capacity of the organizations involved and whether risk tolerances need to be redefined. Assess the project's risks using the Risk Register to ascertain the aggregated risk exposure for the project and identify the current key risks that affect the Business Case. This should include an assessment that the aggregated risk exposure remains within risk tolerances

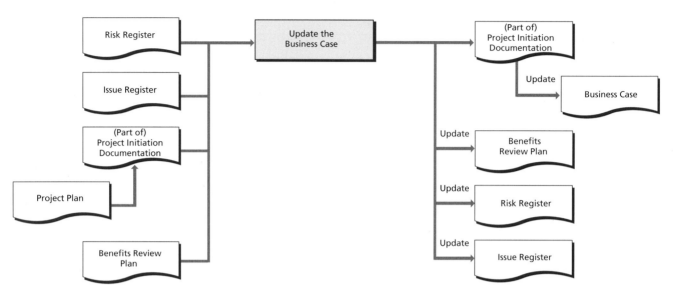

Figure 17.4 Update the Business Case: activity summary

- Update the Benefits Review Plan with the results from any benefits reviews undertaken during the stage
- Examine and review:
  - The Benefits Review Plan for the results of any benefits reviews undertaken during the stage compared with the expected results
  - The impact of approved changes as these may affect the projected benefits
  - The project risk profile and key risks
  - The Issue Register for any issues that may affect the Business Case
  - The Project Plan to see whether the final implementation date of the project has changed (for better or worse), which might affect some or all of the projected benefits
  - The Project Plan to see whether the cost of delivering the project's products has changed, which may affect the cost/benefit analysis

Table 17.3 Update the Business Case: responsibilities

Producer – responsible for product's production

Reviewer – ideally independent of production

Approver – confirms approval

Product	Action	Corporate/Programme	Executive	Senior User	Senior Supplier	Project Manager	Team Manager	Project Assurance	Project Support	Product Description available
Business Case	Update	(R)	(A)	(A)	(A)	P		R		A2
Benefits Review Plan	Update	(R)	(A)	(A)	(A)	P		R		A1
Risk Register	Update					P		R		A25
Issue Register	Update					P		R		A12

- The corporate or programme environment into which the project's products will be delivered, as it may have changed
- Whether any benefits reviews are required in the next management stage

■ Revise the Business Case and, if necessary, the Benefits Review Plan, ready for Project Board approval

■ Update the Risk Register and Issue Register as necessary.

Table 17.3 shows the responsibilities for this activity.

17.4.4 Report stage end

The results of a stage should be reported back to the Project Board so that progress is clearly visible to the project management team.

The Project Manager gives a view on the continuing ability of the project to meet the Project Plan and Business Case, and assesses the overall risk situation.

This activity should happen as close as possible to the actual end of a stage.

Figure 17.5 shows the inputs to, and outputs from, this activity.

PRINCE2 recommends the following actions:

■ For an Exception Plan:
- Depending on the point within the stage when the exception occurred, it may be appropriate to produce an End Stage Report for the activities to date. Whether this is required will be advised by the Project Board in response to the Exception Report. If an

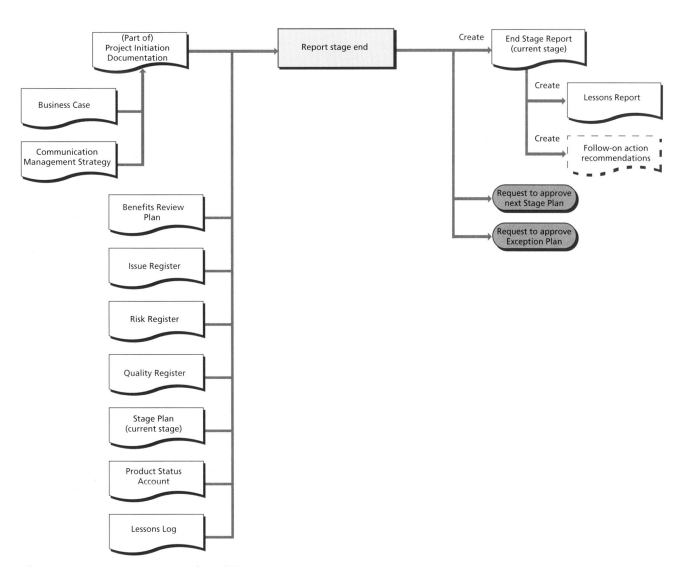

Figure 17.5 Report stage end: activity summary

End Stage Report is required, then follow the guidance for a Stage Plan below

- For a Stage Plan:
  - Review the status of the updated Business Case and, in particular, the achievement of any benefits anticipated for the stage. Confirm that any activities in the Benefits Review Plan for the current stage have been completed
  - Review the Stage Plan to ensure that the objectives of the stage have been met, and the Project Plan to ensure that the project objectives are still achievable
  - Review the team performance for the stage
  - Review the product performance for the stage by reference to the Product Status Account (provided by Project Support):
    - Review the quality management activities for the stage and their results
    - Ensure that all the products identified within the Stage Plan for the current stage are complete and approved, or have been carried forward into the next stage
    - If a phased handover of products occurred during the stage, confirm user acceptance and operational and maintenance acceptance of the products transferred to customer ownership. Identify any follow-on action recommendations for the products handed over

- Review the issues and risks raised during the stage and any risk response actions taken. Include a summary of the current aggregated risk exposure
- Prepare an End Stage Report for the current stage
- It may be appropriate to create a Lessons Report at this time, particularly for longer projects, where interim reviews of lessons, or the project itself, may benefit corporate or programme management. Check the Lessons Log for appropriate lessons to report
- Seek approval from the Project Board of the Exception Plan or Stage Plan (and, if appropriate, the revised Project Plan, the revised Benefits Review Plan and the revised Business Case [see Chapter 13])
- Review the Communication Management Strategy to see whether there is a requirement to send copies of the End Stage Report (and, if appropriate, the Lessons Report) to external interested parties at this time.

Table 17.4 shows the responsibilities for this activity.

17.4.5 Produce an Exception Plan

If a stage or the project is forecast to deviate beyond its agreed tolerances, it no longer has the approval of the Project Board.

Table 17.4 Report stage end: responsibilities

Producer – responsible for product's production
Reviewer – ideally independent of production
Approver – confirms approval

Product	Action	Corporate/Programme	Executive	Senior User	Senior Supplier	Project Manager	Team Manager	Project Assurance	Project Support	Product Description available
End Stage Report	Create		(A)	(A)	(A)	P		R		A9
Lessons Report	Create		(A)	(A)	(A)	P		R		A15
Follow-on action recommendations	Create		(A)	(A)	(A)	P		R		

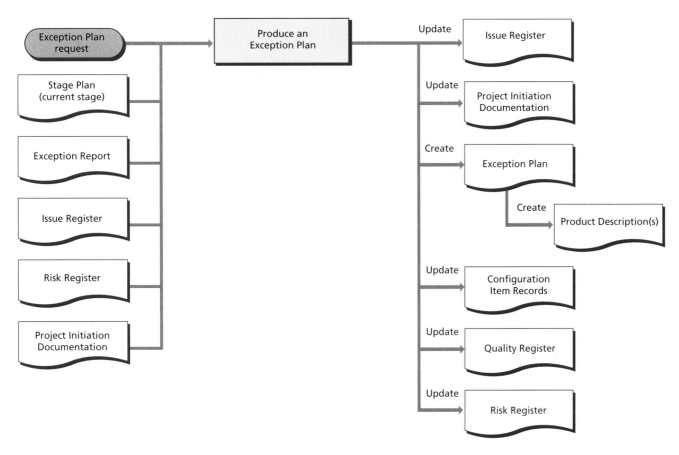

Figure 17.6 Produce an Exception Plan: activity summary

Exception Plans are requested by the Project Board in response to an Exception Report. Although an Exception Plan will be produced prior to the planned stage boundary, its approval by the Project Board marks a stage boundary for the revised stage.

Planning is not an activity undertaken in isolation. The Project Manager will need to consult with Project Board members, Project Assurance, Team Managers and possibly other stakeholders in order to create a viable plan. The more people involved in planning, the more robust the plan will be. See Chapter 7 for more details on planning.

Figure 17.6 shows the inputs to, and outputs from, this activity.

PRINCE2 recommends the following actions:

- Update the Issue Register (and, if necessary, the Issue Report) to record the Project Board's request for an Exception Plan

- Review and, if needed, update the Project Initiation Documentation. It may be necessary to consult with the Project Board regarding any required changes. The following should be reviewed:

- The customer's quality expectations – do they remain unchanged?

- The relevance and suitability of the project approach, the strategies and controls

- Any change in the project management team or their role descriptions (in particular the situation with regard to external resources or suppliers as these may affect the Exception Plan)

- Produce the Exception Plan:

- Examine the Stage Plan to define the products required for the stage

- Examine the Exception Report for details (such as recommended actions) that will contribute to the Exception Plan

- If the Exception Plan requires new products to be created, then examine the Quality Management Strategy for the quality standards and procedures required

- Update the product breakdown structure, Product Descriptions and product flow diagram for the products to be delivered by the Exception Plan

Table 17.5 Produce an Exception Plan: responsibilities

Producer – responsible for product's production

Reviewer – ideally independent of production

Approver – confirms approval

Product	Action	Corporate/Programme	Executive	Senior User	Senior Supplier	Project Manager	Team Manager	Project Assurance	Project Support	Product Description available
Project Initiation Documentation	Update	(R)	(A)	(A)	(A)	P		R		A20
Exception Plan	Create		(A)	(A)	(A)	P		R		A16
Configuration Item Records	Create/update					R		R	P	A5
Risk Register	Update					P		R		A25
Issue Register	Update					P		R		A12
Quality Register	Update					R	(R)	R	P	A23

- Update the Quality Register for planned quality management activities
- Create (or update) Configuration Item Records for products to be produced by the Exception Plan
- Update the Issue Register and Risk Register if any new issues or risks have been identified (or if existing ones need to be modified)
- Update the Quality Register for planned quality management activities. This should include target review and approval dates for the products.

Table 17.5 shows the responsibilities for this activity.

Closing a Project 18

18 Closing a Project

18.1 PURPOSE

The purpose of the Closing a Project process is to provide a fixed point at which acceptance for the project product is confirmed, and to recognize that objectives set out in the original Project Initiation Documentation have been achieved (or approved changes to the objectives have been achieved), or that the project has nothing more to contribute.

18.2 OBJECTIVE

The objective of the Closing a Project process is to:

- Verify user acceptance of the project's products
- Ensure that the host site is able to support the products when the project is disbanded
- Review the performance of the project against its baselines

- Assess any benefits that have already been realized, update the forecast of the remaining benefits, and plan for a review of those unrealized benefits
- Ensure that provision has been made to address all open issues and risks, with follow-on action recommendations.

18.3 CONTEXT

One of the defining features of a PRINCE2 project is that it is finite – it has a start and an end. If the project loses this distinctiveness, it loses some of its advantages over purely operational management approaches.

A clear end to a project:

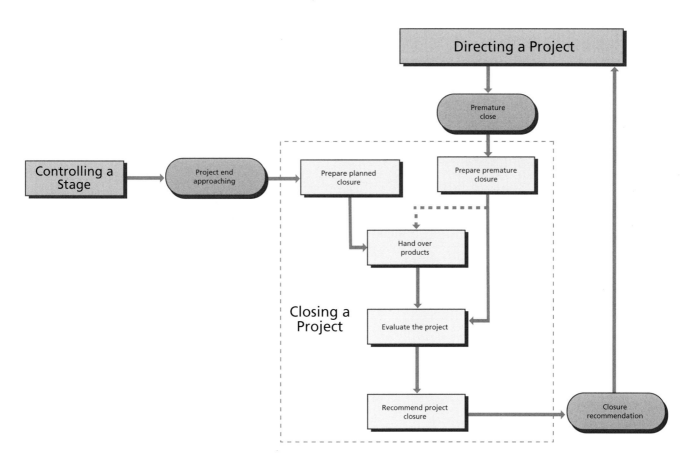

Figure 18.1 Overview of Closing a Project

- Is always more successful than a slow drift into use as it is a recognition by all concerned that:
  - The original objectives have been met (subject to any approved changes)
  - The current project has run its course
  - Either the operational regime must now take over the products from this project, or the products become inputs into some subsequent project or into some larger programme
  - The project management team can be disbanded
  - Project costs should no longer be incurred
- Provides an opportunity to ensure that all unachieved goals and objectives are identified so that they can be addressed in the future
- Transfers ownership of the products to the customer and terminates the responsibility of the project management team.

Closure activities should be planned as part of the Stage Plan for the final management stage. When closing a project, work is required to prepare input to the Project Board in order to obtain its authorization to close the project. Subsequently, the Executive should also notify corporate or programme management that the project has closed (see Chapter 13).

It is also possible that the Project Board may wish to trigger a premature closure of the project under some circumstances (for example, if the Business Case is no longer valid). If the project is being brought to a premature close, this process will still need to be executed, but may have to be tailored to the actual project situation.

A number of actions specific to the project's products may be required after the project, and these should be documented and planned for as follow-on action recommendations. These may have different audiences and therefore may need to be issued individually. The needs of the recipient will determine the format and content – some may want a formal report, some a log entry on a system, and others a meeting.

18.4 ACTIVITIES

The activities within the Closing a Project process are Project-Manager-oriented and are to:

- Prepare planned closure
- Prepare premature closure
- Hand over products
- Evaluate the project
- Recommend project closure.

18.4.1 Prepare planned closure

Before closure of the project can be recommended, the Project Manager must ensure that the expected results have all been achieved and delivered.

Figure 18.2 shows the inputs to, and outputs from, this activity.

PRINCE2 recommends the following actions:

- Update the Project Plan with actuals from the final stage
- Request a Product Status Account from Project Support. From the Product Status Account, ensure that the project's products:

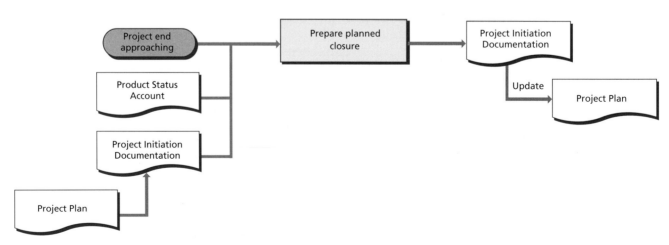

Figure 18.2 Prepare planned closure: activity summary

Table 18.1 Prepare planned closure: responsibilities

Producer – responsible for product's production

Reviewer – ideally independent of production

Approver – confirms approval

Product	Action	Corporate/Programme	Executive	Senior User	Senior Supplier	Project Manager	Team Manager	Project Assurance	Project Support	Product Description available
Project Plan	Update					P		R		A16
Product Status Account	Create					R		R	P	A18

- Have been approved by the authorities identified in their Product Descriptions
- Meet all the quality criteria, or are covered by approved concessions
- Confirm that the project has delivered what is defined in the Project Product Description, and that the acceptance criteria have been met
- Seek approval to give notice to corporate or programme management that resources can be (or are about to be) released.

Table 18.1 shows the responsibilities for this activity.

18.4.2 Prepare premature closure

In some situations, the Project Board may have instructed the Project Manager to close the project prematurely. In such circumstances, the Project Manager must ensure that work in progress is not simply abandoned, but that the project salvages anything of value created to date and checks that any gaps left by the cancellation of the project are raised to corporate or programme management.

Figure 18.3 shows the inputs to, and outputs from, this activity.

PRINCE2 recommends the following actions:

- Update the Issue Register (and, if necessary, the Issue Report) to record the premature closure request

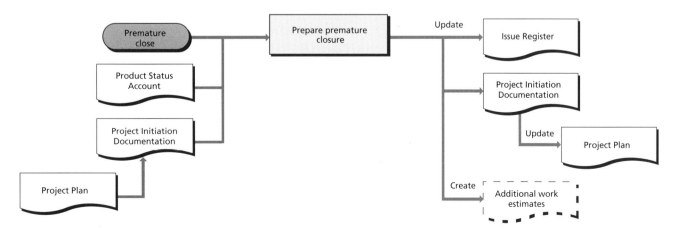

Figure 18.3 Prepare premature closure: activity summary

- Update the Project Plan with actuals from the final stage
- Request a Product Status Account from Project Support. From this, determine which of the project's products:
  - Have been approved by the authorities identified in their Product Descriptions
  - Are currently in development (and which of those need to be completed)
  - Are covered by approved concessions
  - Have yet to be started
  - Need to be made safe
  - May be useful to other projects
- Agree the means for recovering products that have been completed or are in progress (if appropriate). This will need Project Board consultation and may include additional work to create, make safe or complete products that might be useful to other projects (for example, making a part-built building safe and weatherproof). In some cases, the additional work may require an Exception Plan
- Seek approval to give notice to corporate or programme management that resources can be (or are about to be) released early.

Table 18.2 shows the responsibilities for this activity.

18.4.3 Hand over products

The project's products must be passed to an operational and maintenance environment prior to the project being closed. This may happen as a single release at the end of the project, or the project approach may include phased delivery where products are handed over in a number of releases.

In the case of a premature closure, there may be some products that have been approved but not yet handed over and, depending on the Project Board guidance, the ownership of some or all of those products may need to be transferred to the customer.

When handing over products, the Benefits Review Plan may need to be updated to include the post-project benefits review(s) of the performance of the project's products in operational use. Such benefits reviews may identify whether there have been any side-effects (beneficial or adverse) that could provide useful lessons for other projects.

It is not a project activity to undertake benefits reviews post-project, only to plan for such benefits reviews to occur. If the project is part of a programme, then the post-project benefits reviews need to be covered by the programme's benefits management activities.

Figure 18.4 shows the inputs to, and outputs from, this activity.

Table 18.2 Prepare premature closure: responsibilities

Producer – responsible for product's production

Reviewer – ideally independent of production

Approver – confirms approval

Product	Action	Corporate/Programme	Executive	Senior User	Senior Supplier	Project Manager	Team Manager	Project Assurance	Project Support	Product Description available
Issue Register	Update					P				A12
Project Plan	Update					P		R		A16
Product Status Account	Create					R		R	P	A18
Additional work estimates	Create		(A)	(A)	(A)	P		R		

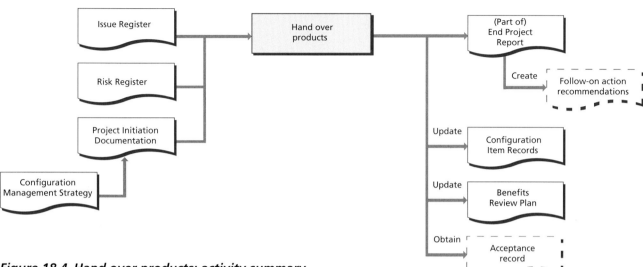

Figure 18.4 Hand over products: activity summary

PRINCE2 recommends the following actions:

■ In consultation with the project management team, prepare follow-on action recommendations for the project's products to include any uncompleted work, issues and risks. There could be separate follow-on action recommendations for each product or distinct user group (for example, human resources, finance, operations)

■ Check that the Benefits Review Plan includes post-project activities to confirm benefits that cannot be measured until after the project's products have been in operational use for some time (for example, reliability requirements)

■ The Configuration Management Strategy should be examined in order to confirm how products are to be handed over to those who will maintain them in their operational life:

● Confirm that the correct operational and maintenance environment is in place

● Consider the early life-support requirements of each product being handed over because the early life of a product is often the period of peak demand on the support organization

● Where a product requires a lot of potentially expensive support and maintenance, the Project Manager should ensure that a suitable service agreement or contract has

Table 18.3 Hand over products: responsibilities

Producer – responsible for product's production

Reviewer – ideally independent of production

Approver – confirms approval

Product	Action	Corporate/Programme	Executive	Senior User	Senior Supplier	Project Manager	Team Manager	Project Assurance	Project Support	Product Description available
Follow-on action recommendations	Create/update		(A)	(A)	(A)	P		R		
Configuration Item Records	Update					A		R	P	A5
Benefits Review Plan	Update	(A)	(R)	(R)	(R)	P		R		A1
Acceptance record	Obtain		(A)	(A)	(A)	P		R		

been drawn up between the operations and maintenance organizations and the end-users. In such instances, the service agreement should be included as a product to be delivered as part of the plan

- Confirm acceptance from the operations and maintenance organizations
- Request and obtain acceptance records
- Transfer the responsibility for the products from the project to the operations and maintenance organizations and update the products' Configuration Item Records.

Table 18.3 shows the responsibilities for this activity.

18.4.4 Evaluate the project

Successful organizations learn from their experiences with projects. When evaluating the project, the objective is to assess how successful or unsuccessful the project has been. It may also be possible to improve the estimation for future projects by analysing the estimates and actual progress metrics for this project.

Figure 18.5 shows the inputs to, and outputs from, this activity.

PRINCE2 recommends the following actions:

- Review the project's original intent as agreed in the initiation stage and defined by the Project Initiation Documentation baselined at that time
- Review the approved changes as defined by the current version of the components of the Project Initiation Documentation
- In consultation with the project management team, prepare an End Project Report to include:
  - The Project Manager's summary of how the project performed
  - An assessment of the results of the project against the expected benefits in the Business Case
  - A review of how the project performed against its planned targets and tolerances
  - A review of team performance
  - A review of the project's products (which should include a summary of any follow-on action recommendations)
  - If necessary, the documented reasons why a project was brought to a premature close
- In consultation with the project management team, prepare a Lessons Report for lessons that could be applied to future projects and seek the

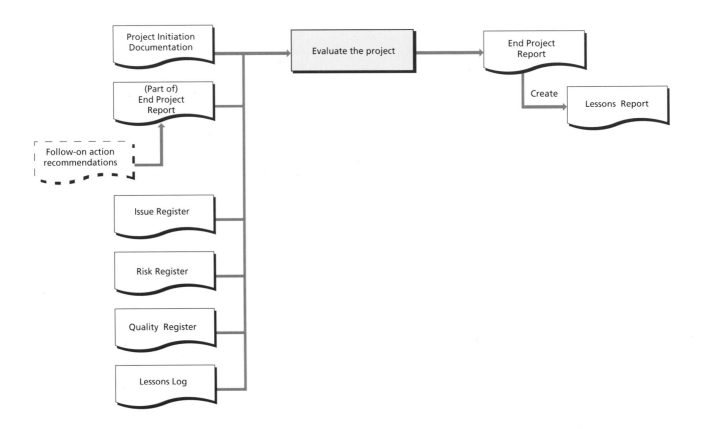

Figure 18.5 Evaluate the project: activity summary

Table 18.4 Evaluate the project: responsibilities

Producer – responsible for product's production

Reviewer – ideally independent of production

Approver – confirms approval

Product	Action	Corporate/Programme	Executive	Senior User	Senior Supplier	Project Manager	Team Manager	Project Assurance	Project Support	Product Description available
End Project Report	Create		(A)	(A)	(A)	P		R		A8
Lessons Report	Create	(A)	(R)	(R)	(R)	P		R		A15

Project Board's approval to send it to corporate or programme management. The report should include:

- A review of what went well, what went badly and any recommendations for corporate or programme management consideration – in particular, the project management method, any specialist methods used, project strategies and controls, and any abnormal events that caused deviation
- A review of useful measurements such as: how much effort was required to create the products; how effective was the Quality Management Strategy in designing, developing and delivering fit-for-purpose products (for example, how many errors were found after products had passed quality inspections); and statistics on issues and risks
- Any useful knowledge gained regarding the tailoring of PRINCE2 for the particular project environment.

Table 18.4 shows the responsibilities for this activity.

18.4.5 Recommend project closure

Once the Project Manager has confirmed that the project can be closed, a closure recommendation should be raised to the Project Board.

Figure 18.6 shows the inputs to, and outputs from, this activity.

PRINCE2 recommends the following actions:

- Use the Communication Management Strategy to identify any organization or interested party who needs to know that the project is closing. Consider also communication activities for public relations and marketing opportunities at this point
- Close the project's Issue Register, Risk Register, Quality Register, Daily Log and Lessons Log
- All project information should be secured and archived (in accordance with the Configuration Management Strategy) in order to permit any future audit of the project management team's decisions, actions and performance
- Prepare and send a draft project closure notification for review by the Project Board, stating that the project has closed.

Table 18.5 shows the responsibilities for this activity.

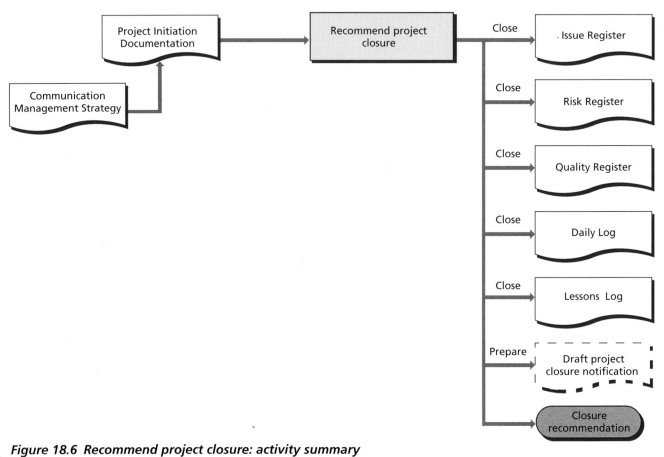

Figure 18.6 Recommend project closure: activity summary

Table 18.5 Recommend project closure: responsibilities

Producer – responsible for product's production

Reviewer – ideally independent of production

Approver – confirms approval

Product	Action	Corporate/Programme	Executive	Senior User	Senior Supplier	Project Manager	Team Manager	Project Assurance	Project Support	Product Description available
Issue Register	Close					P				A12
Risk Register	Close					P				A25
Quality Register	Close					P				A23
Daily Log	Close					P				A7
Lessons Log	Close					P				A14
Draft project closure notification	Prepare		(A)	(A)	(A)	P		R		

Tailoring PRINCE2 to the project environment

19

19 Tailoring PRINCE2 to the project environment

19.1 WHAT IS TAILORING?

PRINCE2 can be used whatever the project scale, complexity, geography or culture, or whether it is part of a programme or is being managed as a 'stand-alone' project. Indeed, it is a principle that a PRINCE2 project tailors the method to suit such contexts.

Tailoring refers to the appropriate use of PRINCE2 on any given project, ensuring that there is the correct amount of planning, control, governance and use of the processes and themes, whereas the adoption of PRINCE2 across an organization is known as embedding. Table 19.1 sets out the difference between embedding and tailoring.

19.2 GENERAL APPROACH TO TAILORING

Some projects may claim that they do not need 'full PRINCE2' and therefore have only implemented portions of the method. This can reveal a flawed understanding of PRINCE2 because the method is designed to be tailored. So tailoring PRINCE2 appropriately *is* 'full PRINCE2'.

Tailoring does not consist of omitting elements of PRINCE2. The method is not a series of isolated silos whereby any element can be omitted with no effect on the others. PRINCE2 is a web of interlinking elements: themes are used in processes;

techniques are undertaken to bring themes to life; and individuals fulfilling project roles create management products. If the practitioner omits an element, project management for the project is weakened.

Therefore tailoring is about adapting the method to external factors (such as any corporate standards that need to be applied) and the project factors to consider (such as the scale of the project). The goal is to apply a level of project management that does not overburden the project but provides an appropriate level of control given the external and project factors.

The danger of not tailoring PRINCE2 is that it can lead to 'robotic' project management if every process activity is followed and every management product is produced without question. This is a common trap in template-driven project management.

Tailoring, therefore, is about thinking how to apply the method and then using it with a lightness of touch. Figure 19.1 shows how the environmental and project factors are evaluated in order to tailor the method.

19.2.1 Applying the principles

As PRINCE2's principles are universal, they will always apply and are not tailored. By looking at

Table 19.1 Embedding and tailoring

Embedding	Tailoring
Done by the organization to adopt PRINCE2.	Done by the project management team to adapt the method to the context of a specific project.
Focus on: ■ Process responsibilities ■ Scaling rules/guidance (e.g. score card) ■ Standards (templates, definitions) ■ Training and development ■ Integration with business processes ■ Tools ■ Process assurance.	Focus on: ■ Adapting the themes (through the strategies and controls) ■ Incorporating specific terms/language ■ Revising the Product Descriptions for the management products ■ Revising the role descriptions for the PRINCE2 project roles ■ Adjusting the processes to match the above.
Guidance in *PRINCE2 Maturity Model*.	Guidance in this manual.

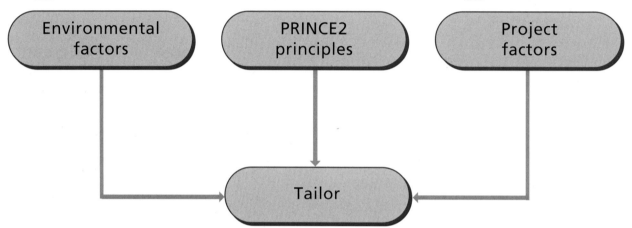

- Multi-organization
- External customer/supplier
- Corporate standards
- Within a programme
- Organization maturity
  (e.g. centre of excellence)
- Terms and language
- Geography
- Organization culture
- Project priority
- etc.

- Scale
- Solution complexity
- Team maturity
- Project type and lifecycle model
- etc.

Environmental factors

PRINCE2 principles

Project factors

Tailor

- Adapt the themes (through the strategies and controls)
- Revise terms and language
- Revise Product Descriptions for the management products
- Revise role descriptions
- Adjust processes to match the above
- Record in the Project Initiation Documentation

Figure 19.1 Influences on the tailoring requirement

the principles, the practitioner can understand how to adapt the theme to the environmental and project factors without losing its value.

19.2.2 Adapting the themes

Adapting a theme does not necessarily mean modifying the method. In most cases, the environmental and project factors are incorporated into the project's strategies and controls. Relevant corporate or programme policies and standards are captured and documented in the project's Risk Management Strategy, Quality Management Strategy, Configuration Management Strategy and Communication Management Strategy. These management products will describe the procedures to be used on the project that fulfil the requirements of the corporate or programme organization. The level of control required will influence the formality and frequency of monitoring, reviewing and reporting.

19.2.3 Applying the organization's terms and language

The method may need to be adapted to incorporate the terms and language of the corporate or programme organization. For example, if the corporate or programme organization uses the term 'investment case' rather than 'Business Case', it may be appropriate to substitute the term within all of the project's documentation if that improves understanding.

19.2.4 Adapting the management products

PRINCE2 provides Product Description outlines for those management products that require particular purpose or composition for their use by the themes and processes. In tailoring PRINCE2, the management products may be adapted, in which case it may be necessary to modify their Product Descriptions or to provide a template for them. For everyone involved in the project, it should remain clear as to what the purpose of the management product is, what it should comprise and what the quality criteria are. For example, in a commercial environment, the Work Package may need to include purchase order details and accompanying terms and conditions.

19.2.5 Adapting the roles

PRINCE2's organization structure needs to be carefully considered for all projects. Standard role description outlines are provided in Appendix C, but it is expected that these will need to be adapted to match individuals' actual capability and authority in the context of the project role they will be assigned. For example, for a project in a programme environment, the responsibility for the Benefits Review Plan may lie with the programme. Therefore, this responsibility should be removed from the Executive's role description.

19.2.6 Adapting the processes

All the PRINCE2 process activities need to be done; it is just that the responsibilities for performing the activities may change (if any roles have been adapted) and any references to the management products may need to change (if any management products have been adapted).

19.3 EXAMPLES OF TAILORING PRINCE2

Sections 19.4–19.10 provide some examples of how PRINCE2 can be tailored.

The examples cover some of the environmental and project factors that are faced by many projects:

- Projects in a programme environment
- Project scale
- Commercial customer/supplier environment
- Multi-organization projects
- Project type
- Sector differences
- Project management Bodies of Knowledge.

The environmental and project factors shown are not exhaustive as the application of PRINCE2 is limitless. Only general guidance is provided to illustrate considerations to take into account and some tactics that can be applied. The guidance

should not be interpreted as the definitive approach to tailoring as it is not specific to a particular project. The practitioner should consider the pros and cons of the tailoring choices as they relate to the specific project context.

For an organization that has embedded PRINCE2, the embedded version of the method still requires tailoring.

19.4 PROJECTS IN A PROGRAMME ENVIRONMENT

A **programme** is a temporary flexible organization structure created to coordinate, direct and oversee the implementation of a set of related projects and activities in order to deliver outcomes and benefits relating to an organization's strategic objectives. A programme may have a life that spans several years.

The distinction between projects and programmes is that projects typically produce or change something and are then disbanded. The benefits of the undertaking are likely to be accrued after the project is completed. Programmes are typically used to help transform organizations. Therefore, the temporary programme organization tends to have a lifespan that covers the realization of the benefits – which could be several years. This is illustrated in Figure 19.2.

Projects operating in a programme environment benefit from a number of advantages, and there are a number of ways in which PRINCE2 can be tailored for use within a programme.

The following sections explain how PRINCE2 can be tailored when working in a programme environment (using OGC's Managing Successful Programmes framework) by looking at how to adapt the themes, processes and management products.

19.4.1 Themes

19.4.1.1 Business Case

The programme will define the standards that the project will need to use when developing the Business Case.

The project Business Case will be aggregated into the overall programme Business Case and is likely

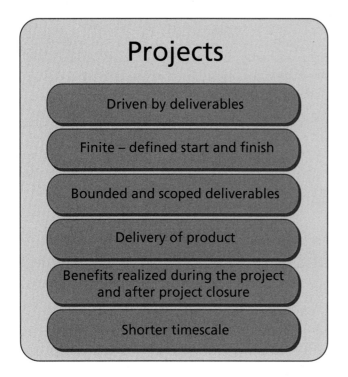

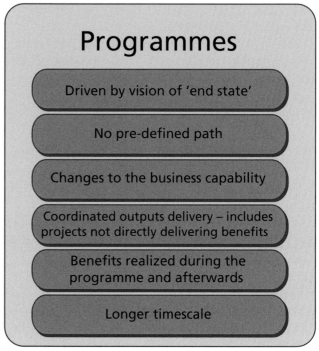

Figure 19.2 Comparison between projects and programmes

to be reduced in content. It may comprise just the details of the budget, a list of benefits (and the benefits tolerance), and a statement as to how the project is contributing to the programme blueprint, with the justification aspects of the project Business Case sitting in the programme Business Case.

In some cases, the Business Case might be produced and maintained by the programme and even exist in detail prior to initiating the project.

Benefits will be defined, tracked and managed by the programme management team, and the project's Benefits Review Plan will be part of the programme's benefits realization plan.

19.4.1.2 Organization

OGC's Managing Successful Programmes (MSP) framework defines a programme board that comprises a programme Senior Responsible Owner (SRO), a programme manager, one or more business change managers, representatives of corporate functions as necessary (e.g. human resources, finance), the lead supplier, and the project Executives of the projects within the programme.

The programme SRO is the single individual with overall responsibility for ensuring that a programme will meet its objectives and deliver the

projected benefits. It is likely that the programme SRO will confirm the appointment of the project Executive.

The programme manager is responsible for the set-up and day-to-day management and delivery of the programme on behalf of the programme SRO.

The business change manager is responsible for benefits definition and management throughout the programme. This role provides the bridge between the programme and business operations to ensure that the capabilities delivered by the projects are adopted by the organization in order to achieve the desired outcome and their subsequent benefits.

The programme and project management team structures need to be integrated such that:

- There are clear lines of responsibility from top to bottom (i.e. everyone is accountable to someone)
- Duplication is avoided
- Reports and reviews are efficient (e.g. four projects within a programme have common Project Board members and by aligning stage boundaries they meet collectively to conduct end stage assessments for all four projects as part of a programme review).

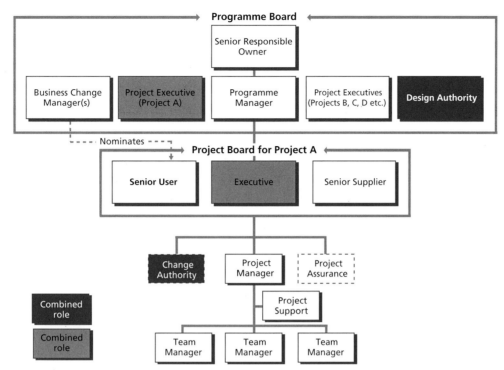

Figure 19.3 Organization structure with the Executive being a member of the programme board and the Senior User being nominated by the relevant business change manager

The integration of roles may include:

- The programme manager being the Executive for one or more of the projects
- A business change manager from the programme fulfilling the project role of Senior User (or having input in the appointment of the Senior User) for one or more of the projects, or being the project Executive for one or more of the projects
- Project Support being provided by the programme
- The programme's design authority (if used) fulfilling the project role of Change Authority or Project Assurance for one or more of the projects as the purpose of a design authority at a programme level is to ensure that there is appropriate alignment and control when changes are being planned and implemented.

The choice of structure and appointments will depend on the scale and complexity of the programme. The pros and cons of the choice of organization structure and appointments need to be evaluated along with their consequences. For example, in Figure 19.4, where the programme manager is also the Executive of one of the projects within the programme, consideration should

be given as to how exceptions will be escalated between the project and the programme, and whether any additional assurance mechanisms need to be established.

See Figures 19.3 and 19.4 for two examples.

The project's Communication Management Strategy will be derived from the programme's stakeholder engagement strategy, with communications being controlled and scheduled as part of the programme communications plan. Stakeholder analysis for the project may be performed by the programme, or the programme may require the project to take a lead with certain stakeholder groups with which it has good engagement.

19.4.1.3 Quality

The project's Quality Management Strategy is derived from the programme's Quality Management Strategy.

Quality assurance and quality control activities may be carried out by members of the programme management team.

The programme's design authority may provide advice and guidance to the Project Manager on any quality methods to be used.

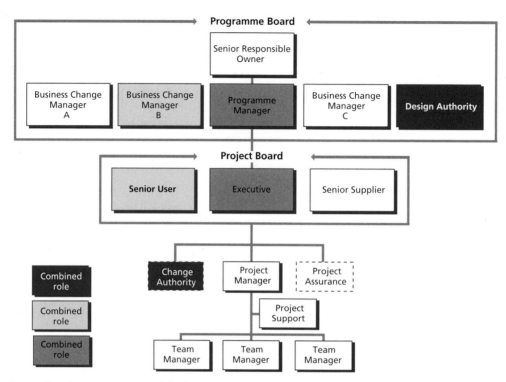

Figure 19.4 Organization structure with the programme manager as the project Executive and the Senior User role on the project being undertaken by the relevant business change manager

19.4.1.4 Plans

Any specific standards that the project planners should work to will be described in the programme monitoring and control strategy. The project planning activity to design the plan will ensure that such standards and tools are adopted by the project.

The programme may have dedicated planners that can help the Project Manager prepare and maintain the Project Plan and Stage Plans.

The programme dependency network will detail how each project's deliverables are being used by other projects within the programme. Any dependencies to or from the project should be incorporated into the project's plans.

19.4.1.5 Risk

The project's Risk Management Strategy will be derived from the programme's Risk Management Strategy. This will include defining a common set of risk categories, risk scales (for probability, impact and proximity), any risk evaluation techniques (such as expected monetary value), the project-level risk tolerance, and the mechanisms to escalate risks to the programme level.

19.4.1.6 Change

The project's Configuration Management Strategy will be derived from the programme's information management strategy. The information management strategy defines how interfaces between projects should be maintained (e.g. so that any changes within this project that may affect one or more other projects are captured and escalated).

The project's issue and change control procedure will be derived from the programme's issue resolution strategy. This will define how scope or delivery changes that take the project out of tolerance, or affect the programme benefits or programme plan, are escalated to the programme level.

The project's Change Authority may include the programme's design authority.

19.4.1.7 Progress

The programme's monitoring and control strategy may influence the formality, frequency and content of the project's reviews and reports, and any project management standards that are to be complied with.

Project-level time and cost tolerances will be defined by the programme.

The number and length of management stages will be influenced by the programme plan. It may be desirable or necessary to align end stage assessments to programme milestones (for example, the end of a tranche). The programme may even define a set of standard management stages that all projects within the programme comply with.

19.4.2 Processes

Within OGC's MSP framework, the Delivering the Capability process within Managing the Tranches is entirely focused on starting, monitoring and closing projects within the programme. This process does not need to be tailored when working with PRINCE2.

The PRINCE2 process most affected by working in a programme will be Starting up a Project.

This process could be undertaken almost entirely by the programme. The programme will: appoint the Executive and Project Manager, review previous lessons, design and appoint the project management team, and probably prepare the Project Brief. The Project Manager will, however, be responsible for preparing the Initiation Stage Plan. In this context, it is not so much that the Starting up a Project process is not done, just that it is now done mainly by the programme.

19.4.3 Management products

Confusingly, there are numerous management products that exist for both the project and programme, for example a Quality Management Strategy. When in a programme environment, it may be desirable to prefix the management product with 'project' and 'programme' to distinguish the difference. Another consideration is to make the project and programme document templates look very different in style so that it is immediately obvious where they apply.

Consideration should be given to whether the project's logs and registers will be maintained locally to the project, or centrally by the programme. For example, a choice needs to be made as to whether there is a single Risk Register, administered by the programme for the programme-level risks and all the risks for each project within the programme, or whether each project should maintain its own Risk Register. If the latter is chosen the project's Risk Management Strategy should define how programme-level risks that are identified and captured by the project are promoted to the programme Risk Register. Likewise, the programme's Risk Management Strategy should define mechanisms for project risks that are identified and captured by the programme level to be demoted to the project Risk Register.

19.5 PROJECT SCALE

PRINCE2 can be used regardless of the scale of the project. A project's scale is relative to the size and experience of the organization hosting the project – e.g. a £10 million project could be a simple project to one organization or a daunting project to another. Scale is related not just to the size of the project (often measured in terms of time, money and people) but also to the context of the project's complexity, risk and importance.

Organizations should consider calibrating the scale of their projects. Table 19.2 illustrates a simple approach to categorizing projects and provides some suggestions about how PRINCE2 could be tailored.

Section 19.5.1 provides guidance on tailoring PRINCE2 for a simple project.

19.5.1 Simple project

As has been stated above, the scale of a project is relative to the organization and context. Nevertheless, there are some pointers that are useful to consider for a project that an organization considers is simple.

A question often asked is: which elements of PRINCE2 can be relaxed on simple projects? There is no easy answer to this. Even simple projects vary enormously in type and style.

First of all, it is important to remember that even simple projects should adhere to the seven PRINCE2 principles if the project is to be managed using PRINCE2. It is in the way the themes, processes and management products are used that PRINCE2 is 'tailored'.

Overall, the purpose of PRINCE2 can be regarded as reducing the risk of project failure. Thus, whenever any element of PRINCE2 is relaxed, this should be regarded as taking a risk.

Table 19.2 Examples of projects of different scales

Project scale		Characteristic	Applying PRINCE2
High ↑ Low ↓	Programme	Business transformation	A programme management framework such as OGC's *Managing Successful Programmes* should be used. PRINCE2 may be used to manage projects within the programme.
	Daunting project	High risk, cost, importance, visibility Multiple organizations Multi-disciplinary (e.g. construction, IT and business change) International	Multiple delivery stages Extended Project Board (e.g. user/supplier groups) Team Managers as a separate role likely Project Support as a separate role likely Individual management products
	Normal project	Medium risk, cost, importance, visibility Commercial customer/supplier relationship Multiple sites	One or more delivery stages Standard Project Board Team Managers as a separate role optional Project Support as a separate role optional Some management products combined
	Simple project	Low risk, cost, importance, visibility Single organization Single site	Single delivery stage Simple Project Board The Project Manager fulfils the Team Manager role The Project Manager fulfils the Project Support role Combined management products
	Task	If there is a single-person Project Board (and typically the Executive is the Project Manager's line manager) then it could normally be treated as a task. The Project Manager may also be the person doing the work. The costs may be within the 'business as usual' budget. Straightforward business justification – e.g. responding to an instruction.	Treat as a Work Package that delivers one or more products. Use Work Packages, Product Descriptions, Logs/Registers and Checkpoint Reports.

19.5.1.1 Themes

The theme most affected by simple projects is the Organization theme:

- Scaling the project management team is primarily about role and function consolidation. Roles can be combined but should not be eliminated
- As the Executive and Senior User roles are both from the customer environment, these can often be combined
- As the Project Manager is likely to be much closer to the Project Board than on larger more complex projects, members of the Project Board are often in a better position to carry out their own Project Assurance rather than appointing another individual to fulfil this role
- For small teams it may not be necessary to appoint Team Managers. The Project Manager of a small project can carry out those responsibilities
- The Project Manager may undertake the role of Project Support and be a team member. In this case, the Project Manager must balance the effort of managing the project against the effort of doing any project work.

Of the other themes, the minimum requirements are:

- **Business Case** Some form of business justification, no matter how this is documented
- **Plans** Product Descriptions for the key deliverables and a simple plan, in the form of a schedule of who is involved in producing, reviewing and approving products, together with key milestones. This is often referred to as a product checklist (see the Product Description outline for a Plan in Appendix A for an example)
- **Quality** An understanding of the levels of quality required in the project, and of the project products
- **Risk** An analysis of the risks facing the project, actions that will be taken to implement risk responses, and communicating risk status via Checkpoint and Highlight Reports
- **Change** A simple method of controlling changes to the project and managing the configuration of the products being delivered – for example, simple product identification and version control standards with secure arrangements for the storage of products

- **Progress** Some form of agreed controls and reporting requirements (whether written or oral).

19.5.1.2 Processes

All processes remain relevant even in simple projects. However, the Starting up a Project process can usually be handled in a less formal manner. The Executive and Project Manager should, however, avoid the temptation to bypass it altogether. In some cases it may be appropriate to combine the Starting up a Project and Initiating a Project processes (i.e. creating the Project Initiation Documentation straight from the mandate and skipping the production of a Project Brief).

19.5.1.3 Management products

The choice of format of the management product can help reduce the project management effort for a small project, for example:

- The Project Board may decide to receive some, or all, reports orally or have a verbal exchange of information and decisions instead of formal meetings. In such cases, the Project Manager should, as a minimum, document the exchange in the Daily Log since people's recollection of a verbal agreement can differ weeks, or even days, later
- Reports could be in the form of an email
- The Project Initiation Documentation could be a set of presentation slides.

Consideration should be given to creating documents that physically include more than one management product. It is possible to manage a small PRINCE2 project with just four sets of documentation:

- The Project Initiation Documentation, which includes:
  - Project Brief
  - Business Case
  - Risk Management Strategy
  - Quality Management Strategy
  - Configuration Management Strategy
  - Communication Management Strategy
  - Project Plan, which includes:
    - Project Product Description
    - Product Descriptions
  - Benefits Review Plan
- Highlight Reports, which include:

- Product Status Account
- The Daily Log, which includes:
  - Issues
  - Risks
  - Lessons
  - Planned and actual quality management activities
  - Configuration Item Records
- End Project Report, which includes:
  - Lessons Report.

The following management products may not be needed:

- **Stage Plan** If there is only one delivery stage, then the Stage Plan details can be included in the Project Plan
- **Checkpoint Reports** If there are no Team Managers, there may be no need for Checkpoint Reports (although the Project Manager may request individual team members to provide them)
- **Work Packages** May only be appropriate when the project has Team Managers. When there is only the Project Manager, then the Stage Plan may suffice. However, even in such cases, the Project Manager may choose to use Work Packages as a control for individual team members
- **End Stage Report** If there is only one delivery stage, then the end of that stage is also the end of the project and only an End Project Report is required
- **Issue Report** If the details of the issue are adequately captured in the Issue Register (or Daily Log), there may be no need for an Issue Report.

19.6 COMMERCIAL CUSTOMER/SUPPLIER ENVIRONMENT

PRINCE2 is based on a customer/supplier environment. It assumes that there will be a customer who will specify the desired result and probably pay for the project, and a supplier who will provide the resources and skills to deliver that result. If the relationship between the customer and the supplier(s) is a commercial one, then additional considerations apply. The main consideration is to recognize that there are at least two sets of:

> **Management products example**
>
> Having decided to combine the Starting up a Project and Initiating a Project processes for a small project, no Project Brief was produced; instead, the project management team used the project mandate to produce simple Project Initiation Documentation. The Project Initiation Documentation included a basic Project Plan, with several Product Descriptions and the details of all the strategies and controls to be applied. The Project Manager elected to use the Daily Log to record risks, issues, lessons and quality results.
>
> Following the initiation stage there was just one more stage, during which a small number of Work Packages were authorized. As these were being managed, the Project Manager held regular checkpoints, which allowed the production of the regular Highlight Reports to the Project Board.
>
> At the end of that stage (and hence the project) an End Project Report was produced that also included the information for the Lessons Report, follow-on action recommendations and Benefits Review Plan.

- Reasons for undertaking the project
- Management systems (including project management methods)
- Governance structures (possibly requiring disclosure of different sorts of project data at different points in the project's life)
- Corporate cultures (e.g. formality, risk taking etc.).

19.6.1 Themes

19.6.1.1 Business Case

In a commercial context, there are at least two Business Cases – the customer's Business Case and the supplier's Business Case. For a successful project, both must demonstrate continued business justification. If the project is no longer viable, desirable or achievable for one party, then the project will struggle and most likely fail regardless of how attractive the Business Case is for the other party.

The customer's Business Case covers the benefits to that customer in contrast to its whole-life costs and risks. The costs should include the internal costs (of customer project resources, and ongoing operations and maintenance resources) and external costs (of suppliers' goods and services). The risks should include the project risks and the ongoing operational risks.

The supplier's Business Case covers the supplier part of the customer project. It should include more than simply making a target margin. Consideration should be given to how the project will contribute to the supplier's:

- Sales objective
- Account plan objectives
- Sales territory objectives
- Market sector objectives.

Example of other considerations in a supplier's Business Case

A sales team request the supplier's senior management to grant discount levels beyond that which they are authorized. The reason for requesting the additional discount is to win the pilot (this project) in order to increase the likelihood of winning a wider roll-out. In this case, the supplier's Business Case should go beyond fulfilling the contractual requirements and cover costs for activities to ensure that the supplier maximizes its sales opportunity for the roll-out.

Each party's Business Case may be private or partly private from the other. Often, the closest a supplier may get to seeing the customer's Business Case is a list of 'reasons' in a request for change. However, depending on the cultural compatibility of the customer and supplier organizations, making the key reasons for undertaking the project (i.e. the benefits) visible to each other will usually lead to a greater yield for both parties.

19.6.1.2 Organization

One of the key decisions to make in a commercial customer/supplier relationship is who should take the role of Senior Supplier. Considerations include:

- Is it appropriate to have a Senior Supplier from an external organization if the Project Board needs to discuss funding of changes or of future work? Or what if the debate is about whether to terminate the contract with the supplier? One option could be to simply exclude

the Senior Supplier from the part of the reviews that involve the sensitive discussions. Another option would be to appoint the person who is responsible for the performance of the supplier contract (e.g. a contracts manager)

- What if there are multiple suppliers? If there are only a few (say three or four), then it is recommended that all of them are on the Project Board as it provides a forum for them to integrate. If there are more than three or four suppliers, then the contracts manager responsible for the performance of all the supplier contracts could sit on the Project Board on their behalf, or it may be appropriate to appoint a prime contractor
- If the project includes a procurement stage, who should fulfil the role of Senior Supplier if the supplier has not been appointed? The project may need a temporary appointment for the Senior Supplier role – perhaps from the customer's procurement department.

Another key decision is who provides the Project Manager. In PRINCE2, the Project Manager will normally come from the customer organization, with the suppliers' Project Manager(s) fulfilling the role of Team Managers for the project. Even though the Team Managers may be called Project Managers in the supplier's organization, the role titles and job titles should not be confused. Remember, there can only be one Project Manager.

There may be projects where the Project Manager comes from the supplier's organization. Customers may choose to stay 'at arm's length' from the working level and expect the supplier to provide the management of the project. The customer is likely to increase the rigour in Project Assurance (and indeed may choose to appoint one of its internal Project Managers to fulfil the role of Project Assurance). In this case it needs to be clear that although the person undertaking Project Assurance may have a job title of Project Manager, that person is not the Project Manager for this project – there can be only one Project Manager. Consideration should be given to the Project Board dynamics if the Project Manager has a project reporting line to the Executive, and a line management (or commercial) reporting line to the Senior Supplier.

The supplier's governance rules may mean that they have to treat their Work Package(s) within the customer's project as a project within the supplier's organization. This may mean establishing a separate supplier Project Board. Consideration should be given to:

- Who fulfils the Senior User role if not someone from the customer's organization (the account manager is a useful proxy as the customer advocate)
- How the customer and supplier Project Board roles relate, i.e. which of the supplier's Project Board members takes the Senior Supplier role on the customer's Project Board. Whoever it is, they need to have authority to make decisions on behalf of the supplier when undertaking the Senior Supplier role on the customer's Project Board.

There are numerous ways to structure the project management team roles in a commercial customer/supplier context. The key objective is to ensure that both organizations establish and maintain sound business justification and that their respective governance rules are adhered to.

19.6.1.3 Quality

The Quality Management Strategy will define whether the project will conform to either the customer's or supplier's quality management systems, or a combination of them.

19.6.1.4 Plans

Can the contract be awarded for the entire project if the Project Board only approves the funding on a stage-by-stage basis? One approach is for the contract to cover the whole project, with purchase orders and milestone payments aligned to each management stage. Such an approach encourages the organizations to consider what will happen in the circumstance where the project is no longer viable for either party and is closed prematurely. It is prudent procurement and sales management to ensure there are break-points in contracts for both sides.

The customer has a choice as to how to manage the procurement activities – either manage them as part of the initiation stage (and consider using the Controlling a Stage and Managing Product Delivery processes to manage them), or add a procurement stage after initiation. Managing the procurement within the initiation stage will reduce the uncertainty in the plans. However, there may not be adequate controls in place if the procurement activities are expensive and time-consuming.

PRINCE2 assumes that Work Packages are agreed between the Project Manager and the Team Manager and that any Team Plan is optional. The Team Plan may be private to the supplier as it may contain other information such as dependencies to or from other client projects, subcontractor costs etc. The Team Manager's Checkpoint Report, containing progress against the milestones agreed in the Work Package, should be sufficient for the Project Manager to maintain the Stage Plan.

19.6.1.5 Risk

In a commercial context there may be a need for more than one Risk Register as some project risks could be unique to only one party, with good reasons for them not to be visible to the other party. Where a joint Risk Register is used, care should be taken as to whose risk it really is, and the risk owner appointed accordingly. For example, on a fixed-price contract any cost overruns will impact the supplier's Business Case, but timescale overruns will typically impact mostly the customer's Business Case.

19.6.1.6 Change

The change control procedure in the Configuration Management Strategy and any provisions for changes in the contract must be aligned. If a change budget is used, it will need to be aligned to the customer's purchasing procedures and the supplier's business approval procedures. (For example, will the customer authorize the change by raising new purchase orders, or variation orders against the original purchase order, or would the original purchase order cover both the project budget and the change budget? Would the supplier's business approval procedure require separate management approval for each request for change, or is it covered by the management approval for the project?)

19.6.1.7 Progress

The frequency, format and formality of reviewing and reporting need to be aligned to the needs of both organizations' governance requirements. For example, Team Managers may need to produce two Checkpoint Reports, one for the customer's Project Manager and one for the supplier's management. The contents of these reports may vary (for example, the Checkpoint Report to the supplier's management may include details of new sales opportunities).

19.6.2 Processes

As PRINCE2 is based on a customer/supplier context from the customer perspective, it is unlikely that the processes need to be tailored from the customer perspective.

From a supplier's perspective, the key change to the processes will be to the Starting up a Project and Initiating a Project processes. The Starting up a Project process will take place pre-contract and is typically in response to the customer's request for a proposal. Some of the Initiating a Project process will be pre-contract as the supplier will need to formulate the strategies, plans and controls in order to assess the viability and desirability of the sale, and the associated costs and prices of the solution being proposed. The Initiating a Project process is not completed, however, until contract negotiation has concluded and the customer's Project Board authorizes the project. Contract negotiation should be managed under change control.

An additional requirement is to align the supplier's business approval processes with the Starting up a Project process (qualifying the opportunity) and the Initiating the Project process (approving the proposal). A tactical approach is to prepare any project documentation to 'final draft' status during pre-contract activities, for it then to be approved as part of the contract award.

19.6.3 Management products

How do the Project Initiation Documentation and Work Packages relate to the contract? One aspect of a contract is to describe who is liable if either party fails to fulfil its contractual obligations. The content of the Project Initiation Documentation should focus on how to make sure that each party's obligations are fulfilled. Therefore they fulfil different purposes. The Project Initiation Documentation could be part of the contract documentation, but care should be taken as it may stifle the project's ability to adapt if the Project Initiation Documentation has to go through legal review for each change.

For an external supplier, the Work Package may take the form of a legally binding contract and may need to be modified to include any required terms and conditions.

19.7 MULTI-ORGANIZATION PROJECTS

Increasingly, the organizational context of projects is becoming more complex. Rather than a simple customer/supplier relationship involving two organizations, projects are being instigated that involve multiple organizations.

Examples are:

- Joint ventures
- Collaborative research
- Inter-departmental projects
- Inter-governmental projects (e.g. the European Union)
- Inter-agency projects (e.g. United Nations Development Programme)
- Alliance contracting
- Bidding consortium
- Partnerships.

There may be one main commissioning authority (or one main customer), but there may be several customers. Likewise there may be several supplier organizations. This may result in a situation where the project is 'multi-owned', in that more than one organization shares ultimate control over the decision-making process. Failure to agree the basis for this 'multi-ownership' puts the project at risk and increases the chance of project failure.

The guidance to using PRINCE2 in a multi-owned project is similar to the commercial customer/supplier context with respect to tailoring the themes with any reference to 'contract' being substituted for 'agreement'. However, arrangements catering for multi-organization projects can become extremely complex. Project Boards, for example, can have more members than can practically make effective decisions. If no single party holds sway over the others, a consensus has to be built on each decision. Large consensual Project Boards work very slowly and the pace of their projects is likely to suffer. Alternatively, Project Managers begin to take decisions that are beyond their remit. Consideration should then be given to adopting the organizational structures of programme management to assist with benefits management and stakeholder engagement.

19.8 PROJECT TYPE

19.8.1 Lifecycle models

Many industries or professions have developed lifecycle models for particular types of projects, such as waterfall or agile methods. PRINCE2 works well with such models as they primarily focus on the activities to create and verify the project's specialist products – the aspect of projects that PRINCE2 deliberately does not address.

Tailoring PRINCE2 to work with specialist lifecycle models principally involves:

- Aligning the management stages to the development lifecycle – e.g. design, build, test, transition

- Using tolerances to match the development focus – e.g. agile projects that use an iterative and incremental approach tend to fix timescale and quality (narrow tolerance) and vary scope (wide tolerance)

- Integrating any specialist roles into the project management team structure. For example, if the lifecycle model includes a technical design authority, should this role be a peer of the Project Manager, a Team Manager who reports to the Project Manager, or a form of Project Assurance? As roles are simply a collection of responsibilities, it is not that important what the role is called, but it is important that the responsibilities defined by the roles are assigned to someone within the organization – and that the assignment is clearly understood by all those people involved

- Using PRINCE2 for the project management products (e.g. Project Brief) and using the specialist method to define the purpose, format, composition and quality criteria for the specialist management products (e.g. the solution architecture definition in DSDM Atern). Specialist methods may also provide some project management products, so it is important to identify which of its management products are to help the creation of the specialist products (e.g. a technical design document), and which are to help manage the project. For each of its project management products, a decision should be made as to whether to use the PRINCE2 equivalent or not. The goal is to avoid duplication or gaps

- Providing hooks from the Managing Product Delivery process to the specialist product development processes.

19.8.2 The evolving project

Research funded by the Engineering and Physical Sciences Research Council under the title *Rethinking Project Management* (Winter and Smith, 2006) identified that today's projects tend not to start with a predefined specification, but have specifications that evolve as the project progresses. Furthermore the specifications are often contestable and open to negotiation throughout the project's life. The implication is that because the specification is driven by the Business Case, a project may not start with a predefined Business Case.

PRINCE2 handles the evolving paradigm as the Business Case represents a 'best and agreed forecast' at a particular point in a project's lifecycle, which will evolve as the project moves from discovery to implementation.

The outline Business Case developed pre-project (during the Starting up a Project process) is likely to have a wide-range forecast of desired outcomes (e.g. a 30% to 50% reduction in costs), whereas the detailed Business Case updated mid-project is likely to have a much narrower forecast (e.g. a 35% to 40% reduction in costs). Furthermore, as the project progresses, the set of products required to provide the desired outcomes are also likely to evolve.

The value of the evolving Business Case is that it enables the organization to make an investment commitment that is commensurate with the expected benefits and risks forecast at that time in the project's evolution. The Business Case also provides the basis for the control and impact assessment of requested changes as a result of the 'contestable and open to negotiation throughout the project's life' aspects of modern projects.

Projects involving research and development, the development of a new policy or the undertaking of a feasibility study are typical of the evolving project paradigm. They require specific consideration as they may not yield any direct benefits (only options) and are likely to generate a negative return on investment. It is possible to value options, which means it is possible to compare the

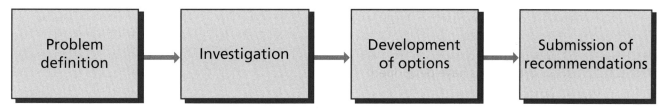

Figure 19.5 An example of a feasibility lifecycle

19.8.3 The feasibility project

In some situations, a feasibility study might be required to investigate the situation and determine options for the way ahead. Using PRINCE2, one approach would be to handle the study as a separate and distinct project.

Figure 19.5 shows the (relatively) simple lifecycle for a feasibility study project. It has one Project Plan, one Business Case, one set of risks and one project product – the recommendation. The possible options may each vary enormously in their costs and timescales. Each option would have a different Project Plan, Business Case and set of risks, but at the end of the feasibility study project there is one recommendation.

If feasibility is treated as a project in its own right, then it is important to recognize that the output is only an option, i.e. the option as to whether to proceed or not. Success should not be judged on whether the idea is feasible but on the ability to make a reliable decision based on the analysis undertaken.

Policy projects are similar to feasibility projects in that the output has no direct value. It is the subsequent implementation of the policy that generates value. As policy projects create products, PRINCE2 is an ideal method to apply. However, a key consideration is the nature of the Business Case. The justification for a policy project may be valid, but it is still important to ensure that the investment in the project provides value for money.

19.9 SECTOR DIFFERENCES

The characteristics of a project apply whether the organization is in the public sector or private sector. The main difference will be the content and nature of the Business Case. However, no tailoring is required as PRINCE2 does not stipulate what makes a Business Case viable, desirable or achievable. These considerations will change from

public sector to private sector but the need for a Business Case, and how it is used by the project, will not.

However, within the UK public sector there are two considerations that may require PRINCE2 to be tailored:

■ Whether the project requires an SRO (see section 19.9.1)
■ Whether the project is subject to OGC Gateway Review (see section 19.9.2).

19.9.1 Senior Responsible Owner

> The **Senior Responsible Owner** is the single individual with overall responsibility for ensuring that a project or programme meets its objectives and delivers the projected benefits.

The Senior Responsible Owner (SRO) role has been introduced widely in the UK government sector for large projects and programmes and is now used increasingly in other sectors and countries. It should be stressed that the SRO is not a PRINCE2 role. However:

■ In the programme context, the Executive would report to the SRO appointed to the programme. It might also be appropriate for the SRO to act as the Executive for major projects within the programme
■ Where an SRO is appointed in the context of a single large project, the person undertaking the SRO role would also undertake the Executive role or appoint the person who will undertake the Executive role.

19.9.2 OGC Gateway Review

The OGC Gateway Review examines projects at key decision points in their lifecycle. It looks ahead to provide assurance that they can progress successfully to the next stage; the process is best practice in UK central civil government, the health sector, local government and defence, and has been adopted by numerous other countries for procurement-based projects using public money.

OGC Gateway Review delivers a 'peer review' in which independent practitioners from outside the project use their experience and expertise to examine the progress and likelihood of successful delivery of the project. It is used to provide a valuable additional perspective on the issues facing the internal team, and an external challenge to the robustness of plans and processes.

Gateway review takes place at different points in a project's lifecycle and the review team will need to consider the relative importance of the individual aspects of delivery confidence given the stage the project has reached. When a project is being set up and has yet to complete its Business Case, the clarity of any scope, the viability of the governance structure and senior management buy-in may dominate the assessment. While those factors are likely to be some of the key determinants of success for any project, later in its lifecycle the appropriateness of processes being used, and the skills and capabilities available to the project, will acquire more weight.

Gateway review can align with PRINCE2 as follows:

- **Review 1: Business justification** This review focuses on the business justification of the project prior to the key decision to approve project initiation. It aligns with the Directing a Project activity of authorizing initiation
- **Reviews 2 and 3: Delivery strategy and investment decision** These reviews align with the Directing a Project activity of authorizing a Stage or Exception Plan, and they focus on ensuring that the project is still required, offers value for money and has a clear delivery strategy

- **Review 4: Readiness for service** This focuses on the readiness of the organization to implement the project and aligns with the Directing a Project activity of authorizing a Stage or Exception Plan.

Another way of considering the alignment would be to organize the project's stages to align to the reviews: initiation (Review 1), procurement stage (Review 2), outline design stage (Review 3), detailed design stage (Review 4), implementation stage, and handover stage.

A gateway review is not the same as a 'gate' or decision point (such as the end stage assessment), but a means of providing added assurance as input to the actual end stage assessment on whether the project is able to meet its objectives. The cost and time of conducting gateway reviews should be included in the Project Plan and Stage Plans.

19.10 PROJECT MANAGEMENT BODIES OF KNOWLEDGE

PRINCE2 should not be confused with a Body of Knowledge (BoK):

- PRINCE2 is an integrated project management method providing a set of processes and themes that can be applied to manage a project from start to finish
- A Body of Knowledge covers the broad spectrum of project management competencies and techniques that Project Managers may need to apply, such as leadership and negotiation.

The comparison between PRINCE2 and a Body of Knowledge (BoK), such as the Association for Project Management's Body of Knowledge, the Project Management Institute's PMBoK or the

Table 19.3 Comparison between PRINCE2 and a Body of Knowledge

PRINCE2	Body of Knowledge
A project management method	A broad collection of 'good practices' for project management
Prescriptive	Non-prescriptive
An integrated set of processes and themes (they are not isolated silos that can be selectively applied)	Each topic area can be referred to in isolation from others
Covers all project management roles	Targeted at Project Managers
Does not cover interpersonal skills	Covers interpersonal skills
References techniques	Describes techniques

International Project Management Association's Competency Baselines, can be seen in Table 19.3.

The differences between PRINCE2 (a method) and a BoK make them highly complementary.

PRINCE2 provides a framework of **what** needs to be done, by **whom** and by **when**. The BoK provides a range of techniques of **how** those things can be done. For example, in PRINCE2 a critical step in creating a plan is estimating. PRINCE2 does not say how estimating should be done as there are a number of techniques that can be applied depending on the project context, whereas a BoK provides an explanation and analysis of the range of estimating techniques available so that the planner can judge which one is most suitable to use.

Tailoring PRINCE2 if the organization is aligned to any particular BoK should include:

- Agreeing a single set of terms to apply. For example, in the Association for Project Management's Body of Knowledge, the steering group is equivalent to PRINCE2's Project Board
- Aligning PRINCE2's management products with any management products recommended by the BoK. For example, in PMBoK the project charter is equivalent to PRINCE2's Project Brief.

Appendix A: Product Description outlines

Appendix A: Product Description outlines

This appendix contains Product Description outlines for PRINCE2's defined management products. These are not full Product Descriptions as defined by Product Description in section A.17, as some elements, such as quality method, will vary depending on the project's needs. Format examples are provided, but these are not exhaustive. The contents of a Product Description for a management product should be tailored to the requirements and environment of each project. There are three types of management product: baselines, records and reports.

Baseline management products are those that define aspects of the project and, once approved, are subject to change control. These are:

- A.1 Benefits Review Plan
- A.2 Business Case
- A.4 Communication Management Strategy
- A.6 Configuration Management Strategy
- A.16 Plan (covers Project, Stage and, optionally, Team Plans)
- A.17 Product Description
- A.19 Project Brief
- A.20 Project Initiation Documentation
- A.21 Project Product Description
- A.22 Quality Management Strategy
- A.24 Risk Management Strategy
- A.26 Work Package.

Records are dynamic management products that maintain information regarding project progress. These are:

- A.5 Configuration Item Records
- A.7 Daily Log
- A.12 Issue Register
- A.14 Lessons Log
- A.23 Quality Register
- A.25 Risk Register.

Reports are management products providing a snapshot of the status of certain aspects of the project. These are:

- A.3 Checkpoint Report
- A.8 End Project Report
- A.9 End Stage Report
- A.10 Exception Report
- A.11 Highlight Report
- A.13 Issue Report
- A.15 Lessons Report
- A.18 Product Status Account.

Although records and reports are not subject to change control, they are still subject to other aspects of configuration management, such as version control, safe storage, access rights etc.

Management products are not necessarily documents, they are information sets that are used by the PRINCE2 processes so that certain roles can take action and/or make decisions.

Most of the baseline products evolve during pre-project and initiation stage activities as shown in Figure A.1. The baseline products are then reviewed and (possibly) updated at the end of each stage. Management products nested within higher-level management products are illustrated in the composition of each management product by reference to their appendix heading (e.g. if a Lessons Report is nested in another report, there will be a cross-reference to section A.15).

A.1 BENEFITS REVIEW PLAN

A.1.1 Purpose

A Benefits Review Plan is used to define how and when a measurement of the achievement of the project's benefits, expected by the Senior User, can be made. The plan is presented to the Executive during the Initiating a Project process, updated at each stage boundary, and used during the Closing a Project process to define any post-project benefits reviews that are required.

The plan has to cover the activities to find out whether the expected benefits of the products have been realized and how the products have performed when in operational use. Each expected benefit has to be assessed for the level of its achievement and whether any additional time is needed to assess the residual benefits. Use of the project's products may have brought unexpected

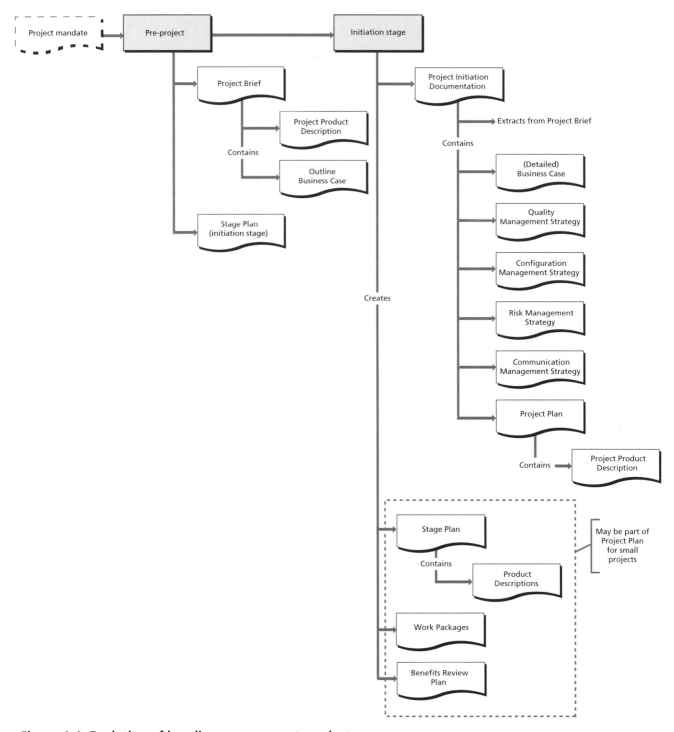

Figure A.1 Evolution of baseline management products

side-effects, either beneficial or adverse. Time and effort have to be allowed to identify and analyse why these side-effects were not foreseen.

If the project is part of a programme, the Benefits Review Plan may be contained within the programme's benefits realization plan and executed at the programme level. Post-project, the

Benefits Review Plan is maintained and executed by corporate or programme management.

A.1.2 Composition

- The scope of the Benefits Review Plan covering what benefits are to be measured
- Who is accountable for the expected benefits

- How to measure achievement of expected benefits, and when they can be measured
- What resources are needed to carry out the review work
- Baseline measures from which the improvements will be calculated
- How the performance of the project's product will be reviewed.

A.1.3 Derivation

- Business Case
- Project Product Description (and the acceptance criteria in particular)
- The programme's benefits realization plan (if part of a programme)
- Corporate performance monitoring function (such as a centre of excellence), if one exists.

A.1.4 Format and presentation

A Benefits Review Plan can take a number of formats, including:

- Document, spreadsheet or presentation slides
- Entry in a project management tool.

A.1.5 Quality criteria

- Covers all benefits stated in the Business Case
- The benefits are measurable and baseline measures have been recorded
- Describes suitable timing for measurement of benefits, together with reasons for the timing
- Identifies the skills or individuals who will be needed to carry out the measurements
- The effort and cost to undertake the benefits reviews is realistic when compared with the value of the anticipated benefits
- Consideration is given to whether dis-benefits should be measured and reviewed.

A.2 BUSINESS CASE

A.2.1 Purpose

A Business Case is used to document the justification for the undertaking of a project, based on the estimated costs (of development, implementation and incremental ongoing operations and maintenance costs) against the anticipated benefits to be gained and offset by any associated risks. It should outline how and when the anticipated benefits can be measured.

The outline Business Case is developed in the Starting up a Project process and refined by the Initiating a Project process. The Directing a Project process covers the approval and re-affirmation of the Business Case.

The Business Case is used by the Controlling a Stage process when assessing impacts of issues and risks. It is reviewed and updated at the end of each management stage by the Managing a Stage Boundary process, and at the end of the project by the Closing a Project process.

A.2.2 Composition

- **Executive summary** Highlights the key points in the Business Case, which should include important benefits and the return on investment (ROI)
- **Reasons** Defines the reasons for undertaking the project and explains how the project will enable the achievement of corporate strategies and objectives
- **Business options** Analysis and reasoned recommendation for the base business options of: do nothing, do the minimum or do something
- **Expected benefits** The benefits that the project will deliver expressed in measurable terms against the situation as it exists prior to the project. Benefits should be both qualitative and quantitative. They should be aligned to corporate or programme benefits. Tolerances should be set for each benefit and for the aggregated benefit. Any benefits realization requirements should be stated
- **Expected dis-benefits** Outcomes perceived as negative by one or more stakeholders. Dis-benefits are actual consequences of an activity whereas, by definition, a risk has some uncertainty about whether it will materialize. For example, a decision to merge two elements of an organization onto a new site may have benefits (e.g. better joint working), costs (e.g. expanding one of the two sites) and dis-benefits (e.g. drop in productivity during the merger). Dis-benefits need to be valued and incorporated into the investment appraisal
- **Timescale** Over which the project will run (summary of the Project Plan) and the period over which the benefits will be realized. This information is subsequently used to help timing

decisions when planning (Project Plan, Stage Plan and Benefits Review Plan)

■ **Costs** A summary of the project costs (taken from the Project Plan), the ongoing operations and maintenance costs and their funding arrangements

■ **Investment appraisal** Compares the aggregated benefits and dis-benefits to the project costs (extracted from the Project Plan) and ongoing incremental operations and maintenance costs. The analysis may use techniques such as cash flow statement, ROI, net present value, internal rate of return and payback period. The objective is to be able to define the value of a project as an investment. The investment appraisal should address how the project will be funded

■ **Major risks** Gives a summary of the key risks associated with the project together with the likely impact and plans should they occur.

A.2.3 Derivation

■ Project mandate and Project Brief – reasons
■ Project Plan – costs and timescales
■ The Senior User(s) – expected benefits
■ The Executive – value for money
■ Risk Register
■ Issue Register.

A.2.4 Format and presentation

A Business Case can take a number of formats, including:

■ Document, spreadsheet or presentation slides
■ Entry in a project management tool.

A.2.5 Quality criteria

■ The reasons for the project must be consistent with the corporate or programme strategy
■ The Project Plan and Business Case must be aligned
■ The benefits should be clearly identified and justified
■ It should be clear how the benefits will be realized
■ It should be clear what will define a successful outcome
■ It should be clear what the preferred business option is, and why

■ Where external procurement is required, it should be clear what the preferred sourcing option is, and why
■ It should be clear how any necessary funding will be obtained
■ The Business Case includes non-financial, as well as financial, criteria
■ The Business Case includes operations and maintenance costs and risks, as well as project costs and risks
■ The Business Case conforms to organizational accounting standards (e.g. break-even analysis and cash flow conventions)
■ The major risks faced by the project are explicitly stated, together with any proposed responses.

A.3 CHECKPOINT REPORT

A.3.1 Purpose

A Checkpoint Report is used to report, at a frequency defined in the Work Package, the status of the Work Package.

A.3.2 Composition

■ **Date** The date of the checkpoint
■ **Period** The reporting period covered by the Checkpoint Report
■ **Follow-ups** From previous reports, for example action items completed or issues outstanding
■ **This reporting period:**
  ● The products being developed by the team during the reporting period
  ● The products completed by the team during the reporting period
  ● Quality management activities carried out during the period
  ● Lessons identified
■ **Next reporting period:**
  ● The products being developed by the team in the next reporting period
  ● The products planned to be completed by the team in the next reporting period
  ● Quality management activities planned for the next reporting period
■ **Work Package tolerance status** How execution of the Work Package is performing against its tolerances (e.g. cost/time/scope actuals and forecast)

- **Issues and risks** Update on issues and risks associated with the Work Package.

A.3.3 Derivation

- Work Package
- Team Plan and actuals
- Previous Checkpoint Report.

A.3.4 Format and presentation

A Checkpoint Report can take a number of formats, including:

- Oral report to the Project Manager (could be in person or over the phone)
- Presentation at a progress review (physical meeting or conference call)
- Document or email issued to the Project Manager
- Entry in a project management tool.

A.3.5 Quality criteria

- Prepared at the frequency required by the Project Manager
- The level and frequency of progress assessment is right for the stage and/or Work Package
- The information is timely, useful, objective and accurate
- Every product in the Work Package, for that period, is covered by the report
- Includes an update on any unresolved issues from the previous report.

A.4 COMMUNICATION MANAGEMENT STRATEGY

A.4.1 Purpose

A Communication Management Strategy contains a description of the means and frequency of communication to parties both internal and external to the project. It facilitates engagement with stakeholders through the establishment of a controlled and bi-directional flow of information.

A.4.2 Composition

- **Introduction** States the purpose, objectives and scope, and identifies who is responsible for the strategy
- **Communication procedure** A description of (or reference to) any communication methods to be used. Any variance from corporate or

programme management standards should be highlighted, together with a justification for the variance

- **Tools and techniques** Refers to any communication tools to be used, and any preference for techniques that may be used, for each step in the communication process
- **Records** Definition of what communication records will be required and where they will be stored (for example, logging of external correspondence)
- **Reporting** Describes any reports on the communication process that are to be produced, including their purpose, timing and recipients (for example, performance indicators)
- **Timing of communication activities** States when formal communication activities are to be undertaken (for example, at the end of a stage) including performance audits of the communication methods
- **Roles and responsibilities** Describes who will be responsible for what aspects of the communication process, including any corporate or programme management roles involved with communication
- **Stakeholder analysis:**
  - Identification of the interested party (which may include accounts staff, user forum, internal audit, corporate or programme quality assurance, competitors etc.)
  - Current relationship
  - Desired relationship
  - Interfaces
  - Key messages
- **Information needs for each interested party:**
  - Information required to be provided from the project
  - Information required to be provided to the project
  - Information provider and recipient
  - Frequency of communication
  - Means of communication
  - Format of the communication.

A.4.3 Derivation

- Corporate communications policies (e.g. rules for disclosure for publicly listed companies)
- The programme's information management strategy

- Other components of the Project Initiation Documentation (in particular the project management team structure, the Risk Management Strategy, Quality Management Strategy and Configuration Management Strategy)
- Facilitated workshops/informal discussions with stakeholders
- Stakeholder analysis.

A.4.4 Format and presentation

A Communication Management Strategy can take a number of formats, including:

- Stand-alone product or a section of the Project Initiation Documentation
- Document, spreadsheet or mindmap
- Entry in a project management tool.

A.4.5 Quality criteria

- All stakeholders have been identified and consulted for their communication requirements
- There is agreement from all stakeholders about the content, frequency and method of communication
- A common standard for communication has been considered
- The time, effort and resources required to carry out the identified communications have been allowed for in Stage Plans
- The formality and frequency of communication is reasonable for the project's importance and complexity
- For projects that are part of a programme, the lines of communication, and the reporting structure between the project and programme, have been made clear in the Communication Management Strategy
- The Communication Management Strategy incorporates corporate communications facilities where appropriate (e.g. using the marketing communications department for distributing project bulletins).

A.5 CONFIGURATION ITEM RECORD

A.5.1 Purpose

To provide a record of such information as the history, status, version and variant of each configuration item, and any details of important relationships between them.

The set of Configuration Item Records for a project is often referred to as a configuration library.

A.5.2 Composition

The composition of a Configuration Item Record will be defined in the project's Configuration Management Strategy.

There follows a suggested list of components for each Configuration Item Record (note that the first three uniquely identify the configuration item):

- **Project identifier** A unique reference. It will typically be a numeric or alpha-numeric value
- **Item identifier** A unique reference. It will typically be a numeric or alpha-numeric value
- **Current version** Typically an alpha-numeric value
- **Item title** The description of the item (for a product this should be as it appears in the product breakdown structure)
- **Date of last status change**
- **Owner** The person or group who will take ownership of the product when it is handed over
- **Location** Where the item is stored
- **Copy holders** (if relevant) Who currently has the product?
- **Item type** Component, product, release (see section 9.2.2)
- **Item attributes** As defined by the Configuration Management Strategy. These are used to specify a subset of products when producing a Product Status Account, such as the management stage in which the product is created, the type of product (e.g. hardware/software), product destination etc.
- **Stage** When the product will be developed
- **Users** The person or group who will use the item
- **Status** As defined by the Configuration Management Strategy, e.g. pending development, in development, in review, approved or handed over
- **Product state** (if used) As defined by the Product Description, e.g. dismantled machinery, moved machinery, reassembled machinery (see section 7.3.3.2)
- **Variant** (if used) for example, language variants

- **Producer** The person or team responsible for creating or obtaining the item
- **Date allocated** To the producer
- **Source** For example, in house, or purchased from a third-party company
- **Relationship with other items** Those items that:
  - Would be affected if this item changed
  - If changed, would affect this item
- **Cross-references:**
  - Issues and risks
  - Documentation that defines requirements, design, build, production and verification for the item (specifically this will include the Product Description).

A.5.3 Derivation

- Configuration Management Strategy
- Product breakdown structure
- Stage Plan and Work Package
- Quality Register, Issue Register and Risk Register.

A.5.4 Format and presentation

Configuration Item Records can take a number of formats, including:

- Document, spreadsheet or database
- Entry in a project management tool

Configuration Item Records may be part of a Configuration Management Database for those organizations that have a corporate or programme configuration management system.

A.5.5 Quality criteria

- The records reflect the status of the products accurately
- The records are kept together in a secure location
- Version numbers match the actual products
- Configuration Item Records show products' version histories
- A process exists by which the Configuration Item Records are defined and updated.

A.6 CONFIGURATION MANAGEMENT STRATEGY

A.6.1 Purpose

A Configuration Management Strategy is used to identify how, and by whom, the project's products will be controlled and protected.

It answers the questions:

- How and where the project's products will be stored
- What storage and retrieval security will be put in place
- How the products and the various versions and variants of these will be identified
- How changes to products will be controlled
- Where responsibility for configuration management will lie.

A.6.2 Composition

- **Introduction** States the purpose, objectives and scope, and identifies who is responsible for the strategy
- **Configuration management procedure** A description of (or reference to) the configuration management procedure to be used. Any variance from corporate or programme management standards should be highlighted, together with a justification for the variance. The procedure should cover activities such as planning, identification, control (including storage/retrieval, product security, handover procedures etc.), status accounting, and verification and audit
- **Issue and change control procedure** A description (or reference to) the issue and change control procedures to be used. Any variance from corporate or programme management standards should be highlighted, together with a justification for the variance. The procedure should cover activities such as capturing, examining, proposing, deciding and implementing
- **Tools and techniques** Refers to any configuration management systems or tools to be used and any preference for techniques that may be used for each step in the configuration management procedure
- **Records** Definition of the composition and format of the Issue Register and Configuration Item Records

- **Reporting** Describes the composition and format of the reports that are to be produced (Issue Report, Product Status Account), their purpose, timing and chosen recipients. This should include reviewing the performance of the procedures
- **Timing of configuration management and issue and change control activities** States when formal activities (for example, configuration audits) are to be undertaken
- **Roles and responsibilities** Describes who will be responsible for what aspects of the procedures, including any corporate or programme management roles involved with the configuration management of the project's products. Describes whether a Change Authority and/or change budget will be established
- **Scales for priority and severity** For prioritizing requests for change and off-specifications and for determining the level of management that can make decisions on severity of issue.

A.6.3 Derivation

- The customer's quality expectations
- Corporate configuration management system (e.g. any configuration management software in use or mandated by the user)
- Programme Quality Management Strategy and information management strategy (if applicable)
- The user's quality management system
- The supplier's quality management system
- Specific needs of the project's product(s) and environment
- Project management team structure (to identify those with configuration management responsibilities)
- Facilitated workshops and informal discussions.

A.6.4 Format and presentation

A Configuration Management Strategy can take a number of formats, including:

- Stand-alone document or a section of the Project Initiation Documentation
- Entry in a project management tool.

A.6.5 Quality criteria

- Responsibilities are clear and understood by both user and supplier

- The key identifier for the project's product(s) is defined
- The method and circumstances of version control are clear
- The strategy provides the Project Manager with all the product information required
- The corporate or programme strategy for configuration management has been considered
- The retrieval system will produce all required information in an accurate, timely and usable manner
- The project files provide the information necessary for any audit requirements
- The project files provide the historical records required to support any lessons
- The chosen Configuration Management Strategy is appropriate for the size and nature of the project
- Resources are in place to administer the chosen method of configuration management
- The requirements of the operational group (or similar group to whom the project's product will be transitioned) should be considered.

A.7 DAILY LOG

A.7.1 Purpose

A Daily Log is used to record informal issues, required actions or significant events not caught by other PRINCE2 registers or logs. It acts as the project diary for the Project Manager.

It can also be used as a repository for issues and risks during the Starting up a Project process if the other registers have not been set up.

There may be more than one Daily Log as Team Managers may elect to have one for their Work Packages, separate from the Project Manager's Daily Log.

A.7.2 Composition

A Daily Log is in free form but likely to include:

- Date of entry
- Problem, action, event or comment
- Person responsible
- Target date
- Results.

A.7.3 Derivation

Entries are made when the Project Manager or Team Manager feels it is appropriate to log some event. Often entries are based on thoughts, conversations and observations.

A.7.4 Format and presentation

A Daily Log can take a number of formats, including:

- Document or spreadsheet
- Desk diary or log book
- Electronic diary/calendar/task lists
- Entry in a project management tool.

A.7.5 Quality criteria

- Entries are sufficiently documented to be understandable later (a short note might make sense at the time, but will it in several months' time?)
- Date, person responsible and target date are always filled in
- Consideration has been given to access rights for the Daily Log (e.g. should the Daily Log be visible to everyone working on the project?).

A.8 END PROJECT REPORT

A.8.1 Purpose

An End Project Report is used during project closure to review how the project performed against the version of the Project Initiation Documentation used to authorize it. It also allows the passing on of:

- Any lessons that can be usefully applied to other projects
- Details of unfinished work, ongoing risks or potential product modifications to the group charged with future support of the project's products in their operational life.

A.8.2 Composition

- **Project Manager's report** Summarizing the project's performance
- **Review of the Business Case** Summarizing the validity of the project's Business Case:
  - Benefits achieved to date
  - Residual benefits expected (post-project)
  - Expected net benefits
  - Deviations from the approved Business Case
- **Review of project objectives** Review of how the project performed against its planned targets and tolerances for time, cost, quality, scope, benefits and risk. Review the effectiveness of the project's strategies and controls
- **Review of team performance** In particular, providing recognition for good performance
- **Review of products:**
  - **Quality records** Listing the quality activities planned and completed
  - **Approval records** Listing the products and their requisite approvals
  - **Off-specifications** Listing any missing products or products that do not meet the original requirements, and confirmation of any concessions granted
  - **Project product handover** Confirmation (in the form of acceptance records) by the customer that operations and maintenance functions are ready to receive the project's product
  - **Summary of follow-on action recommendations** Request for Project Board advice about who should receive each recommended action. The recommended actions are related to unfinished work, ongoing issues and risks, and any other activities needed to take the products to the next phase of their life
- **Lessons Report** (see section A.15) A review of what went well, what went badly, and any recommendations for corporate or programme management consideration (and if the project was prematurely closed, then the reasons should be explained).

A.8.3 Derivation

- Project Initiation Documentation
- Business Case
- Project Plan
- Benefits Review Plan
- Issue Register, Quality Register and Risk Register
- Lessons Report
- End Stage Reports (and Exceptions Reports, if applicable).

A.8.4 Format and presentation

An End Project Report can take a number of formats, including:

- Presentation to the Project Board (physical meeting or conference call)
- Document or email issued to the Project Board
- Entry in a project management tool.

A.8.5 Quality criteria

- Any abnormal situations are described, together with their impact
- At the end of the project, all issues should either be closed or become the subject of a follow-on action recommendation
- Any available useful documentation or evidence should accompany the follow-on action recommendation(s)
- Any appointed Project Assurance roles should agree with the report.

A.9 END STAGE REPORT

A.9.1 Purpose

An End Stage Report is used to give a summary of progress to date, the overall project situation, and sufficient information to ask for a Project Board decision on what to do next with the project.

The Project Board uses the information in the End Stage Report in tandem with the next Stage Plan to decide what action to take with the project: for example, authorize the next stage, amend the project scope, or stop the project.

A.9.2 Composition

- **Project Manager's report** Summarizing the stage performance
- **Review of the Business Case** Summarizing the validity of the project's Business Case:
  - Benefits achieved to date
  - Residual benefits expected (remaining stages and post-project)
  - Expected net benefits
  - Deviations from approved Business Case
  - Aggregated risk exposure
- **Review of project objectives** Review of how the project has performed to date against its planned targets and tolerances for time, cost, quality, scope, benefits and risk. Review the effectiveness of the project's strategies and controls
- **Review of stage objectives** Review of how the specific stage performed against its planned targets and tolerances for time, cost, quality, scope, benefits and risk
- **Review of team performance** In particular, providing recognition for good performance
- **Review of products:**
  - **Quality records** Listing the quality activities planned and completed in the stage
  - **Approval records** Listing the products planned for completion in the stage and their requisite approvals
  - **Off-specifications** Listing any missing products or products that do not meet the original requirements, and confirmation of any concessions granted
  - **Phased handover (if applicable)** Confirmation by the customer that operations and maintenance functions are ready to receive the release
  - **Summary of follow-on action recommendations (if applicable)** Request for Project Board advice for who should receive each recommended action. The recommended actions are related to unfinished work, ongoing issues and risks, and any other activities needed to take the products handed over to the next phase of their life
- **Lessons Report** (if appropriate) (see section A.15) A review of what went well, what went badly, and any recommendations for corporate or programme management consideration
- **Issues and risks** Summary of the current set of issues and risks affecting the project
- **Forecast** The Project Manager's forecast for the project and next stage against planned targets and tolerances for time, cost, quality, scope, benefits and risk.

Where the End Stage Report is being produced at the end of the initiation stage, not all of the above content may be appropriate or necessary.

A.9.3 Derivation

- Current Stage Plan and actuals
- Project Plan
- Benefits Review Plan
- Risk Register, Quality Register and Issue Register

- Exception Report (if applicable)
- Lessons Report
- Completed/slipped Work Packages
- Updated Business Case.

A.9.4 Format and presentation

An End Stage Report can take a number of formats, including:

- Presentation to the Project Board (physical meeting or conference call)
- Document or email issued to the Project Board
- Entry in a project management tool.

A.9.5 Quality criteria

- The report clearly shows stage performance against the plan
- Any abnormal situations are described, together with their impact
- Any appointed Project Assurance roles agree with the report.

A.10 EXCEPTION REPORT

A.10.1 Purpose

An Exception Report is produced when a Stage Plan or Project Plan is forecast to exceed tolerance levels set. It is prepared by the Project Manager in order to inform the Project Board of the situation, and to offer options and recommendations for the way to proceed.

A.10.2 Composition

- **Exception title** An overview of the exception being reported
- **Cause of the exception** A description of the cause of a deviation from the current plan
- **Consequences of the deviation** What the implications are if the deviation is not addressed for:
  - The project
  - Corporate or programme management
- **Options** What are the options that are available to address the deviation and what would the effect of each option be on the Business Case, risks and tolerances
- **Recommendation** Of the available options, what is the recommendation, and why?
- **Lessons** What can be learned from the exception, on this project or future projects.

A.10.3 Derivation

- Current plan and actuals
- Issue Register, Risk Register and Quality Register
- Highlight Reports, Issue Reports (for stage/project-level deviations) or Checkpoint Reports (for team-level deviations)
- Project Board advice of an external event that affects the project.

A.10.4 Format and presentation

An Exception Report can take a number of formats, including:

- Issue raised at a minuted progress review (physical meeting or conference call)
- Document or email issued to the next-higher level of management
- Entry in a project management tool.

For urgent exceptions, it is recommended that the Exception Report is oral in the first instance, and then followed up in the agreed format.

A.10.5 Quality criteria

- The current plan must accurately show the status of time and cost performance
- The reason(s) for the deviation must be stated, the exception clearly analysed, and any impacts assessed and fully described
- Implications for the Business Case have been considered and the impact on the overall Project Plan has been calculated
- Options are analysed (including any risks associated with them) and recommendations are made for the most appropriate way to proceed
- The Exception Report is given in a timely and appropriate manner.

A.11 HIGHLIGHT REPORT

A.11.1 Purpose

A Highlight Report is used to provide the Project Board (and possibly other stakeholders) with a summary of the stage status at intervals defined by them. The Project Board uses the report to monitor stage and project progress. The Project Manager also uses it to advise the Project Board of any potential problems or areas where the Project Board could help.

A.11.2 Composition

- **Date** The date of the report
- **Period** The reporting period covered by the Highlight Report
- **Status summary** An overview of the status of the stage at this time
- **This reporting period:**
  - Work Packages – pending authorization, in execution, and completed in the period (if the Work Packages are being performed by external suppliers, this information may be accompanied by purchase order and invoicing data)
  - Products completed in the period
  - Products planned but not started or completed in the period (providing an early warning indicator or potential breach of time tolerance)
  - Corrective actions taken during the period
- **Next reporting period:**
  - Work Packages – to be authorized, in execution, and to be completed during the next period (if the Work Packages are being performed by external suppliers, this information may be accompanied by purchase order and invoicing data)
  - Products to be completed in the next period
  - Corrective actions to be completed during the next period
- **Project and stage tolerance status** How execution of the project and stage are performing against their tolerances (e.g. cost/time actuals and forecast)
- **Requests for change** Raised, approved/rejected and pending
- **Key issues and risks** Summary of actual or potential problems and risks
- **Lessons Report** (if appropriate) (see section A.15) A review of what went well, what went badly, and any recommendations for corporate or programme management consideration.

A.11.3 Derivation

- Project Initiation Documentation
- Checkpoint Reports
- Issue Register, Quality Register and Risk Register
- Stage Plan and actuals
- Communication Management Strategy.

A.11.4 Format and presentation

A Highlight Report can take a number of formats, including:

- Presentation to the Project Board (physical meeting or conference call)
- Document or email issued to the Project Board
- Entry in a project management tool.

A.11.5 Quality criteria

- The level and frequency of progress reporting required by the Project Board is right for the stage and/or project
- The Project Manager provides the Highlight Report at the frequency, and with the content, required by the Project Board
- The information is timely, useful, accurate and objective
- The report highlights any potential problem areas.

A.12 ISSUE REGISTER

A.12.1 Purpose

The purpose of the Issue Register is to capture and maintain information on all of the issues that are being formally managed. The Issue Register should be monitored by the Project Manager on a regular basis.

A.12.2 Composition

For each entry in the Issue Register, the following should be recorded:

- **Issue identifier** Provides a unique reference for every issue entered into the Issue Register. It will typically be a numeric or alpha-numeric value
- **Issue type** Defines the type of issue being recorded, namely:
  - Request for change
  - Off-specification
  - Problem/concern
- **Date raised** The date on which the issue was originally raised
- **Raised by** The name of the individual or team who raised the issue
- **Issue Report author** The name of the individual or team who created the Issue Report

- **Issue description** A statement describing the issue, its cause and impact
- **Priority** This should be given in terms of the project's chosen categories. Priority should be re-evaluated after impact analysis
- **Severity** This should be given in terms of the project's chosen scale. Severity will indicate what level of management is required to make a decision on the issue
- **Status** The current status of the issue and the date of the last update
- **Closure date** The date the issue was closed.

A.12.3 Derivation

- The format and composition of the Issue Register will be defined in the Configuration Management Strategy
- Entries are initially made on the Issue Register once a new issue has been raised
- The Issue Register is updated as the issue is progressed. Once the issue has been resolved, the entry in the Issue Register is closed.

A.12.4 Format and presentation

An Issue Register can take a number of formats, including:

- Document, spreadsheet or database
- Stand-alone register or a carry forward in progress review minutes
- Entry in a project management tool
- Part of an integrated project register for all risks, actions, decisions, assumptions, issues, lessons etc.

A.12.5 Quality criteria

- The status indicates whether action has been taken
- The issues are uniquely identified, including information about which product they refer to
- A process is defined by which the Issue Register is to be updated
- Entries on the Issue Register that, upon examination, are in fact risks, are transferred to the Risk Register and the entries annotated accordingly
- Access to the Issue Register is controlled and the register is kept in a safe place.

A.13 ISSUE REPORT

A.13.1 Purpose

An Issue Report is a report containing the description, impact assessment and recommendations for a request for change, off-specification or a problem/concern. It is only created for those issues that need to be handled formally.

The report is initially created when capturing the issue, and updated both after the issue has been examined and when proposals are identified for issue resolution. The Issue Report is later amended further in order to record what option was decided upon, and finally updated when the implementation has been verified and the issue is closed.

A.13.2 Composition

- **Issue identifier** As shown in the Issue Register (provides a unique reference for every Issue Report)
- **Issue type** Defines the type of issue being recorded, namely:
  - Request for change
  - Off-specification
  - Problem/concern
- **Date raised** The date on which the issue was originally raised
- **Raised by** The name of the individual or team who raised the issue
- **Issue Report author** The name of the individual or team who created the Issue Report
- **Issue description** A statement describing the issue in terms of its cause and impact
- **Impact analysis** A detailed analysis of the likely impact of the issue. This may include, for example, a list of products impacted
- **Recommendation** A description of what the Project Manager believes should be done to resolve the issue (and why)
- **Priority** This should be given in terms of the project's chosen scale. It should be re-evaluated after impact analysis
- **Severity** This should be given in terms of the project's chosen scale. Severity will indicate what level of management is required to make a decision on the issue
- **Decision** The decision made (accept, reject, defer or grant concession)

- **Approved by** A record of who made the decision
- **Decision date** The date of the decision
- **Closure date** The date that the issue was closed.

A.13.3 Derivation

- The format and composition of the Issue Report will be defined in the Configuration Management Strategy
- Highlight Report(s), Checkpoint Report(s) and End Stage Report(s)
- Stage Plan, together with actual values and events
- Users and supplier teams working on the project
- The application of quality controls
- Observation and experience of the processes
- Quality Register, Risk Register and Lessons Log
- Completed Work Packages.

A.13.4 Format and presentation

An Issue Report can take a number of formats, including:

- Document, spreadsheet or database
- Entry in a project management tool.

Not all entries in the Issue Register will need a separately documented Issue Report.

A.13.5 Quality criteria

- The issue stated is clear and unambiguous
- A detailed impact analysis has occurred
- All implications have been considered
- The issue has been examined for its effect on the tolerances
- The issue has been correctly registered in the Issue Register
- Decisions are accurately and unambiguously described.

A.14 LESSONS LOG

A.14.1 Purpose

The Lessons Log is a project repository for lessons that apply to this project or future projects. Some lessons may originate from other projects and should be captured on the Lessons Log for input to the project's strategies and plans. Some lessons may originate from within the project – where new experience (both good and bad) can be passed on to others via a Lessons Report.

A.14.2 Composition

For each entry in the Lessons Log, the following should be recorded:

- **Lesson type** Defines the type of lesson being recorded:
  - Project – to be applied to this project
  - Corporate or programme – to be passed on to the corporate or programme management
  - Both project and corporate or programme management
- **Lesson detail** The detail may include:
  - Event
  - Effect (e.g. positive/negative financial impact)
  - Causes/trigger
  - Whether there were any early warning indicators
  - Recommendations
  - Whether it was previously identified as a risk (threat or opportunity)
- **Date logged** The date on which the lesson was originally logged
- **Logged by** The name of the person or team who raised the lesson
- **Priority** In terms of the project's chosen categories.

A.14.3 Derivation

- Lessons Reports from other projects
- Project mandate or Project Brief
- Daily Log, Issue Register, Quality Register and Risk Register
- Checkpoint Reports and Highlight Reports
- Completed Work Packages
- Stage Plans with actuals
- Observation and experience of the project's processes.

A.14.4 Format and presentation

A Lessons Log can take a number of formats, including:

- Document, spreadsheet or database
- Stand-alone log or a carry forward in progress review minutes

- Entry in a project management tool
- Part of an integrated project register for all risks, actions, decisions, assumptions, issues, lessons etc.

A.14.5 Quality criteria

- The status indicates whether action has been taken
- Lessons are uniquely identified, including to which product they refer
- A process is defined by which the Lessons Log is to be updated
- Access to the Lessons Log is controlled
- The Lessons Log is kept in a safe place.

A.15 LESSONS REPORT

A.15.1 Purpose

The Lessons Report is used to pass on any lessons that can be usefully applied to other projects.

The purpose of the report is to provoke action so that the positive lessons become embedded in the organization's way of working, and that the organization is able to avoid any negative lessons on future projects.

A Lessons Report can be created at any time in a project and should not necessarily wait until the end. Typically it should be included as part of the End Stage Report and End Project Report. It may be appropriate (and necessary) for there to be several Lessons Reports specific to the particular organization (e.g. user, supplier, corporate or programme).

The data in the report should be used by the corporate group that is responsible for the quality management system, in order to refine, change and improve the standards. Statistics on how much effort was needed for products can help improve future estimating.

A.15.2 Composition

- Executive summary
- Scope of the report (e.g. stage or project)
- A review of what went well, what went badly and any recommendations for corporate or programme management consideration. In particular:
  - Project management method (including the tailoring of PRINCE2)

  - Any specialist methods used
  - Project strategies (risk management, quality management, communications management and configuration management)
  - Project controls (and the effectiveness of any tailoring)
  - Abnormal events causing deviations
- A review of useful measurements such as:
  - How much effort was required to create the products
  - How effective was the Quality Management Strategy in designing, developing and delivering fit-for-purpose products (for example, how many errors were found after products had passed quality inspections?)
  - Statistics on issues and risks
- For significant lessons it may be useful to provide additional details on:
  - Event
  - Effect (e.g. positive/negative financial impact)
  - Causes/trigger
  - Whether there were any early-warning indicators
  - Recommendations
  - Whether the triggered event was previously identified as a risk (threat or opportunity).

A.15.3 Derivation

- Project Initiation Documentation (for the baseline position)
- Lessons Log (for identification of lessons)
- Quality Register, Issue Register and Risk Register (for statistical analysis)
- Quality records (for statistical analysis)
- Communication Management Strategy (for the distribution list).

A.15.4 Format and presentation

A Lessons Report can take a number of formats, including:

- Oral report to the Project Board (could be in person or over the phone)
- Presentation at a progress review (physical meeting or conference call)
- Document or email issued to the Project Board
- Entry in a project management tool.

A.15.5 Quality criteria

- Every management control has been examined
- Statistics of estimates versus actuals are provided
- Statistics of the success of quality controls used are included
- Any appointed Project Assurance roles agree with the report
- Unexpected risks are reviewed to determine whether they could have been anticipated
- Recommended actions are provided for each lesson (note that lessons are not 'learned' until action is taken).

A.16 PLAN

A.16.1 Purpose

A plan provides a statement of how and when objectives are to be achieved, by showing the major products, activities and resources required for the scope of the plan. In PRINCE2, there are three levels of plan: project, stage and team. Team Plans are optional and may not need to follow the same composition as a Project Plan or Stage Plan.

An Exception Plan is created at the same level as the plan that it is replacing.

A Project Plan provides the Business Case with planned costs, and it identifies the management stages and other major control points. It is used by the Project Board as a baseline against which to monitor project progress.

Stage Plans cover the products, resources, activities and controls specific to the stage and are used as a baseline against which to monitor stage progress.

Team Plans (if used) could comprise just a schedule appended to the Work Package(s) assigned to the Team Manager.

A plan should cover not just the activities to create products but also the activities to manage product creation – including activities for assurance, quality management, risk management, configuration management, communication and any other project controls required.

A.16.2 Composition

- **Plan description** Covering a brief description of what the plan encompasses (i.e. project, stage, team, exception) and the planning approach
- **Plan prerequisites** Containing any fundamental aspects that must be in place, and remain in place, for the plan to succeed
- **External dependencies** That may influence the plan
- **Planning assumptions** Upon which the plan is based
- **Lessons incorporated** Details of relevant lessons from previous similar projects, which have been reviewed and accommodated within this plan
- **Monitoring and control** Details of how the plan will be monitored and controlled
- **Budgets** Covering time and cost, including provisions for risks and changes
- **Tolerances** Time, cost and scope tolerances for the level of plan (which may also include more specific stage- or team-level risk tolerances)
- **Product Descriptions** (see section A.17) Covering the products within the scope of the plan (for the Project Plan this will include the project's product; for the Stage Plan this will be the stage products; and for a Team Plan this should be a reference to the Work Package assigned). Quality tolerances will be defined in each Product Description
- **Schedule** Which may include graphical representations of:
  - Gantt or bar chart
  - Product breakdown structure (see Appendix D for an example)
  - Product flow diagram (see Appendix D for an example)
  - Activity network
  - Table of resource requirements – by resource type (e.g. four engineers, one test manager, one business analyst)
  - Table of requested/assigned specific resources – by name (e.g. Nikki, Jay, Francesca).

A.16.3 Derivation

- Project Brief
- Quality Management Strategy (for quality management activities to be included in the plan)
- Risk Management Strategy (for risk management activities to be included in the plan)

- Communication Management Strategy (for communication management activities to be included in the plan)
- Configuration Management Strategy (for configuration management activities to be included in the plan)
- Resource availability
- Registers and logs.

A.16.4 Format and presentation

A plan can take a number of formats, including:

- A stand-alone document or a section of the Project Initiation Documentation
- Document, spreadsheet, presentation slides or mindmap
- Entry in a project management tool.

The schedule may be in the form of a product checklist (which is a list of the products to be delivered within the scope of the plan, together with key status dates such as draft ready, quality inspected, approved etc.) or the output from a project planning tool.

A.16.5 Quality criteria

- The plan is achievable
- Estimates are based on consultation with the resources, who will undertake the work, and/or historical data
- Team Managers agree that their part of the plan is achievable
- It is planned to an appropriate level of detail (not too much, not too little)

- The plan conforms to required corporate or programme standards
- The plan incorporates lessons from previous projects
- The plan incorporates any legal requirements
- The plan covers management and control activities (such as quality) as well as the activities to create the products in scope
- The plan supports the Quality Management Strategy, Configuration Management Strategy, Risk Management Strategy, Communication Management Strategy and project approach
- The plan supports the management controls defined in the Project Initiation Documentation.

A.17 PRODUCT DESCRIPTION

A.17.1 Purpose

A Product Description is used to:

- Understand the detailed nature, purpose, function and appearance of the product
- Define who will use the product
- Identify the sources of information or supply for the product
- Identify the level of quality required of the product
- Enable identification of activities to produce, review and approve the product
- Define the people or skills required to produce, review and approve the product.

Table A.1 Example of a product checklist

Product identifier	Product title	Product Description approved		Draft ready		Final quality check completed		Approved		Handed over (if applicable)	
		Plan	Actual	Plan	Actual	Plan	Actual	Plan	Actual	Plan	Actual
...											
121	Test Plan	02/01	02/01	07/02	07/02	14/02	21/02	21/02	28/02	NA	NA
124	Water Pump	02/01	02/01	13/03	13/03	14/06		30/06		14/07	
...											

A.17.2 Composition

- **Identifier** Unique key, probably allocated by the configuration management method and likely to include the project name, item name and version number
- **Title** Name by which the product is known
- **Purpose** This defines the purpose that the product will fulfil and who will use it. Is it a means to an end or an end in itself? It is helpful in understanding the product's functions, size, quality, complexity, robustness etc.
- **Composition** This is a list of the parts of the product. For example, if the product were a report, this would be a list of the expected chapters or sections
- **Derivation** What are the source products from which this product is derived? Examples are:
  - A design is derived from a specification
  - A product is bought in from a supplier
  - A statement of the expected benefits is obtained from the user
  - A product is obtained from another department or team
- **Format and presentation** The characteristics of the product – for example, if the product were a report, this would specify whether the report should be a document, presentation slides or an email
- **Development skills required** An indication of the skills required to develop the product or a pointer to which area(s) should supply the development resources. Identification of the actual people may be left until planning the stage in which the product is to be created
- **Quality criteria** To what quality specification must the product be produced, and what quality measurements will be applied by those inspecting the finished product? This might be a simple reference to one or more common standards that are documented elsewhere, or it might be a full explanation of some yardstick to be applied. If the product is to be developed and approved in different states (e.g. dismantled machinery, moved machinery and reassembled machinery), then the quality criteria should be grouped into those that apply for each state
- **Quality tolerance** Details of any range in the quality criteria within which the product would be acceptable

- **Quality method** The kinds of quality method – for example, design verification, pilot, test, inspection or review – that are to be used to check the quality or functionality of the product
- **Quality skills required** An indication of the skills required to undertake the quality method or a pointer to which area(s) should supply the checking resources. Identification of the actual people may be left until planning the stage in which the quality inspection is to be done
- **Quality responsibilities** Defining the producer, reviewer(s) and approver(s) for the product.

A.17.3 Derivation

- Product breakdown structure
- The end-users of the product
- Quality Management Strategy
- Configuration Management Strategy.

A.17.4 Format and presentation

A Product Description can take a number of formats, including:

- Document, presentation slides or mindmap
- Entry in a project management tool.

A.17.5 Quality criteria

- The purpose of the product is clear and is consistent with other products
- The product is described to a level of detail sufficient to plan and manage its development
- The Product Description is concise yet sufficient to enable the product to be produced, reviewed and approved
- Responsibility for the development of the product is clearly identified
- Responsibility for the development of the product is consistent with the roles and responsibilities described in the project management team organization and the Quality Management Strategy
- The quality criteria are consistent with the project quality standards, standard checklists and acceptance criteria
- The quality criteria can be used to determine when the product is fit for purpose
- The types of quality inspection required are able to verify whether the product meets its stated quality criteria

- The Senior User(s) confirms that their requirements of the product, as defined in the Product Description, are accurately defined
- The Senior Supplier(s) confirms that the requirements of the product, as defined in the Product Description, can be achieved.

A.18 PRODUCT STATUS ACCOUNT

A.18.1 Purpose

The Product Status Account provides information about the state of products within defined limits. The limits can vary. For example, the report could cover the entire project, a particular stage, a particular area of the project, or the history of a specific product. It is particularly useful if the Project Manager wishes to confirm the version number of products.

A.18.2 Composition

- **Report scope** Describing the scope of the report (e.g. for the entire project, by stage, by product type, by supplier etc. The product's attribute can be used to select the subset of products for the report)
- **Date produced** The date the report was generated
- **Product status** For each product within the scope of the report, the report may include:
  - Product identifier and title
  - Version
  - Status and date of status change
  - Product state
  - Owner
  - Copy-holders
  - Location
  - User(s)
  - Producer and date allocated to producer
  - Planned and actual date Product Description was baselined
  - Planned and actual date product was baselined
  - Planned date for the next baseline
  - List of related items
  - List of related issues (including changes pending and approved) and risks.

A.18.3 Derivation

- Configuration Item Records

- Stage Plan.

A.18.4 Format and presentation

A Product Status Account can take a number of formats, including:

- Document, spreadsheet or report from a database
- Output from a project management tool.

A.18.5 Quality criteria

- The details and dates match those in the Stage Plan
- The product name is consistent with the product breakdown structure and the name in the Configuration Item Record.

A.19 PROJECT BRIEF

A.19.1 Purpose

A Project Brief is used to provide a full and firm foundation for the initiation of the project and is created in the Starting up a Project process.

In the Initiating a Project process, the contents of the Project Brief are extended and refined in the Project Initiation Documentation, after which the Project Brief is no longer maintained.

A.19.2 Composition

- **Project definition** Explaining what the project needs to achieve. It should include:
  - Background
  - Project objectives (covering time, cost, quality, scope, risk and benefit performance goals)
  - Desired outcomes
  - Project scope and exclusions
  - Constraints and assumptions
  - Project tolerances
  - The user(s) and any other known interested parties
  - Interfaces
- **Outline Business Case** (see section A.2) Reasons why the project is needed and the business option selected. This will later be developed into a detailed Business Case during the Initiating a Project process
- **Project Product Description** (see section A.21) Including the customer's quality expectations,

user acceptance criteria, and operations and maintenance acceptance criteria

- **Project approach** To define the choice of solution that will be used within the project to deliver the business option selected from the Business Case, taking into consideration the operational environment into which the solution must fit
- **Project management team structure** A chart showing who will be involved with the project
- **Role descriptions** For the project management team and any other key resources identified at this time
- **References** To any associated documents or products.

A.19.3 Derivation

- A project mandate supplied at the start of the project
- Programme management – if the project is part of a programme, the Project Brief is likely to be supplied by the programme, and therefore it will not have to be derived from a project mandate
- Discussions with corporate management regarding corporate strategy and any policies and standards that apply
- Discussions with the Project Board and users if the project mandate is incomplete or if no project mandate is provided
- Discussions with the operations and maintenance organization (if applicable)
- Discussion with the (potential) suppliers regarding specialist development lifecycles that could be used
- Lessons Log.

A.19.4 Format and presentation

A Project Brief can take a number of formats, including:

- Document or presentation slides
- Entry in a project management tool.

A.19.5 Quality criteria

- It is brief because its purpose at this point is to provide a firm basis on which to initiate a project. It will later be refined and expanded as part of the Project Initiation Documentation

- The Project Brief accurately reflects the project mandate and the requirements of the business and the users
- The project approach considers a range of solutions, such as: bespoke or off-the-shelf; contracted out or developed in-house; designed from new or a modified existing product
- The project approach has been selected which maximizes the chance of achieving overall success for the project
- The project objectives, project approach and strategies are consistent with the organization's corporate social responsibility directive
- The project objectives are Specific, Measurable, Achievable, Realistic and Time-bound (SMART).

A.20 PROJECT INITIATION DOCUMENTATION

A.20.1 Purpose

The purpose of the Project Initiation Documentation is to define the project, in order to form the basis for its management and an assessment of its overall success. The Project Initiation Documentation gives the direction and scope of the project and (along with the Stage Plan) forms the 'contract' between the Project Manager and the Project Board.

The three primary uses of the Project Initiation Documentation are to:

- Ensure that the project has a sound basis before asking the Project Board to make any major commitment to the project
- Act as a base document against which the Project Board and Project Manager can assess progress, issues and ongoing viability questions
- Provide a single source of reference about the project so that people joining the 'temporary organization' can quickly and easily find out what the project is about, and how it is being managed.

The Project Initiation Documentation is a living product in that it should always reflect the current status, plans and controls of the project. Its component products will need to be updated and re-baselined, as necessary, at the end of each stage, to reflect the current status of its constituent parts.

The version of the Project Initiation Documentation that was used to gain authorization for the project is preserved as the basis against which performance will later be assessed when closing the project.

A.20.2 Composition

There follows a contents list for the Project Initiation Documentation. Note that the first two items (project definition and project approach) are extracted from the Project Brief.

- **Project definition** Explaining what the project needs to achieve. It should include:
  - Background
  - Project objectives and desired outcomes
  - Project scope and exclusions
  - Constraints and assumptions
  - The user(s) and any other known interested parties
  - Interfaces
- **Project approach** To define the choice of solution that will be used in the project to deliver the business option selected from the Business Case, taking into consideration the operational environment into which the solution must fit
- **Business Case** (see section A.2) Describing the justification for the project based on estimated costs, risks and benefits
- **Project management team structure** A chart showing who will be involved with the project
- **Role descriptions** For the project management team and any other key resources
- **Quality Management Strategy** (see section A.22) Describing the quality techniques and standards to be applied, and the responsibilities for achieving the required quality levels
- **Configuration Management Strategy** (see section A.6) Describing how and by whom the project's products will be controlled and protected
- **Risk Management Strategy** (see section A.24) Describing the specific risk management techniques and standards to be applied, and the responsibilities for achieving an effective risk management procedure
- **Communication Management Strategy** (see section A.4) To define the parties interested in the project and the means and frequency of communication between them and the project
- **Project Plan** (see section A.16) Describing how and when the project's objectives are to be achieved, by showing the major products,

activities and resources required on the project. It provides a baseline against which to monitor the project's progress stage by stage

- **Project controls** Summarizing the project-level controls such as stage boundaries, agreed tolerances, monitoring and reporting
- **Tailoring of PRINCE2** A summary of how PRINCE2 will be tailored for the project.

A.20.3 Derivation

- Project Brief
- Discussions with user, business and supplier stakeholders for input on methods, standards and controls.

A.20.4 Format and presentation

The Project Initiation Documentation could be:

- A single document
- An index for a collection of documents
- A document with cross-references to a number of other documents
- A collection of information in a project management tool.

A.20.5 Quality criteria

- The Project Initiation Documentation correctly represents the project
- It shows a viable, achievable project that is in line with corporate strategy or overall programme needs
- The project management team structure is complete, with names and titles. All the roles have been considered and are backed up by agreed role descriptions. The relationships and lines of authority are clear. If necessary, the project management team structure says to whom the Project Board reports
- It clearly shows a control, reporting and direction regime that can be implemented, appropriate to the scale, risk and importance of the project to corporate or programme management
- The controls cover the needs of the Project Board, Project Manager and Team Managers and satisfy any delegated assurance requirements
- It is clear who will administer each control
- The project objectives, approach and strategies are consistent with the organization's corporate social responsibility directive, and the project

controls are adequate to ensure that the project remains compliant with such a directive

■ Consideration has been given to the format of the Project Initiation Documentation. For small projects a single document is appropriate. For large projects it is more appropriate for the Project Initiation Documentation to be a collection of stand-alone documents. The volatility of each element of the Project Initiation Documentation should be used to assess whether it should be stand-alone, e.g. elements that are likely to change frequently are best separated out.

A.21 PROJECT PRODUCT DESCRIPTION

A.21.1 Purpose

The Project Product Description is a special form of Product Description that defines what the project must deliver in order to gain acceptance. It is used to:

■ Gain agreement from the user on the project's scope and requirements

■ Define the customer's quality expectations

■ Define the acceptance criteria, method and responsibilities for the project.

The Product Description for the project product is created in the Starting up a Project process as part of the initial scoping activity, and is refined during the Initiating a Project process when creating the Project Plan. It is subject to formal change control and should be checked at stage boundaries (during Managing a Stage Boundary) to see if any changes are required. It is used by the Closing a Project process as part of the verification that the project has delivered what was expected of it, and that the acceptance criteria have been met.

A.21.2 Composition

■ **Title** Name by which the project is known

■ **Purpose** This defines the purpose that the project's product will fulfil and who will use it. It is helpful in understanding the product's functions, size, quality, complexity, robustness etc.

■ **Composition** A description of the major products to be delivered by the project

■ **Derivation** What are the source products from which this product is derived? Examples are:

● Existing products to be modified
● Design specifications
● A feasibility report
● Project mandate

■ **Development skills required** An indication of the skills required to develop the product, or a pointer to which area(s) should supply the development resources

■ **Customer's quality expectations** A description of the quality expected of the project's product and the standards and processes that will need to be applied to achieve that quality. They will impact on every part of the product development, and thus on time and cost. The quality expectations are captured in discussions with the customer. Where possible, expectations should be prioritized

■ **Acceptance criteria** A prioritized list of criteria that the project's product must meet before the customer will accept it – i.e. measurable definitions of the attributes that must apply to the set of products to be acceptable to key stakeholders (and, in particular, the users and the operational and maintenance organizations). Examples are: ease of use, ease of support, ease of maintenance, appearance, major functions, development costs, running costs, capacity, availability, reliability, security, accuracy or performance

■ **Project-level quality tolerances** Specifying any tolerances that may apply for the acceptance criteria

■ **Acceptance method** Stating the means by which acceptance will be confirmed. This may simply be a case of confirming that all the project's products have been approved or may involve describing complex handover arrangements for the project's product, including any phased handover of the project's products

■ **Acceptance responsibilities** Defining who will be responsible for confirming acceptance.

A.21.3 Derivation

■ Project mandate

■ Discussions with the Senior User and Executive – possibly via scoping workshops

■ Request for proposal (if in a commercial customer/supplier environment).

A.21.4 Format and presentation

A Product Description for the project product can take a number of formats, including:

- Document, presentation slides or mindmap
- Entry in a project management tool.

A.21.5 Quality criteria

- The purpose is clear
- The composition defines the complete scope of the project
- The acceptance criteria form the complete list against which the project will be assessed
- The acceptance criteria address the requirements of all the key stakeholders (e.g. operations and maintenance)
- The Project Product Description defines how the users and the operational and maintenance organizations will assess the acceptability of the finished product(s):
  - All criteria are measurable
  - Each criterion is individually realistic
  - The criteria are realistic and consistent as a set. For example, high quality, early delivery and low cost may not go together
  - All criteria can be proven within the project life (e.g. the maximum throughput of a water pump), or by proxy measures that provide reasonable indicators as to whether acceptance criteria will be achieved post-project (e.g. a water pump that complies with design and manufacturing standards of reliability)
- The quality expectations have considered:
  - The characteristics of the key quality requirements (e.g. fast/slow, large/small, national/global)
  - The elements of the customer's quality management system that should be used
  - Any other standards that should be used
  - The level of customer/staff satisfaction that should be achieved if surveyed.

A.22 QUALITY MANAGEMENT STRATEGY

A.22.1 Purpose

A Quality Management Strategy is used to define the quality techniques and standards to be applied, and the various responsibilities for achieving the required quality levels, during the project.

A.22.2 Composition

- **Introduction** States the purpose, objectives and scope, and identifies who is responsible for the strategy
- **Quality management procedure** A description of (or reference to) the quality management procedure to be used. Any variance from corporate or programme management quality standards should be highlighted, together with a justification for the variance. The procedure should cover:
  - Quality planning
  - Quality control: the project's approach to quality control activities. This may include:
    - Quality standards
    - Templates and forms to be employed (e.g. Product Description(s), Quality Register)
    - Definitions of types of quality methods (e.g. inspection, pilot)
    - Metrics to be employed in support of quality control
  - Quality assurance: the project's approach to quality assurance activities. This may include:
    - Responsibilities of the Project Board
    - Compliance audits
    - Corporate or programme management reviews
- **Tools and techniques** Refers to any quality management systems or tools to be used, and any preference for techniques which may be used for each step in the quality management procedure
- **Records** Definition of what quality records will be required and where they will be stored, including the composition and format of the Quality Register
- **Reporting** Describes any quality management reports that are to produced, their purpose, timing and recipients
- **Timing of quality management activities** States when formal quality management activities are to be undertaken – for example, audits (where this may involve reference to the Quality Register)
- **Roles and responsibilities** Defines the roles and responsibilities for quality management activities, including those with quality responsibilities from corporate or programme management.

A.22.3 Derivation

- Project Board
- Project Brief:
  - Project management team structure (for roles and responsibilities)
  - Project Product Description (for the customer's quality expectations and acceptance criteria)
- Organizational standards
- Supplier and customer quality management systems
- Configuration management requirements
- Change control requirements
- Corporate or programme strategies
- Facilitated workshops and informal discussions.

A.22.4 Format and presentation

A Quality Management Strategy can take a number of formats, including:

- Stand-alone document or a section of the Project Initiation Documentation
- Entry in a project management tool.

A.22.5 Quality criteria

- The strategy clearly defines ways in which the customer's quality expectations will be met
- The defined ways are sufficient to achieve the required quality
- Responsibilities for quality are defined up to a level that is independent of the project and Project Manager
- The strategy conforms to the supplier's and customer's quality management systems
- The strategy conforms to the corporate or programme quality policy
- The approaches to assuring quality for the project are appropriate in the light of the standards selected.

A.23 QUALITY REGISTER

A.23.1 Purpose

A Quality Register is used to summarize all the quality management activities that are planned or have taken place, and provides information for the End Stage Reports and End Project Report. Its purpose is to:

- Issue a unique reference for each quality activity
- Act as a pointer to the quality records for a product
- Act as a summary of the number and type of quality activities undertaken.

A.23.2 Composition

For each entry in the Quality Register, the following should be recorded:

- **Quality identifier** Provides a unique reference for every quality activity entered into the Quality Register. It will typically be a numeric or alpha-numeric value
- **Product identifier(s)** Unique identifier(s) for the product(s) that the quality activity relates to
- **Product title(s)** The name(s) by which the product(s) is known
- **Method** The method employed for the quality activity (e.g. pilot, quality review, audit etc.)
- **Roles and responsibilities** The person or team responsible for the quality management activities (e.g. auditor or, for quality reviews, presenter, reviewer(s), chair, administrator)
- **Dates** Planned, forecast and actual dates for:
  - The quality activity
  - Sign-off that the quality activity is complete
- **Result** The result of the quality activity. If a product fails a quality review, then any re-assessment should be listed as a separate entry in the register, as the original quality activity has been completed (in deciding that the result is a 'fail')
- **Quality records** References to the quality inspection documentation, such as a test plan or the details of any actions required to correct errors and omissions of the products being inspected.

A.23.3 Derivation

- The format and composition of the Quality Register will be defined in the Quality Management Strategy
- Entries are made when a quality activity is entered on a Stage Plan for the current management stage. It may be updated when a Team Plan is created
- The remaining information comes from the actual performance of the quality activity

- The sign-off date is when all corrective action items have been signed off.

A.23.4 Format and presentation
A Quality Register can take a number of formats, including:

- Document, spreadsheet or database
- Stand-alone register or a carry forward in progress review minutes
- Entry in a project management tool
- Part of an integrated project register for all risks, actions, decisions, assumptions, issues, lessons etc.

A.23.5 Quality criteria
- A procedure is in place that will ensure that every quality activity is entered on the Quality Register
- Responsibility for the Quality Register has been allocated
- Actions are clearly described and assigned
- Entries are uniquely identified, including to which product they refer
- Access to the Quality Register is controlled
- The Quality Register is kept in a safe place
- All quality activities are at an appropriate level of control.

A.24 RISK MANAGEMENT STRATEGY

A.24.1 Purpose
A Risk Management Strategy describes the specific risk management techniques and standards to be applied and the responsibilities for achieving an effective risk management procedure.

A.24.2 Composition
- **Introduction** States the purpose, objectives and scope, and identifies who is responsible for the strategy
- **Risk management procedure** A description of (or reference to) the risk management procedure to be used. Any variance from corporate or programme management standards should be highlighted, together with a justification for the variance. The procedure should cover activities such as:
  - Identify
  - Assess

  - Plan
  - Implement
  - Communicate
- **Tools and techniques** Refers to any risk management systems or tools to be used, and any preference for techniques which may be used for each step in the risk management procedure
- **Records** Definition of the composition and format of the Risk Register and any other risk records to be used by the project
- **Reporting** Describes any risk management reports that are to be produced, including their purpose, timing and recipients
- **Timing of risk management activities** States when formal risk management activities are to be undertaken – for example, at end stage assessments
- **Roles and responsibilities** Defines the roles and responsibilities for risk management activities
- **Scales** Defines the scales for estimating probability and impact for the project to ensure that the scales for cost and time (for instance) are relevant to the cost and timeframe of the project. These may be shown in the form of probability impact grids giving the criteria for each level within the scale, e.g. for 'very high', 'high', 'medium', 'low' and 'very low'
- **Proximity** Guidance on how proximity for risk events is to be assessed. Proximity reflects the fact that risks will occur at particular times and the severity of their impact will vary according to when they occur. Typical proximity categories will be: imminent, within the stage, within the project, beyond the project
- **Risk categories** Definition of the risk categories to be used (if at all). These may be derived from a risk breakdown structure or prompt list. If no risks have been recorded against a category, this may suggest that the risk identification has not been as thorough as it should have been
- **Risk response categories** Definition of the risk response categories to be used, which themselves depend on whether a risk is a perceived threat or an opportunity
- **Early-warning indicators** Definition of any indicators to be used to track critical aspects of the project so that if certain predefined levels are reached, corrective action will be triggered. They will be selected for their relevance to the project objectives

■ **Risk tolerance** Defining the threshold levels of risk exposure, which, when exceeded, require the risk to be escalated to the next level of management. (For example, a project-level risk tolerance could be set as any risk that, should it occur, would result in loss of trading. Such risks would need to be escalated to corporate or programme management.) The risk tolerance should define the risk expectations of corporate or programme management and the Project Board

■ **Risk budget** Describing whether a risk budget is to be established and, if so, how it will be used.

A.24.3 Derivation
■ Project Brief
■ Business Case
■ The corporate or programme management's risk management guide, strategy or policy.

A.24.4 Format and presentation
A Risk Management Strategy can take a number of formats, including:

■ Stand-alone document or a section of the Project Initiation Documentation
■ Entry in a project management tool.

A.24.5 Quality criteria
■ Responsibilities are clear and understood by both customer and supplier
■ The risk management procedure is clearly documented and can be understood by all parties
■ Scales, expected value and proximity definitions are clear and unambiguous
■ The chosen scales are appropriate for the level of control required
■ Risk reporting requirements are fully defined.

A.25 RISK REGISTER

A.25.1 Purpose
A Risk Register provides a record of identified risks relating to the project, including their status and history. It is used to capture and maintain information on all of the identified threats and opportunities relating to the project.

A.25.2 Composition
For each entry in the Risk Register, the following should be recorded:

■ **Risk identifier** Provides a unique reference for every risk entered into the Risk Register. It will typically be a numeric or alpha-numeric value
■ **Risk author** The person who raised the risk
■ **Date registered** The date the risk was identified
■ **Risk category** The type of risk in terms of the project's chosen categories (e.g. schedule, quality, legal etc.)
■ **Risk description** In terms of the cause, event (threat or opportunity) and effect (description in words of the impact)
■ **Probability, impact and expected value** It is helpful to estimate the *inherent* values (pre-response action) and *residual* values (post-response action). These should be recorded in accordance with the project's chosen scales
■ **Proximity** This would typically state how close to the present time the risk event is anticipated to happen (e.g. imminent, within stage, within project, beyond project). Proximity should be recorded in accordance with the project's chosen scales
■ **Risk response categories** How the project will treat the risk in terms of the project's chosen categories. For example:
  ● **For threats:** avoid, reduce, fallback, transfer, accept, share
  ● **For opportunities:** enhance, exploit, reject, share
■ **Risk response** Actions to resolve the risk, and these actions should be aligned to the chosen response categories. Note that more than one risk response may apply to a risk
■ **Risk status** Typically described in terms of whether the risk is active or closed
■ **Risk owner** The person responsible for managing the risk (there can be only one risk owner per risk)
■ **Risk actionee** The person(s) who will implement the action(s) described in the risk response. This may or may not be the same person as the risk owner.

A.25.3 Derivation

- The composition, format and presentation of the Risk Register will be derived from the Risk Management Strategy
- Entries are made on the Risk Register once a new risk has been identified
- There may be one or more risks inherent in the project mandate
- New risks may be discovered when creating the Project Brief, designing and appointing the project management team, establishing the project's controls and developing its plans, when issuing Work Packages, when reviewing Work Package status, or when reviewing stage status
- Daily Log/Issue Register – often issues raised to the Project Manager and captured in the Daily Log or Issue Register are actually risks and only identified as such after further examination.

A.25.4 Format and presentation

A Risk Register can take a number of formats, including:

- Document, spreadsheet or database
- Stand-alone register or a carry forward in progress review minutes
- Entry in a project management tool
- Part of an integrated project register for all risks, actions, decisions, assumptions, issues, lessons etc.

A.25.5 Quality criteria

- The status indicates whether action has been taken
- Risks are uniquely identified, including information about which product they refer to
- Access to the Risk Register is controlled and it is kept in a safe place.

A.26 WORK PACKAGE

A.26.1 Purpose

A Work Package is a set of information about one or more required products collated by the Project Manager to pass responsibility for work or delivery formally to a Team Manager or team member.

A.26.2 Composition

Although the content may vary greatly according to the relationship between the Project Manager and the recipient of the Work Package, it should cover:

- **Date** The date of the agreement between the Project Manager and the Team Manager/person authorized
- **Team Manager or person authorized** The name of the Team Manager or individual with whom the agreement has been made
- **Work Package description** A description of the work to be done
- **Techniques, processes and procedures** Any techniques, tools, standards, processes or procedures to be used in the creation of the specialist products
- **Development interfaces** Interfaces that must be maintained while developing the products. These may be people providing information or those who need to receive information
- **Operations and maintenance interfaces** Identification of any specialist products with which the product(s) in the Work Package will have to interface during their operational life. These may be other products to be produced by the project, existing products, or those to be produced by other projects (for example, if the project is part of a programme)
- **Configuration management requirements** A statement of any arrangements that must be made by the producer for: version control of the products in the Work Package; obtaining copies of other products or their Product Descriptions; submission of the product to configuration management; any storage or security requirements; and who, if anyone, needs to be advised of changes in the status of the Work Package
- **Joint agreements** Details of the agreements on effort, cost, start and end dates, and key milestones for the Work Package
- **Tolerances** Details of the tolerances for the Work Package (the tolerances will be for time and cost but may also include scope and risk)
- **Constraints** Any constraints (apart from the tolerances) on the work, people to be involved, timings, charges, rules to be followed (for example, security and safety) etc.

- **Reporting arrangements** The expected frequency and content of Checkpoint Reports
- **Problem handling and escalation** This refers to the procedure for raising issues and risks
- **Extracts or references** Any extracts or references to related documents, specifically:
  - **Stage Plan extract** This will be the relevant section of the Stage Plan for the current management stage or will be a pointer to it
  - **Product Description(s)** This would normally be an attachment of the Product Description(s) for the products identified in the Work Package (note that the Product Description contains the quality methods to be used)
- **Approval method** The person, role or group who will approve the completed products within the Work Package, and how the Project Manager is to be advised of completion of the products and Work Package.

There should be space on the Work Package to record both its initial authorization and its acceptance and return as a completed Work Package. This can be enhanced to include an assessment of the work and go towards performance appraisal.

Projects with common controls across all Work Packages may simply cross-reference the controls defined in the Project Plan or Stage Plan.

A.26.3 Derivation

- Existing commercial agreements between the customer and supplier (if any)
- Quality Management Strategy
- Configuration Management Strategy
- Stage Plan.

A.26.4 Format and presentation

A Work Package can take a number of formats, including:

- Document
- Oral conversation between the Project Manager and a Team Manager
- Entry in a project management tool.

The Work Package will vary in content and in degree of formality, depending on circumstances.

Where the work is being conducted by a team working directly under the Project Manager, the Work Package may be an oral instruction – although there are good reasons for putting it in writing, such as avoidance of misunderstanding and providing a link to performance assessment. Where the work is being carried out by a supplier under a contract and the Project Manager is part of the customer organization, there is a need for a formal written instruction in line with standards laid down in that contract.

A.26.5 Quality criteria

- The required Work Package is clearly defined and understood by the assigned resource
- There is a Product Description for each required product, with clearly identified and acceptable quality criteria
- The Product Description(s) matches up with the other Work Package documentation
- Standards for the work are agreed
- The defined standards are in line with those applied to similar products
- All necessary interfaces have been defined
- The reporting arrangements include the provision for raising issues and risks
- There is agreement between the Project Manager and the recipient on exactly what is to be done
- There is agreement on the constraints, including effort, cost and targets
- The dates and effort are in line with those shown in the Stage Plan for the current management stage
- Reporting arrangements are defined
- Any requirement for independent attendance at, and participation in, quality activities is defined.

Appendix B:
Governance

B

Appendix B: Governance

The governance of project management concerns those areas of corporate governance that are specifically related to project activities. Effective governance of project management ensures that an organization's project portfolio is aligned to the organization's objectives, is delivered efficiently, and is sustainable. Governance of project management also supports the means by which the corporate board and other major project stakeholders are provided with timely, relevant and reliable information.

Table B.1 The Association for Project Management's governance of project management principles

Governance of project management principles	Addressed by PRINCE2?
The board has overall responsibility for governance of project management.	This governance principle relates to the main board of the corporate organization and is outside the scope of PRINCE2.
The roles, responsibilities and performance criteria for the governance of project management are clearly defined.	Partially. The project has clearly defined roles, responsibilities and performance criteria for governance, but PRINCE2 does not extend into the governance responsibilities of the corporate roles.
Disciplined governance arrangements, supported by appropriate methods and controls, are applied throughout the project lifecycle.	Fully.
A coherent and supportive relationship is demonstrated between the overall business strategy and the project portfolio.	Partially. Each PRINCE2 project should demonstrate alignment to corporate strategy through its Business Case. PRINCE2 does not provide guidance on portfolio management.
All projects have an approved plan containing authorization points at which the Business Case is reviewed and approved. Decisions made at authorization points are recorded and communicated.	Fully.
Members of delegated authorization bodies have sufficient representation, competence, authority and resources to enable them to make appropriate decisions.	Partially. PRINCE2 provides the framework for effective delegation. The competence of project personnel is outside the scope of PRINCE2.
The project Business Case is supported by relevant and realistic information that provides a reliable basis for making authorization decisions.	Fully.
The board, or its delegated agents, decide when independent scrutiny of projects and project management systems is required, and implement such scrutiny accordingly.	Partially. PRINCE2 recommends independent scrutiny by corporate or programme management as part of the Project Assurance responsibilities.
There are clearly defined criteria for reporting project status, and for the escalation of risks and issues to the levels required by the organization.	Fully.
The organization fosters a culture of improvement and of frank internal disclosure of project information.	Partially. PRINCE2 encourages open reporting through its management-by-exception and assurance structures.
Project stakeholders are engaged at a level that is commensurate with their importance to the organization, and in a manner that fosters trust.	Fully.

From *Directing Change: A Guide to Governance of Project Management* (reprinted with minor revisions 2005), APM Governance SIG. © Association for Project Management, 2004. Reproduced with permission.

PRINCE2 provides (if applied within the spirit of its principles) a framework for effective governance. Table B.1 shows how PRINCE2 addresses the governance principles published by the Association for Project Management.

Appendix C: Roles and responsibilities

Appendix C: Roles and responsibilities

C.1 PROJECT BOARD

The Project Board is accountable to corporate or programme management for the success of the project, and has the authority to direct the project within the remit set by corporate or programme management as documented in the project mandate.

The Project Board is also responsible for the communications between the project management team and stakeholders external to that team (e.g. corporate and programme management).

According to the scale, complexity, importance and risk of the project, Project Board members may delegate some Project Assurance tasks to separate individuals. The Project Board may also delegate decisions regarding changes to a Change Authority.

C.1.1 General responsibilities

During start-up and initiation:

- Confirm project tolerances with corporate or programme management
- Approve the Project Brief
- Approve the Stage Plan for the initiation stage
- Authorize project initiation
- Decide whether to use a Change Authority and, if so, agree the level of authority to be delegated
- Set the scale for severity ratings for issues
- Set the scale for priority ratings for requests for change and off-specifications
- Approve the supplier contract (if the relationship between the customer and supplier is a commercial one)
- Approve the Project Initiation Documentation (and its components)
- Authorize the start of the project.

During the project:

- Set tolerances for each stage and approve Stage Plans
- Authorize each management stage and approve the Product Descriptions for each stage
- Approve Exception Plans when stage-level tolerances are forecast to be exceeded

- Communicate with stakeholders as defined in the Communication Management Strategy (including briefing corporate or programme management about project progress)
- Provide overall guidance and direction to the project, ensuring it remains viable and within any specified constraints
- Respond to requests for advice from the Project Manager
- Ensure that risks are being tracked and managed as effectively as possible
- Approve changes (unless delegated to a Change Authority)
- Make decisions on escalated issues
- Approve completed products.

At the end of the project:

- Provide assurance that all products have been delivered satisfactorily
- Provide assurance that all acceptance criteria have been met
- Confirm acceptance of the project product
- Approve the End Project Report and ensure that any issues, lessons and risks are documented and passed on to the appropriate body
- Authorize follow-on action recommendations and Lessons Reports to be distributed to corporate or programme management
- Transfer responsibility for the updated Benefits Review Plan to corporate or programme management
- Authorize project closure and send project closure notification to corporate or programme management.

C.1.2 Competencies

To be successful, the Project Board should:

- Have sufficient authority to make decisions, approve plans and authorize any necessary deviation from Stage Plans
- Have sufficient authority to allocate resources to the project
- Be capable of adequately representing the business, user and supplier interests

- Ideally be able to stay with the project throughout its life.

Key competencies include:

- Decision making
- Delegation
- Leadership
- Negotiation and conflict resolution.

C.2 EXECUTIVE

The Executive is ultimately responsible for the project, supported by the Senior User and Senior Supplier. The Executive's role is to ensure that the project is focused throughout its life on achieving its objectives and delivering a product that will achieve the forecast benefits. The Executive has to ensure that the project gives value for money, ensuring a cost-conscious approach to the project, balancing the demands of the business, user and supplier.

Throughout the project, the Executive is responsible for the Business Case.

The Project Board is not a democracy controlled by votes. The Executive is the ultimate decision maker and is supported in the decision making by the Senior User and Senior Supplier.

C.2.1 Responsibilities

In addition to the Project Board's collective responsibilities, the Executive will:

- Design and appoint the project management team (in particular the Project Manager)
- Oversee the development of the Project Brief and the outline Business Case, ensuring that the project is aligned with corporate strategies (and presenting the outline Business Case to corporate or programme management for approval where required)
- Oversee the development of the detailed Business Case
- Secure the funding for the project
- Approve any additional supplier contracts (if the relationship between the user and supplier is a commercial one)
- Hold the Senior Supplier to account for the quality and integrity of the specialist approach and specialist products created for the project
- Hold the Senior User to account for realizing the benefits defined in the Business Case, ensuring that benefits reviews take place to

monitor the extent to which the Business Case benefits are achieved
- Transfer responsibility for post-project benefits reviews to corporate or programme management
- Monitor and control the progress of the project at a strategic level, in particular reviewing the Business Case regularly
- Escalate issues and risks to corporate or programme management if project tolerance is forecast to be exceeded
- Ensure that risks associated with the Business Case are identified, assessed and controlled
- Make decisions on escalated issues, with particular focus on continued business justification
- Organize and chair Project Board reviews
- Ensure overall business assurance of the project – that it remains on target to deliver products that will achieve the expected business benefits, and that the project will be completed within its agreed tolerances. Where appropriate, delegate some business Project Assurance activities (see section C.7).

C.3 SENIOR USER

The Senior User(s) is responsible for specifying the needs of those who will use the project's products, for user liaison with the project management team, and for monitoring that the solution will meet those needs within the constraints of the Business Case in terms of quality, functionality and ease of use.

The role represents the interests of all those who will use the project's products (including operations and maintenance), those for whom the products will achieve an objective or those who will use the products to deliver benefits. The Senior User role commits user resources and monitors products against requirements. This role may require more than one person to cover all the user interests. For the sake of effectiveness, the role should not be split between too many people.

The Senior User(s) specifies the benefits and is held to account by demonstrating to corporate or programme management that the forecast benefits which were the basis of project approval have in fact been realized. This is likely to involve a commitment beyond the end of the life of the project.

C.3.1 Responsibilities

In addition to the Project Board's collective responsibilities, the Senior User(s) will:

- Provide the customer's quality expectations and define acceptance criteria for the project
- Ensure that the desired outcome of the project is specified
- Ensure that the project produces products that will deliver the desired outcomes, and meet user requirements
- Ensure that the expected benefits (derived from the project's outcomes) are realized
- Provide a statement of actual versus forecast benefits at the benefits reviews
- Resolve user requirements and priority conflicts
- Ensure that any user resources required for the project (e.g. to undertake user quality inspections and product approval) are made available
- Make decisions on escalated issues, with particular focus on safeguarding the expected benefits
- Brief and advise user management on all matters concerning the project
- Maintain business performance stability during transition from the project to business as usual
- Provide the user view on follow-on action recommendations
- Undertake Project Assurance from the user perspective (user assurance) and, where appropriate, delegate user Project Assurance activities (see section C.7).

C.4   SENIOR SUPPLIER

The Senior Supplier represents the interests of those designing, developing, facilitating, procuring and implementing the project's products. This role is accountable for the quality of products delivered by the supplier(s) and is responsible for the technical integrity of the project. If necessary, more than one person may be required to represent the suppliers.

Depending on the particular customer/supplier environment, the customer may also wish to appoint an independent person or group to carry out assurance on the supplier's products (for example, if the relationship between the customer and supplier is a commercial one).

C.4.1 Responsibilities

In addition to the Project Board's collective responsibilities, the Senior Supplier will:

- Assess and confirm the viability of the project approach
- Ensure that proposals for designing and developing the products are realistic
- Advise on the selection of design, development and acceptance methods
- Ensure that the supplier resources required for the project are made available
- Make decisions on escalated issues, with particular focus on safeguarding the integrity of the complete solution
- Resolve supplier requirements and priority conflicts
- Brief non-technical management on supplier aspects of the project
- Ensure quality procedures are used correctly, so that products adhere to requirements
- Undertake Project Assurance from the supplier perspective (supplier assurance) and, where appropriate, delegate supplier Project Assurance activities (see section C.7).

C.5   PROJECT MANAGER

The Project Manager has the authority to run the project on a day-to-day basis on behalf of the Project Board within the constraints laid down by them.

The Project Manager's prime responsibility is to ensure that the project produces the required products within the specified tolerances of time, cost, quality, scope, risk and benefits. The Project Manager is also responsible for the project producing a result capable of achieving the benefits defined in the Business Case.

C.5.1 Responsibilities

The Project Manager's responsibilities include the following:

- Prepare the following baseline management products, in conjunction with any Project Assurance roles, and agree them with the Project Board:
  - Project Brief, including the Project Product Description
  - Benefits Review Plan

- Project Initiation Documentation (and its components)
- Stage/Exception Plans and their Product Descriptions
- Work Packages
- Prepare the following reports:
  - Highlight Reports
  - Issue Reports
  - End Stage Reports
  - Lessons Reports
  - Exception Reports
  - End Project Report
- Maintain the following records:
  - Issue Register
  - Risk Register
  - Daily Log
  - Lessons Log
- Liaise with corporate or programme management to ensure that work is neither overlooked nor duplicated by related projects
- Liaise with any external suppliers or account managers
- Lead and motivate the project management team
- Ensure that behavioural expectations of team members are established
- Manage the information flows between the directing and delivering levels of the project
- Manage the production of the required products, taking responsibility for overall progress and use of resources and initiating corrective action where necessary
- Establish and manage the project's procedures – risk management, issue and change control, configuration management, and communication
- Establish and manage the project controls – monitoring and reporting
- Authorize Work Packages
- Advise the Project Board of any deviations from the plan
- Unless appointed to another person(s), perform the Team Manager role (see section C.6)
- Unless appointed to another person (or corporate/programme function), perform the Project Support role (see section C.9)
- Implement the Configuration Management Strategy

- Ensure project personnel comply with the Configuration Management Strategy
- Schedule configuration audits to check that the physical products are consistent with the Configuration Item Records and initiate any necessary corrective action.

C.5.2 Competencies

Different types of project will require different types of project management skills. To be successful, the Project Manager must be able to balance the different aspects of the Project Manager role for a particular project.

Key competencies include:

- Planning
- Time management
- People management
- Problem solving
- Attention to detail
- Communication
- Negotiation
- Conflict management.

C.6 TEAM MANAGER

The Team Manager's prime responsibility is to ensure production of those products defined by the Project Manager to an appropriate quality, in a set timescale and at a cost acceptable to the Project Board. The Team Manager role reports to, and takes direction from, the Project Manager.

C.6.1 Responsibilities

- Prepare the Team Plan and agree it with the Project Manager
- Produce Checkpoint Reports as agreed with the Project Manager
- Plan, monitor and manage the team's work
- Take responsibility for the progress of the team's work and use of team resources, and initiate corrective action, where necessary, within the constraints laid down by the Project Manager
- Identify and advise the Project Manager of any issues and risks associated with a Work Package
- Advise the Project Manager of any deviations from the plan, recommend corrective action, and help to prepare any appropriate Exception Plans

- Pass back to the Project Manager products that have been completed and approved in line with the agreed Work Package requirements
- Liaise with any Project Assurance and Project Support roles
- Ensure that quality activities relating to the team's work are planned and performed correctly, and are within tolerance
- Ensure that the appropriate entries are made in the Quality Register
- Manage specific issues and risks as directed by the Project Manager
- Assist the Project Manager in examining issues and risks
- Ensure that all assigned issues are properly reported to the person maintaining the Issue Register.

C.6.2 Competencies

Different types of project will require different types of skills from the Team Manager.

Key competencies are similar to that of a Project Manager.

C.7 PROJECT ASSURANCE

Project Assurance covers the primary stakeholder interests (business, user and supplier).

Project Assurance has to be independent of the Project Manager; therefore the Project Board cannot delegate any of its assurance activities to the Project Manager.

C.7.1 Responsibilities

The implementation of the assurance responsibilities needs to answer the question: what is to be assured? A list of possibilities applicable to the business, user and supplier stakeholder interests would include ensuring that:

- Liaison is maintained between the business, user and supplier throughout the project
- Risks are controlled
- The right people are involved in writing Product Descriptions
- The right people are planned to be involved in quality inspection at the correct points in the products' development
- Staff are properly trained in the quality methods

- The quality methods are being correctly followed
- Quality control follow-up actions are dealt with correctly
- An acceptable solution is being developed
- The scope of the project is not changing unnoticed
- Internal and external communications are working
- Applicable standards are being used
- The needs of specialist interests (for example, security) are being observed.

Business assurance responsibilities

- Assist the Project Manager to develop the Business Case and Benefits Review Plan (if it is being prepared by the Project Manager)
- Advise on the selection of project management team members
- Advise on the Risk Management Strategy
- Review the Business Case for compliance with corporate or programme standards
- Verify the Business Case against external events and against project progress
- Check that the Business Case is being adhered to throughout the project
- Check that the project remains aligned to the corporate or programme strategy
- Review project finance on behalf of the customer
- Verify that the solution continues to provide value for money
- Periodically check that the project remains viable
- Assess that the aggregated risk exposure remains within project tolerance
- Check that any supplier and contractor payments are authorized
- Review issues and risks by assessing their impact on the Business Case
- Constrain user and supplier excesses
- Inform the project management team of any changes caused by a programme of which the project is part (this responsibility may be transferred if there is other programme representation on the project management team)
- Monitor stage and project progress against the agreed tolerances.

User assurance responsibilities

- Advise on stakeholder engagement
- Advise on the Communication Management Strategy
- Ensure that the specification of the user's needs is accurate, complete and unambiguous
- Assess whether the solution will meet the user's needs and is progressing towards that target
- Advise on the impact of potential changes from the user's point of view
- Monitor risks to the user
- Ensure that the quality activities relating to products at all stages has appropriate user representation
- Ensure that quality control procedures are used correctly to ensure that products meet user requirements
- Ensure that user liaison is functioning effectively.

Supplier assurance responsibilities

- Review the Product Descriptions
- Advise on the Quality Management Strategy and Configuration Management Strategy
- Advise on the selection of the development strategy, design and methods
- Ensure that any supplier and operating standards defined for the project are met and used to good effect
- Advise on potential changes and their impact on the correctness, completeness and integrity of products against their Product Description from a supplier perspective
- Monitor any risks in the production aspects of the project
- Assess whether quality control procedures are used correctly, so that products adhere to requirements.

C.7.2 Competencies

To be successful, Project Assurance should:

- Be capable of adequately representing the business, user or supplier stakeholder interests
- Have sufficient credibility to ensure that advice and guidance are followed
- Have sufficient specialist knowledge of the business, user or supplier stakeholder areas
- Ideally be able to stay with the project throughout its lifecycle.

Key competencies include:

- Diplomacy
- Thoroughness
- Attention to detail
- Communication.

C.8 CHANGE AUTHORITY

The Project Board may delegate authority for approving responses to requests for change or off-specifications to a separate individual or group, called a Change Authority. The Project Manager could be assigned as the Change Authority for some aspects of the project (e.g. changing baselined Work Packages if it does not affect stage tolerances).

C.8.1 Responsibilities

- Review and approve or reject all requests for change and off-specifications within the delegated limits of authority and change budget set by the Project Board
- Refer to the Project Board if any delegated limits of authority or allocated change budget are forecast to be exceeded.

C.8.2 Competencies

The Change Authority should:

- Be capable of adequately representing the business, user and supplier stakeholder interests
- Have sufficient credibility to ensure that advice and guidance are followed
- Have sufficient specialist knowledge of the business, user or supplier stakeholder areas.

Key competencies include:

- Decision making
- Planning
- Attention to detail
- Problem solving.

C.9 PROJECT SUPPORT

The provision of any Project Support on a formal basis is optional. If it is not delegated to a separate person or function, it will need to be undertaken by the Project Manager.

One support function that must be considered is that of configuration management. Depending on the project size and environment, there may be a need to formalize this and it may become a task with which the Project Manager cannot cope without support.

Project Support functions may be provided by a project office or by specific resources for the project. Refer to OGC's guidance *Portfolio, Programme and Project Support Offices* (2008) for further information on the use of a project office.

C.9.1 Responsibilities

The following is a suggested list of tasks:

- Set up and maintain project files
- Establish document control procedures
- Collect actuals data and forecasts
- Update plans
- Administer or assist the quality review process
- Administer or assist Project Board meetings
- Assist with the compilation of reports
- Contribute expertise in specialist tools and techniques (for example, planning and control tools, risk analysis)
- Maintain the following records
  - Quality Register
  - Configuration Item Records
  - Any other registers/logs delegated by the Project Manager
- Administer the configuration management procedure (these responsibilities may be undertaken by a configuration librarian from corporate or programme management):
  - Administer the receipt, identification, versions, storage and issue of all project products
  - Provide information on the status of all products (by preparing and issuing Product Status Accounts)
  - Archive superseded product copies
  - Ensure the security and preservation of the master copies of all project products
  - Maintain a record of all copies issued
  - Notify holders of any changes to their copies
  - Number, record, store and distribute Issue Reports
  - Conduct configuration audits.

C.9.2 Competencies

Typical competencies for Project Support roles will depend on the type of project and organization.

Key competencies include:

- Administration and organization
- Knowledge of specialist tools and techniques
- Knowledge of corporate or programme management standards applicable to the project.

Appendix D:
Product-based
planning example

Appendix D: Product-based planning example

D.1 SCENARIO

A project is required to organize and run a conference for between 80 and 100 delegates. The date and subject matter are set, and the focus of the conference is to bring members of a particular profession up to date on recent developments in professional procedures and standards. The project team will need to identify a venue, and check its availability, facilities and price before booking it. They will also need to identify suitable speakers and book them, before producing a detailed agenda and programme. A mailing list of delegates is available, and once the venue has been booked, the project team will need to issue a press release based on the agreed programme. Part of the project will involve producing 100 delegate handouts, with a cover reflecting the selected subject matter. These handouts must contain a printed agenda covering the agreed programme, copies of slides and notes used by the speakers, and a feedback form to capture attendee reviews. Booking arrangements for attending the conference, including details of the programme and venue, must be sent out in the mail-shot. The team will need to regularly update the attendance list based on responses to the mail-shot, and make arrangements to recruit staff to help on the day, based on the final attendance list.

D.2 EXAMPLE OF A PROJECT PRODUCT DESCRIPTION

Table D.1 gives an example of a Project Product Description for an annual conference.

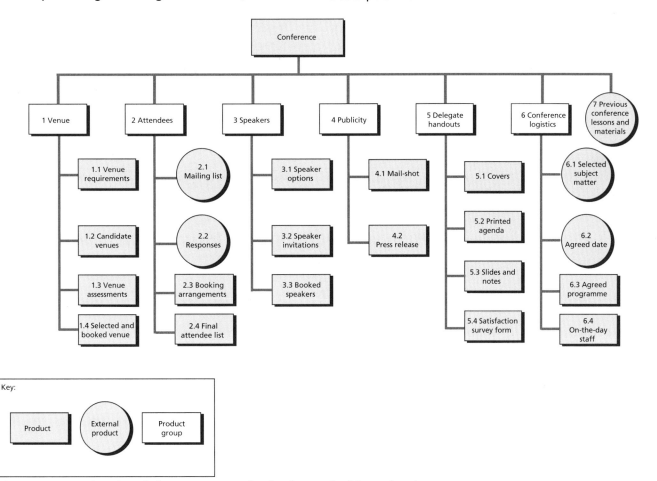

Figure D.1 Product breakdown structure in the form of a hierarchy chart

Table D.1 Example of a Project Product Description for an annual conference

Title	Annual conference
Purpose	The conference is the annual showcase of the profession and provides its members with an opportunity to learn about the latest developments in professional procedures and standards, and to network with fellow members
Composition	■ Conference venue ■ Attendees ■ Speakers ■ Publicity ■ Delegate handouts ■ Conference logistics.
Derivation	■ Selected subject matter ■ Mailing list ■ Previous conference lessons and materials ■ Agreed date.
Development skills required	■ Conference management ■ Marketing ■ Public relations.
Customer's quality expectations	Priority 1: The conference must be ■ Professional in style, funded by attendees and address the needs of the range of members (from beginners to experienced professionals) ■ The event will provide a forum for networking ■ Repeat attendance at future conferences is generated from satisfied members Priority 2: ■ The speakers will be chosen on the basis of their knowledge, experience and expertise. They are not delivering a 'sales pitch' to the members ■ The conference will be interactive in style ■ The conference will be held at a central location, therefore minimizing travel.
Acceptance criteria and project-level quality tolerances	In priority order: ■ The cost of the conference must be covered by the attendance fees ■ Minimum of 80 and maximum of 100 people attend the conference ■ More than 50% of the presentations are interactive (tutorials rather than lectures) ■ The speakers and programme are approved by the editorial board representing the interests of the members ■ The attendees' satisfaction survey indicates that >75% will attend next year's conference and/or recommend it to colleagues. ■ The hotel venue is within three miles of a main line train station
Acceptance method	As the conference cannot be rerun should it prove to be unacceptable, the Project Board will grant: ■ Preliminary acceptance – based on approval of the agreed programme by the editorial board and independent assurance that the attendee numbers and conference costs are forecast to be acceptable ■ Final acceptance – based on the End Project Report providing evidence that the acceptance criteria were met.
Acceptance responsibilities	■ The Senior User and Executive are responsible for confirming acceptance

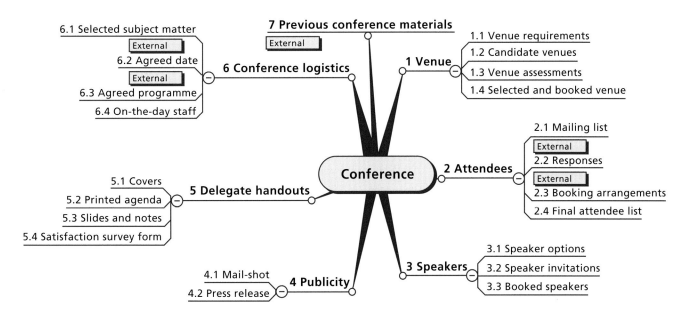

Figure D.2 Product breakdown structure in the form of a mindmap

D.3 EXAMPLES OF A PRODUCT BREAKDOWN STRUCTURE

PRINCE2 does not specify the format in which a product breakdown structure is drawn. Three example formats are provided for the conference project:

- Hierarchy chart (Figure D.1)
- Mindmap (Figure D.2)
- Indented list.

Product breakdown structure in the form of an indented list

Conference

1 Venue
   1.1 Venue requirements
   1.2 Candidate venues
   1.3 Venue assessments
   1.4 Selected and booked venue
2 Attendees
   2.1 Mailing list (external)
   2.2 Responses (external)
   2.3 Booking arrangements
   2.4 Final attendee list
3 Speakers
   3.1 Speaker options
   3.2 Speaker invitations
   3.3 Booked speakers

4 Publicity
   4.1 Mail-shot
   4.2 Press release
5 Delegate handouts
   5.1 Covers
   5.2 Printed agenda
   5.3 Slides and notes
   5.4 Satisfaction survey form
6 Conference logistics
   6.1 Selected subject matter (external)
   6.2 Agreed date (external)
   6.3 Agreed programme
   6.4 On-the-day staff

7 Previous conference lessons and materials (external).

D.4 EXAMPLE OF A PRODUCT DESCRIPTION

Identifier	Conference/4.1/version 1.0
Title	Mail-shot
Purpose	The mail-shot is the primary means of advertising the conference to potential delegates. It will be mailed to a list of professionals working in the industry.
Composition	• Mailing envelope • Letter giving outline explanation of the conference • Leaflet giving detailed explanation of the conference, the venue and how to make a booking • Booking form • Response envelope
Derivation	• Mailing list • Agreed programme • Booking arrangements • Selected venue
Format and presentation	Letter to be A4 on standard branded letterhead Leaflet and booking form to be A5 size Mailing envelope to be C5
Development skills required	Marketing, design and copywriting skills required Knowledge of conference necessary
Quality responsibilities	• **Producer** – Event management company • **Reviewers** – as stated under 'Quality Skills Required' • **Approver** – Membership secretary

Quality criteria	Quality tolerance	Quality method	Quality skills required
Adheres to corporate identity standards	As defined in corporate identity standards	PRINCE2 quality review	Marketing team
Letter and leaflet accurately reflect all agreed details of the conference	None	Inspection	Conference Project Manager
No spelling or grammatical errors in any elements of the mail-shot	None	Word processor spell checker Inspection	Proof reader
The covering letter fits on one side of A4	May extend to reverse of a single sheet of A4	Inspection	Proof reader

D.5 PRODUCT FLOW DIAGRAM

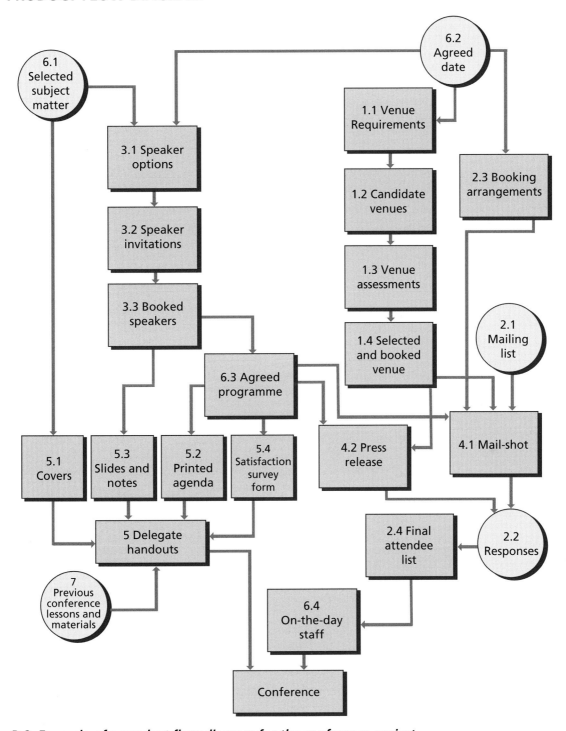

Figure D.3 Example of a product flow diagram for the conference project

Note: Only the project product, releases and products need to be transferred from the product breakdown structure to the product flow diagram. For example, in this scenario the planner has used 'publicity' in the product breakdown structure but the only publicity products that need to be produced are the mail-shot and press release. 'Publicity' is not a product that requires work but a convenient way to describe the products that provide the publicity for the conference, whereas the delegate handout is a product that is created by bringing together the covers, printed agenda, printouts of the conference slides and notes, and the satisfaction survey form products.

Appendix E:
Health check

Appendix E: Health check

The following are process-oriented checklists that can be used at various points in the project to assess that the key aspects of PRINCE2 are adequately addressed. The checklists are not exhaustive but should provide reasonable confidence as to whether a project is being managed in accordance with PRINCE2.

It is important to note that any reference to a management product means 'in accordance with the Product Description in Appendix A' and in particular the quality criteria for those management products should also be reviewed.

E.1 STARTING UP A PROJECT

Question	Yes/No
1 Have project management team roles been allocated for the:	
a Executive?	
b Project Manager?	
c Senior User(s)?	
d Senior Supplier(s) – if appropriate at this point?	
e Project Support?	
f Team Managers – if appropriate at this point?	
g Project Assurance?	
h Change Authority – if appropriate at this point?	
2 Do the Project Board members have sufficient authority, availability and credibility to direct the project?	
3 Are the project's stakeholders sufficiently represented by the Project Board?	
4 Do role descriptions exist for each key appointment?	
5 Have those people appointed confirmed their acceptance?	
6 Has a Daily Log been set up?	
7 Has the Lessons Log been set up?	
8 Have lessons from previous similar projects been identified and, where appropriate, applied?	
9 If the organization has not undertaken a project like this before, have lessons been sought from comparable projects external to the organization?	
10 Has the Project Brief been produced?	
11 Is there an outline Business Case?	
12 Has the Project Product Description been produced?	
13 Has the project approach been decided upon?	
14 Is there a Stage Plan for the initiation stage?	

E.2 DIRECTING A PROJECT

E.2.1 Authorize initiation

Question	Yes/No
15 Has the Project Board approved the Project Brief? Specifically, has it:	
▪ Confirmed the project definition and approach?	
▪ Reviewed and approved the Project Product Description?	
▪ Formally confirmed the appointments to the core project management team?	
▪ Reviewed and approved the outline Business Case, particularly the projected benefits?	
16 Has the Project Board approved the Initiation Stage Plan? Specifically, has it:	
▪ Approved the plan to develop the Project Initiation Documentation?	
▪ Obtained or committed the resources needed by the Stage Plan for the initiation stage?	
▪ Ensured that adequate reporting and control mechanisms are in place for the initiation stage?	
▪ Set tolerances for the initiation stage?	
▪ Requested the necessary logistical support (for example, accommodation, communication facilities, equipment and any Project Support) from corporate or programme management?	
▪ Confirmed that they have understood any risks that affect the decision to authorize the initiation stage?	
▪ Confirmed to the Project Manager that the work defined in the Initiation Stage Plan may start?	
17 Has the Project Board informed corporate or programme management (and other interested parties) that project initiation has been authorized?	

E.2.2 Authorize the project

Question	Yes/No
18 Has the Project Board approved the Project Initiation Documentation? Specifically, has it:	
▪ Confirmed that the Business Case is viable, desirable and achievable and meets corporate or programme management expectations and standards, and approved it?	
▪ Confirmed that lessons from previous similar projects have been reviewed and incorporated?	
▪ Confirmed that the Quality Management Strategy will deliver the quality expectations, and approved it?	
▪ Confirmed that that the Configuration Management Strategy will deliver the approach expected, and approved it?	
▪ Confirmed that that the Risk Management Strategy will safeguard the project, and approved it?	
▪ Confirmed that there has been a risk assessment, and that risk response actions have been planned?	
▪ Confirmed the validity and achievability of the Project Plan and approved it?	
▪ Confirmed that the Benefits Review Plan covers all expected benefits, and approved it?	
▪ Confirmed that all members of the project management team have agreed their roles (the project management team structure, roles and responsibilities)?	
▪ Ensured that the project controls are adequate for the nature of the project?	
▪ Ensured that the information needs and timing of communications, as defined in the Communication Management Strategy, are adequate for the nature of the project, and approved it?	
▪ Reviewed the tolerances for the project provided by corporate or programme management to ensure that they are appropriate and realistic?	

Question	Yes/No
▓ Considered the consistency of the various components and approved the Project Initiation Documentation overall?	
19 Has the Project Board informed corporate or programme management (and other interested parties) that the project has been authorized?	

E.2.3 Authorize a Stage or Exception Plan

Question	Yes/No
20 Has the Project Board reviewed the End Stage Report? Specifically:	
▓ Did the board review the performance status of the project using the End Stage Report for the current management stage?	
▓ Has the board reviewed the benefits achieved and lessons learned during the stage?	
21 Has the Project Board assessed overall project viability? Specifically, has it:	
▓ Reviewed the Project Plan and the position in relation to project tolerances agreed with corporate or programme management?	
▓ Reviewed the Business Case to ensure that the project is still justified?	
▓ Reviewed the key risks to ensure that the exposure level is still acceptable and that response actions are planned?	
▓ Obtained decisions from outside the project for any potential deviations beyond project tolerances? (For example, if this project is part of a programme, then programme management should have examined the impact on the programme, and taken appropriate action.)	
22 Has the Project Board reviewed and approved the next Stage Plan (or Exception Plan)? Specifically, has it:	
▓ Reviewed the plan for which the Project Manager is seeking approval? (This will be a Stage Plan for the next management stage or an Exception Plan.)	
▓ Authorized the Project Manager to proceed with the submitted plan (Stage Plan or Exception Plan) or instructed the Project Manager to prematurely close the project?	
▓ Set the tolerances for the next management stage or (in the case of an Exception Plan) revised the current stage tolerances as necessary?	
23 Has the Project Board informed corporate or programme management (and other interested parties) that the next stage has been authorized (or an exception plan for the current stage has been approved)?	

E.2.4 Give ad hoc direction

Question	Yes/No
24 Has the Project Board responded to the Project Manager's requests? Specifically, has it:	
▓ Reviewed the request? (This could be informal or formal, the latter in the form of an Issue Report.)	
▓ Made a decision – for example, approved, rejected, deferred decision, requested more information?	
▓ Provided guidance to the Project Manager?	
25 Has the Project Board responded to reports? Specifically, has it:	
▓ Reviewed the latest Highlight Report in order to understand the status of the project and satisfied itself, through a dialogue with the Project Manager, that the stage is progressing according to plan?	
▓ Made decisions on Exception Reports – adjusted tolerances or approved responses to the exception as appropriate?	

Question	Yes/No
■ Made decisions on Issue Reports within the board's delegated limits of authority or sought advice from corporate or programme management?	
26 Has the Project Board responded to external influences? Specifically, has it:	
■ Ensured that the project is kept informed of external events that may affect it?	
■ Ensured that the project remains focused on the corporate or programme objectives set, and remains justified in business terms?	
■ Ensured that the Project Manager is notified of any changes in the corporate or programme environment that may impact on the project and that appropriate action is taken?	
27 Has the Project Board informed corporate or programme management (and other interested parties) of the project's progress in accordance with the Communication Management Strategy?	

E.2.5 Authorize project closure

Question	Yes/No
28 Has the Project Board confirmed handover and acceptance? Specifically, has it:	
■ Verified that the handover of the project product was in accordance with the Configuration Management Strategy and in particular that records of all required user acceptance and operational/maintenance acceptance exist?	
■ Ensured that, where appropriate, the resulting changes in the business are supported and sustainable?	
■ Ensured that any customer quality expectations that cannot be confirmed until after the project closes (e.g. performance levels regarding reliability) are included in the Benefits Review Plan as a post-project check?	
29 Has the Project Board Approved the End Project Report? Specifically, has it:	
■ Used the version of the Project Initiation Documentation which was approved at project initiation as the baseline to assess how the project has deviated from its initial basis, and to provide information against which the success of the project can be judged?	
■ Ensured follow-on action recommendations have been recorded correctly in the End Project Report and that the appropriate groups have been made aware of their responsibility for taking them forward?	
■ Approved the End Project Report for distribution to any interested parties, such as corporate or programme management?	
30 Has the Project Board reviewed the Lessons Report and agreed who should receive it? Has the Board ensured that the appropriate groups (for example, corporate or programme management, centre of excellence) have been made aware of their responsibility for taking any recommendations forward?	
31 Has the Project Board confirmed the Business Case? Specifically, has it confirmed the updated Business Case by comparing actual and forecast benefits, costs and risks against the approved Business Case within the Project Initiation Documentation? (It may not be possible to confirm all the benefits as some will not be realized until after the project is closed.)	
32 Has the Project Board approved the updated Benefits Review Plan? Specifically, has it:	
■ Reviewed and gained approval for the updated Benefits Review Plan, ensuring that it addresses the expected benefits that cannot yet be confirmed?	
■ Confirmed that the responsibility for the Benefits Review Plan has been transferred to corporate or programme management?	
33 Has the Project Board issued the project closure notification? Specifically, has it:	
■ Reviewed and issued a project closure notification in accordance with the Communication Management Strategy?	

Question	Yes/No
▨ Advised those who have provided the support infrastructure and resources for the project that these can now be withdrawn?	
▨ Released the resources provided to the project?	
▨ Provided a closing date for costs being charged to the project?	

E.3 INITIATING A PROJECT

Question		Yes/No
34	Have lessons from previous similar projects been identified and, where appropriate, have they been applied?	
35	Has the Risk Management Strategy been defined and documented?	
36	Has the Risk Register been set up and populated?	
37	Has the Configuration Management Strategy been defined and documented?	
38	Have the initial Configuration Item Records been set up?	
39	Has the Issue Register been set up and populated?	
40	Has the Quality Management Strategy been defined and documented?	
41	Has the Quality Register been set up and populated?	
42	Has the Communication Management Strategy been defined and documented?	
43	Have the project controls been determined and established?	
44	Has the Project Plan been created?	
45	Has the project management team structure been updated to reflect any new roles being appointed or any changes to responsibilities of existing roles?	
46	For new appointments, do role descriptions exist and have those people who have been appointed confirmed their acceptance?	
47	Has the outline Business Case been refined into a detailed Business Case?	
48	Has the Benefits Review Plan been created (this may have been done by corporate or programme management)?	
49	Has the Project Initiation Documentation been assembled?	

E.4 CONTROLLING A STAGE

Question		Yes/No
50	Have Work Packages been created and issued?	
51	Have all the Team Managers agreed all their Work Packages?	
52	Have completed products been produced in accordance with the Work Package and Product Description?	
53	Have the relevant Configuration Item Records been created/updated?	
54	Has the Quality Register been maintained?	
55	Were any products handed over as part of a phased delivery? If so, were they handed over in accordance with the Configuration Management Strategy?	
56	Has the Risk Register been maintained?	
57	Has the Issue Register been maintained?	
58	Has the Stage Plan been updated with actuals and revised forecasts?	

Question	Yes/No
59	Has the Daily Log been maintained?	
60	Have Checkpoint Reports been received for each issued Work Package at the frequency and in the format agreed?	
61	Was progress (actual and forecast) checked against agreed tolerances?	
62	If tolerances were forecast to be exceeded, were they escalated to the Project Board?	
63	If corrective actions were required, were they logged, implemented and tracked?	
64	Was the Business Case periodically checked for ongoing viability?	
65	Were Highlight Reports created and issued in accordance with the agreed reporting format and frequency?	
66	Do Issue Reports exist for all issues being handled formally?	
67	Do Exception Reports exist for all exceptions raised to the Project Board?	
68	Has the Lessons Log been updated with any new lessons?	

E.5 MANAGING PRODUCT DELIVERY

Question	Yes/No
69	Did the Work Package and Product Description(s) contain sufficient information, including cross-references, to enable the Team Manager to produce the products required?	
70	Has a Team Plan been created that demonstrates that the Work Package could be completed within agreed tolerances?	
71	Has the Team Plan been updated with actuals and revised forecasts?	
72	Was progress (actual and forecast) checked against agreed tolerances?	
73	If tolerances were forecast to be exceeded, were they escalated to the Project Manager?	
74	Were Checkpoint Reports issued to the Project Manager at the frequency and in the format agreed?	
75	Did the Team Manager notify the Project Manager of any issues and risks?	
76	Do approval records exist for each completed product?	
77	Did the Team Manager notify Project Support of any required updates to Configuration Item Records and the Quality Register?	
78	Did the Team Manager notify the Project Manager that all the products in the Work Package had been delivered?	

E.6 MANAGING A STAGE BOUNDARY

Question	Yes/No
79	Have all products that were planned to be completed within the stage been approved?	
80	Has a Product Status Account been created to verify the status of the stage's products?	
81	If there was a product handover during the stage, were related outstanding issues documented as follow-on action recommendations ready for distribution subject to Project Board approval?	
82	Has the Lessons Log been reviewed and updated?	
83	If required, has a Lessons Report been created ready for distribution, subject to Project Board approval?	
84	Has the Stage Plan been updated with actuals?	
85	Has the Risk Management Strategy been reviewed and (if necessary) updated?	
86	Has the Risk Register been reviewed and updated?	

Question	Yes/No
87	Has the Configuration Management Strategy been reviewed and (if necessary) updated?	
88	Have the Configuration Item Records been reviewed and updated?	
89	Has the Issue Register been reviewed and updated?	
90	Has the Quality Management Strategy been reviewed and (if necessary) updated?	
91	Has the Quality Register been reviewed and updated?	
92	Has the Communication Management Strategy been reviewed and (if necessary) updated?	
93	Have the project controls been reviewed and (if necessary) updated?	
94	Has the Project Plan been reviewed and (if necessary) updated?	
95	Has the project management team structure been updated to reflect any new roles being appointed or any changes to responsibilities of existing roles?	
96	For new appointments, do role descriptions exist and have those people who have been appointed confirmed their acceptance?	
97	Has the Business Case been reviewed and (if necessary) updated?	
98	Has the Benefits Review Plan been reviewed and (if necessary) updated?	
99	Has the Project Initiation Documentation been reviewed and (if necessary) updated?	
100	Has an End Stage Report been produced showing actual against planned performance, and summarizing lessons and follow-on action recommendations?	
101	Has the End Stage Report been issued to the Project Board in accordance with the project controls?	
For the next stage		
102	Has a Stage Plan for the next stage been created?	
103	Have Product Descriptions been created for the next stage's products?	
104	Has the Project Board been requested to authorize the next stage?	
For exceptions		
105	Has an Exception Plan been created (if requested by the Project Board)?	
106	Have Product Descriptions been created/updated for the Exception Plan?	
107	Has the Project Board been requested to approve the Exception Plan?	

E.7 CLOSING A PROJECT

Question	Yes/No
108	Have all products been completed and approved?	
109	Has a Product Status Account been created to verify the status of all the products?	
110	Have all outstanding issues been documented as follow-on action recommendations ready for distribution subject to Project Board approval?	
111	For premature closure, has the means for recovering products that have been completed or are in progress been approved by the Project Board? If requested, was an Exception Plan created and approved?	
112	Is there an acceptance record for the handover of the project product?	
113	Does the acceptance record include operational and maintenance acceptance?	
114	Has the Lessons Log been reviewed and a Lessons Report created ready for distribution subject to Project Board approval?	
115	Has the Project Plan been updated with actuals?	

Question		Yes/No
116	Has the Business Case been updated with actuals?	
117	Has the Benefits Review Plan been updated with actuals?	
118	Has an End Project Report been produced showing actual against planned performance and summarizing lessons and follow-on action recommendations?	
119	Has the End Project Report been issued to the Project Board in accordance with the project controls?	
120	Has a draft project closure notification been created for Project Board approval and onward distribution?	
121	Have all registers and logs been closed?	
122	Has all project documentation been archived?	

Further information

Further information

FROM BEST MANAGEMENT PRACTICE

PRINCE2

PRINCE2 is part of a suite of guidance developed by the Office of Government Commerce (OGC), aimed at helping organizations and individuals manage their projects, programmes and services. Where appropriate, this guidance is supported by a qualification scheme and accredited training and consultancy services.

Managing Successful Projects with PRINCE2 (2009). The Stationery Office, London.

Directing Successful Projects with PRINCE2 (2009). The Stationery Office, London.

Management of Risk (M_o_R)

Projects exist in a fundamentally uncertain world and, as such, effective management of risk is crucial to managing the delivery of the project's products, their outcomes and the ultimate benefits that have been identified. Management of risk (M_o_R) puts the management of project risk into the context of the wider business environment.

Management of Risk: Guidance for Practitioners (2010). The Stationery Office, London.

Managing Successful Programmes (MSP)

Managing Successful Programmes (MSP) represents proven programme management good practice in successfully delivering transformational change across a wide range of public and private sector organizations. It provides a framework to direct and oversee the implementation of a set of related projects and activities in order to deliver outcomes and benefits related to the organization's strategic objectives.

Managing Successful Programmes (2011). The Stationery Office, London.

Management of Portfolios (MoP®)

Portfolio management concerns the twin issues of how to do the 'right' projects and programmes in the context of the organization's strategic objectives, and how to do them 'correctly' in terms of achieving delivery and benefits at a collective level. MoP encompasses consideration of the principles upon which effective portfolio management is based; the key practices in the portfolio definition and delivery cycles, including examples of how they have been applied in real life; and guidance on how to implement portfolio management and sustain progress in a wide variety of organizations.

Management of Portfolios (2011). The Stationery Office, London.

Management of Value (MoV®)

MoV provides a cross-sector and universally applicable guide on how to maximize value in a way that takes account of organizations' priorities, differing stakeholders' needs and, at the same time, uses resources as efficiently and effectively as possible. It will help organizations to put in place effective methods to deliver enhanced value across their portfolio, programmes, projects and operational activities to meet the challenges of ever-more competitive and resource-constrained environments.

Management of Value (2010). The Stationery Office, London.

Portfolio, Programme and Project Management Maturity Model (P3M3®)

The Portfolio, Programme and Project Management Maturity Model (P3M3) is a reference guide for structured best practice. It breaks down the broad disciplines of portfolio, programme and project management into a hierarchy of perspectives.

The hierarchical approach enables organizations to assess their current capability and then plot a roadmap for improvement prioritized by those perspectives that will make the biggest impact on performance.

Portfolio, Programme and Project Offices (P3O)

Portfolio, Programme and Project Offices (P3O) provides guidance on how to define, establish and operate a portfolio, programme or project office. It covers the range of functions and services that P3Os may provide and includes references to the techniques that may be employed.

Portfolio, Programme and Project Offices (2008). The Stationery Office, London.

PRINCE2 Maturity Model (P2MM)

The PRINCE2 Maturity Model (P2MM) describes a set of key process areas (KPAs) required for the effective implementation and use of PRINCE2 within an organization. This is P2MM's core value: while the PRINCE2 manual describes how to manage a single project, it does not include any processes on how to embed PRINCE2, whereas P2MM does.

P2MM describes key practices aligned with the PRINCE2 processes and components to enable repeatable application of the method (Level 2), and goes further to describe the key practices required to institutionalize the method (Level 3) as a standard business process for managing projects.

OGC Gateway Review process

OGC Gateway Review process is a well-established project and programme assurance review process which is mandated for all UK government high-risk programmes and projects. OGC Gateway Review delivers a peer review, in which independent practitioners from outside the individual programme/project use their experience and expertise to examine progress and assess the likelihood of successful delivery of the programme or project. The review process is used to provide a valuable additional perspective on the issues facing the internal team, and an external challenge to the robustness of plans and processes. This service is based on good practice and there are many similar examples across all business sectors of this type of peer review designed to provide assurance to the owner of the programme or project.

Full details of the OGC Gateway Review process are available from The National Archives website.

Achieving Excellence in Construction

Achieving Excellence in Construction procurement guidance is contained within a set of 11 guides and two high-level guides. It builds on UK central government departments' recent experience, supports future strategy and aligns with the OGC Gateway Review process.

Copies of the guides are available for download from The National Archives website.

ITIL® Service Management Practices

ITIL is the most widely accepted approach to IT service management in the world. Providing a cohesive set of best-practice guidance drawn from the public and private sectors across the world, it has recently undergone a major and important refresh project.

IT Service Management (ITSM) derives enormous benefits from a best-practice approach. Because ITSM is driven both by technology and the huge range of organizational environments in which it operates, it is in a state of constant evolution. Best practice, based on expert advice and input from ITIL users, is both current and practical, combining the latest thinking with sound, common-sense guidance.

ITIL Continual Service Improvement (2011). The Stationery Office, London.

ITIL Service Design (2011). The Stationery Office, London.

ITIL Service Operation (2011). The Stationery Office, London.

ITIL Service Strategy (2011). The Stationery Office, London.

ITIL Service Transition (2011). The Stationery Office, London.

FROM THE STATIONERY OFFICE (COMPLEMENTARY PUBLICATIONS)

APMP for PRINCE2 Practitioners

This study guide enables candidates familiar with PRINCE2 to prepare for the APMP exam. It provides APMP exam candidates with a single source of reference material that covers all aspects of the APMP syllabus, including both pre-course and on-course material, whilst aligning it with the PRINCE2 method. This enables PRINCE2 practitioners (or project management staff working within a PRINCE2 environment) to expand their project management knowledge to cover all topics within the APMP syllabus.

APMP for PRINCE2 Practitioners (2008). The Stationery Office, London.

Focus on Skills series suite (set of three books)

The Focus on Skills series suite explores the various 'soft skills' that are demonstrated by effective project and programme managers, as the day-to-day coordination, motivation and communication aspects of project and programme management are very similar.

Leadership Skills for Project and Programme Managers (2008). The Stationery Office, London.

Team Management Skills for Project and Programme Managers (2008). The Stationery Office, London.

Communication Skills for Project and Programme Managers (2008). The Stationery Office, London.

Agile Project Management: Running PRINCE2 Projects with DSDM Atern

This ground-breaking book shows how users can combine the strength of both approaches considered, so that they complement each other and create a new, best-of-breed framework suitable for all project environments. Based on PRINCE2 and DSDM Atern, the two most established and internationally recognized project management approaches, this title explores the differences between the two approaches before showing where they overlap and how they can be integrated. While DSDM Atern is a project management methodology in its own right, this new publication sits within the PRINCE2 suite of titles.

Agile Project Management: Running PRINCE2 Projects with DSDM Atern (2007). The Stationery Office, London.

Improving Project Performance using the PRINCE2 Maturity Model

PRINCE2 is cited as the most widely used project management method worldwide, but, while the PRINCE2 manual describes how to manage a single project, it does not include any guidance on how to embed PRINCE2 into an organization.

Such guidance is now available: this publication describes the organizational processes and practices required for the effective implementation of PRINCE2 as an organizational standard. It includes guidance on assigning ownership, tailoring the method, training, integrating PRINCE2 with other management systems and establishing quality assurance mechanisms to gain a continual improvement capability.

In reading *Improving Project Performance using the PRINCE2 Maturity Model*, you will discover how organizations can gain full value from the PRINCE2 method. It contains practical advice on using the OGC's PRINCE2 Maturity Model (P2MM), and shows how P2MM can be applied in different situations.

Improving Project Performance using the PRINCE2 Maturity Model (2007). The Stationery Office, London.

OTHER SOURCES

The following is a list of useful references, some of which have been cited by the PRINCE2 authors.

Adair, John (2004) *The John Adair Handbook of Management and Leadership*, Thorogood, ISBN 978-1854182043.

APM GoPM Specific Interest Group (2005) *Directing Change: A Guide to the Governance of Project Management,* 2nd edition, Association for Project Management, High Wycombe, ISBN 1-903494-15-X.

Association of Project Management (2006) *APM Body of Knowledge*, 5th edition, High Wycombe, ISBN 978-1903494134.

British Standards Institution (2002) *BS6079–1:2002 A Guide to Project Management*, BSI, London.

Goldratt, Eliyahu M. (1997) *Critical Chain*, Avebury, ISBN 978-0566080388.

International Project Management Association (2006) *ICB-IPMA Competency Baseline, version 3.0*, ISBN 0-9553213-0-1.

Project Management Institute (2004) *A Guide to the Project Management Body of Knowledge: PMBOK Guide*, 3rd edition, ISBN 978-1930699458.

Winter, Mark and Smith, Charles (2006) *Rethinking Project Management*, EPSRC Network 2004–2006.

Glossary

Glossary

accept (risk response)

A risk response to a threat where a conscious and deliberate decision is taken to retain the threat, having discerned that it is more economical to do so than to attempt a risk response action. The threat should continue to be monitored to ensure that it remains tolerable.

acceptance

The formal act of acknowledging that the project has met agreed acceptance criteria and thereby met the requirements of its stakeholders.

acceptance criteria

A prioritized list of criteria that the project product must meet before the customer will accept it, i.e. measurable definitions of the attributes required for the set of products to be acceptable to key stakeholders.

activity

A process, function or task that occurs over time, has recognizable results and is managed. It is usually defined as part of a process or plan.

agile methods

Principally, software development methods that apply the project approach of using short time-boxed iterations where products are incrementally developed. PRINCE2 is compatible with agile principles.

approval

The formal confirmation that a product is complete and meets its requirements (less any concessions) as defined by its Product Description.

approver

The person or group (e.g. a Project Board) who is identified as qualified and authorized to approve a (management or specialist) product as being complete and fit for purpose.

assumption

A statement that is taken as being true for the purposes of planning, but which could change later. An assumption is made where some facts are not yet known or decided, and is usually reserved for matters of such significance that, if they change or turn out not to be true, there will need to be considerable replanning.

assurance

All the systematic actions necessary to provide confidence that the target (system, process, organization, programme, project, outcome, benefit, capability, product output, deliverable) is appropriate. Appropriateness might be defined subjectively or objectively in different circumstances. The implication is that assurance will have a level of independence from that which is being assured. See also 'Project Assurance' and 'quality assurance'.

authority

The right to allocate resources and make decisions (applies to project, stage and team levels).

authorization

The point at which an authority is granted.

avoid (risk response)

A risk response to a threat where the threat either can no longer have an impact or can no longer happen.

baseline

Reference levels against which an entity is monitored and controlled.

baseline management product

A type of management product that defines aspects of the project and, once approved, is subject to change control.

benefit

The measurable improvement resulting from an outcome perceived as an advantage by one or more stakeholders.

Benefits Review Plan

A plan that defines how and when a measurement of the achievement of the project's benefits can be made. If the project is being managed within a programme, this information may be created and maintained at the programme level.

benefits tolerance

The permissible deviation in the expected benefit that is allowed before the deviation needs to be escalated to the next level of management. Benefits tolerance is documented in the Business Case. See also 'tolerance'.

Business Case

The justification for an organizational activity (project), which typically contains costs, benefits, risks and timescales, and against which continuing viability is tested.

centre of excellence

A corporate coordinating function for portfolios, programmes and projects providing standards, consistency of methods and processes, knowledge management, assurance and training.

Change Authority

A person or group to which the Project Board may delegate responsibility for the consideration of requests for change or off-specifications. The Change Authority may be given a change budget and can approve changes within that budget.

change budget

The money allocated to the Change Authority available to be spent on authorized requests for change.

change control

The procedure that ensures that all changes that may affect the project's agreed objectives are identified, assessed and either approved, rejected or deferred.

checkpoint

A team-level, time-driven review of progress.

Checkpoint Report

A progress report of the information gathered at a checkpoint, which is given by a team to the Project Manager and which provides reporting data as defined in the Work Package.

closure notification

Advice from the Project Board to inform all stakeholders and the host sites that the project resources can be disbanded and support services, such as space, equipment and access, demobilized. It should indicate a closure date for costs to be charged to the project.

closure recommendation

A recommendation prepared by the Project Manager for the Project Board to send as a project closure notification when the board is satisfied that the project can be closed.

Communication Management Strategy

A description of the means and frequency of communication between the project and the project's stakeholders.

concession

An off-specification that is accepted by the Project Board without corrective action.

configuration item

An entity that is subject to configuration management. The entity may be a component of a product, a product, or a set of products in a release.

Configuration Item Record

A record that describes the status, version and variant of a configuration item, and any details of important relationships between them.

configuration management

Technical and administrative activities concerned with the creation, maintenance and controlled change of configuration throughout the life of a product.

Configuration Management Strategy

A description of how and by whom the project's products will be controlled and protected.

configuration management system

The set of processes, tools and databases that are used to manage configuration data. Typically, a project will use the configuration management system of either the customer or supplier organization.

constraints

The restrictions or limitations that the project is bound by.

contingency

Something that is held in reserve typically to handle time and cost variances, or risks. PRINCE2 does not advocate the use of contingency because estimating variances are managed by setting tolerances, and risks are managed through appropriate risk responses (including the fallback response that is contingent on the risk occurring).

corporate or programme standards

These are over-arching standards that the project must adhere to. They will influence the four project strategies (Communication Management Strategy, Configuration Management Strategy, Quality Management Strategy and Risk Management Strategy) and the project controls.

corrective action

A set of actions to resolve a threat to a plan's tolerances or a defect in a product.

cost tolerance

The permissible deviation in a plan's cost that is allowed before the deviation needs to be escalated to the next level of management. Cost tolerance is documented in the respective plan. See also 'tolerance'.

customer

The person or group who commissioned the work and will benefit from the end results.

customer's quality expectations

A statement about the quality expected from the project product, captured in the Project Product Description.

Daily Log

Used to record problems/concerns that can be handled by the Project Manager informally.

deliverable

See 'output'.

dependencies (plan)

The relationship between products or activities. For example, the development of Product C cannot start until Products A and B have been completed. Dependencies can be internal or external.

Internal dependencies are those under the control of the Project Manager. External dependencies are those outside the control of the Project Manager – for example, the delivery of a product required by this project from another project.

dis-benefit

An outcome that is perceived as negative by one or more stakeholders. It is an actual consequence of an activity whereas, by definition, a risk has some uncertainty about whether it will materialize.

DSDM Atern

An agile project delivery framework developed and owned by the DSDM consortium. Atern uses a time-boxed and iterative approach to product development and is compatible with PRINCE2.

embedding (PRINCE2)

What an organization needs to do to adopt PRINCE2 as its corporate project management method. See also, in contrast, 'tailoring', which defines what a project needs to do to apply the method to a specific project environment.

End Project Report

A report given by the Project Manager to the Project Board, that confirms the handover of all products and provides an updated Business Case and an assessment of how well the project has done against the original Project Initiation Documentation.

end stage assessment

The review by the Project Board and Project Manager of the End Stage Report to decide whether to approve the next Stage Plan. According to the size and criticality of the project, the review may be formal or informal. The authority to proceed should be documented as a formal record.

End Stage Report

A report given by the Project Manager to the Project Board at the end of each management stage of the project. This provides information about the project performance during the stage and the project status at stage end.

enhance (risk response)

A risk response to an opportunity where proactive actions are taken to enhance both the probability of the event occurring and the impact of the event should it occur.

event-driven control

A control that takes place when a specific event occurs. This could be, for example, the end of a stage, the completion of the Project Initiation Documentation, or the creation of an Exception Report. It could also include organizational events that may affect the project, such as the end of the financial year.

exception

A situation where it can be forecast that there will be a deviation beyond the tolerance levels agreed between Project Manager and Project Board (or between Project Board and corporate or programme management).

exception assessment

This is a review by the Project Board to approve (or reject) an Exception Plan.

Exception Plan

This is a plan that often follows an Exception Report. For a Stage Plan exception, it covers the period from the present to the end of the current stage. If the exception were at project level, the Project Plan would be replaced.

Exception Report

A description of the exception situation, its impact, options, recommendation and impact of the recommendation. This report is prepared by the Project Manager for the Project Board.

Executive

The single individual with overall responsibility for ensuring that a project meets its objectives and delivers the projected benefits. This individual should ensure that the project maintains its business focus, that it has clear authority, and that the work, including risks, is actively managed. The Executive is the chair of the Project Board. He or she represents the customer and is responsible for the Business Case.

exploit (risk response)

A risk response to an opportunity by seizing the opportunity to ensure that it will happen and that the impact will be realized.

fallback (risk response)

A risk response to a threat by putting in place a fallback plan for the actions that will be taken to reduce the impact of the threat should the risk occur.

follow-on action recommendations

Recommended actions related to unfinished work, ongoing issues and risks, and any other activities needed to take a product to the next phase of its life. These are summarized and included in the End Stage Report (for phased handover) and End Project Report.

governance (corporate)

The ongoing activity of maintaining a sound system of internal control by which the directors and officers of an organization ensure that effective management systems, including financial monitoring and control systems, have been put in place to protect assets, earning capacity and the reputation of the organization.

governance (project)

Those areas of corporate governance that are specifically related to project activities. Effective governance of project management ensures that an organization's project portfolio is aligned to the organization's objectives, is delivered efficiently and is sustainable.

handover

The transfer of ownership of a set of products to the respective user(s). The set of products is known as a release. There may be more than one handover in the life of a project (phased delivery). The final handover takes place in the Closing a Project process.

Highlight Report

A time-driven report from the Project Manager to the Project Board on stage progress.

host site

A site where project work is being undertaken (for example, an office or construction site).

impact (of risk)

The result of a particular threat or opportunity actually occurring, or the anticipation of such a result.

inherent risk

The exposure arising from a specific risk before any action has been taken to manage it.

initiation stage

The period from when the Project Board authorizes initiation to when they authorize the project (or decide not to go ahead with the project). The detailed planning and establishment of the project management infrastructure is covered by the Initiating a Project process.

issue

A relevant event that has happened, was not planned, and requires management action. It can be any concern, query, request for change, suggestion or off-specification raised during a project. Project issues can be about anything to do with the project.

Issue Register

A register used to capture and maintain information on all of the issues that are being managed formally. The Issue Register should be monitored by the Project Manager on a regular basis.

Issue Report

A report containing the description, impact assessment and recommendations for a request for change, off-specification or a problem/concern. It is only created for those issues that need to be handled formally.

Lessons Log

An informal repository for lessons that apply to this project or future projects.

Lessons Report

A report that documents any lessons that can be usefully applied to other projects. The purpose of the report is to provoke action so that the positive lessons from a project become embedded in the organization's way of working and that the organization is able to avoid the negative lessons on future projects.

logs

Informal repositories managed by the Project Manager that do not require any agreement by the Project Board on their format and composition. PRINCE2 has two logs: the Daily Log and the Lessons Log.

management product

A product that will be required as part of managing the project, and establishing and maintaining quality (for example, Highlight Report, End Stage Report etc.). The management products stay constant, whatever the type of project, and can be used as described, or with any relevant modifications, for all projects. There are three types of management product: baselines, records and reports.

management stage

The section of a project that the Project Manager is managing on behalf of the Project Board at any one time, at the end of which the Project Board will wish to review progress to date, the state of the Project Plan, the Business Case and risks, and the next Stage Plan in order to decide whether to continue with the project.

milestone

A significant event in a plan's schedule, such as completion of key Work Packages, a technical stage, or a management stage.

off-specification

Something that should be provided by the project, but currently is not (or is forecast not to be) provided. This might be a missing product or a product not meeting its specifications. It is one type of issue.

operational and maintenance acceptance

A specific type of acceptance by the person or group who will support the product once it is handed over into the operational environment.

outcome

The result of change, normally affecting real-world behaviour and/or circumstances. Outcomes are desired when a change is conceived. They are achieved as a result of the activities undertaken to effect the change.

output

A specialist product that is handed over to a user(s). Note that management products are not outputs but are created solely for the purpose of managing the project.

performance targets

A plan's goals for time, cost, quality, scope, benefits and risk.

plan

A detailed proposal for doing or achieving something which specifies the what, when, how and by whom. In PRINCE2 there are only the following types of plan: Project Plan, Stage Plan, Team Plan, Exception Plan and Benefits Review Plan.

planned closure

The PRINCE2 activity to close a project.

planning horizon

The period of time for which it is possible to accurately plan.

portfolio

All the programmes and stand-alone projects being undertaken by an organization, a group of organizations, or an organizational unit.

premature closure

The PRINCE2 activity to close a project before its planned closure. The Project Manager must ensure that work in progress is not simply abandoned, but that the project salvages any value created to date, and checks that any gaps left by the cancellation of the project are raised to corporate or programme management.

prerequisites (plan)

Any fundamental aspects that must be in place, and remain in place, for a plan to succeed.

PRINCE2 principles

The guiding obligations for good project management practice that form the basis of a project being managed using PRINCE2.

PRINCE2 project

A project that applies the PRINCE2 principles.

probability

This is the evaluated likelihood of a particular threat or opportunity actually happening, including a consideration of the frequency with which this may arise.

problem/concern

A type of issue (other than a request for change or off-specification) that the Project Manager needs to resolve or escalate.

procedure

A series of actions for a particular aspect of project management established specifically for the project – for example, a risk management procedure.

process

A structured set of activities designed to accomplish a specific objective. A process takes one or more defined inputs and turns them into defined outputs.

producer

The person or group responsible for developing a product.

product

An input or output, whether tangible or intangible, that can be described in advance, created and tested. PRINCE2 has two types of products – management products and specialist products.

product breakdown structure

A hierarchy of all the products to be produced during a plan.

product checklist

A list of the major products of a plan, plus key dates in their delivery.

Product Description

A description of a product's purpose, composition, derivation and quality criteria. It is produced at planning time, as soon as possible after the need for the product is identified.

product flow diagram

A diagram showing the sequence of production and interdependencies of the products listed in a product breakdown structure.

Product Status Account

A report on the status of products. The required products can be specified by identifier or the part of the project in which they were developed.

product-based planning

A technique leading to a comprehensive plan based on the creation and delivery of required outputs. The technique considers prerequisite products, quality requirements and the dependencies between products.

programme

A temporary flexible organization structure created to coordinate, direct and oversee the implementation of a set of related projects and activities in order to deliver outcomes and benefits related to the organization's strategic objectives. A programme is likely to have a life that spans several years.

project

A temporary organization that is created for the purpose of delivering one or more business products according to an agreed Business Case.

project approach

A description of the way in which the work of the project is to be approached. For example, are we building a product from scratch or buying in a product that already exists?

Project Assurance

The Project Board's responsibilities to assure itself that the project is being conducted correctly. The Project Board members each have a specific area of focus for Project Assurance, namely business assurance for the Executive, user assurance for the Senior User(s), and supplier assurance for the Senior Supplier(s).

project authorization notification

Advice from the Project Board to inform all stakeholders and the host sites that the project has been authorized and to request any necessary logistical support (e.g. communication facilities, equipment and any project support) sufficient for the duration of the project.

Project Brief

Statement that describes the purpose, cost, time and performance requirements, and constraints for a project. It is created pre-project during the Starting up a Project process and is used during the Initiating a Project process to create the Project Initiation Documentation and its components. It is superseded by the Project Initiation Documentation and not maintained.

Project Initiation Documentation

A logical set of documents that brings together the key information needed to start the project on a sound basis and that conveys the information to all concerned with the project.

project initiation notification

Advice from the Project Board to inform all stakeholders and the host sites that the project is being initiated and to request any necessary logistical support (e.g. communication facilities, equipment and any project support) sufficient for the initiation stage.

project lifecycle

The period from the start-up of a project to the acceptance of the project product.

project management

The planning, delegating, monitoring and control of all aspects of the project, and the motivation of those involved, to achieve the project objectives within the expected performance targets for time, cost, quality, scope, benefits and risks.

project management team

The entire management structure of the Project Board, and Project Manager, plus any Team Manager, Project Assurance and Project Support roles.

project management team structure

An organization chart showing the people assigned to the project management team roles to be used, and their delegation and reporting relationships.

Project Manager

The person given the authority and responsibility to manage the project on a day-to-day basis to deliver the required products within the constraints agreed with the Project Board.

project mandate

An external product generated by the authority commissioning the project that forms the trigger for Starting up a Project.

project office

A temporary office set up to support the delivery of a specific change initiative being delivered as a project. If used, the project office undertakes the responsibility of the Project Support role.

Project Plan

A high-level plan showing the major products of the project, when they will be delivered and at what cost. An initial Project Plan is presented as part of the Project Initiation Documentation. This is revised as information on actual progress appears. It is a major control document for the Project Board to measure actual progress against expectations.

project product

What the project must deliver in order to gain acceptance.

Project Product Description

A special type of Product Description used to gain agreement from the user on the project's scope and requirements, to define the customer's quality expectations, and to define the acceptance criteria for the project.

Project Support

An administrative role in the project management team. Project Support can be in the form of advice and help with project management tools, guidance, administrative services such as filing, and the collection of actual data.

proximity (of risk)

The time factor of risk, i.e. when the risk may occur. The impact of a risk may vary in severity depending on when the risk occurs.

quality

The totality of features and inherent or assigned characteristics of a product, person, process, service and/or system that bears on its ability to show that it meets expectations or satisfies stated needs, requirements or specifications.

quality assurance

An independent check that products will be fit for purpose or meet requirements.

quality control

The process of monitoring specific project results to determine whether they comply with relevant standards and of identifying ways to eliminate causes of unsatisfactory performance.

quality criteria

A description of the quality specification that the product must meet, and the quality measurements that will be applied by those inspecting the finished product.

quality inspection

A systematic, structured assessment of a product carried out by two or more carefully selected people (the review team) in a planned, documented and organized fashion.

quality management

The coordinated activities to direct and control an organization with regard to quality.

Quality Management Strategy

A strategy defining the quality techniques and standards to be applied, and the various responsibilities for achieving the required quality levels, during a project.

quality management system

The complete set of quality standards, procedures and responsibilities for a site or organization. In the project context, 'sites' and 'organizations' should be interpreted as the permanent or semi-permanent organization(s) sponsoring the project work, i.e. they are 'external' to the project's temporary organization. A programme, for instance, can be regarded as a semi-permanent organization that sponsors projects – and it may have a documented quality management system.

quality records

Evidence kept to demonstrate that the required quality assurance and quality control activities have been carried out.

Quality Register

A register containing summary details of all planned and completed quality activities. The Quality Register is used by the Project Manager and Project Assurance as part of reviewing progress.

quality review

See 'quality inspection'.

quality review technique

A quality inspection technique with defined roles and a specific structure. It is designed to assess whether a product that takes the form of a document (or similar, e.g. a presentation) is complete, adheres to standards and meets the quality criteria agreed for it in the relevant Product Description. The participants are drawn from those with the necessary competence to evaluate its fitness for purpose.

quality tolerance

The tolerance identified for a product for a quality criterion defining an acceptable range of values. Quality tolerance is documented in the Project Product Description (for the project-level quality tolerance) and in the Product Description for each product to be delivered.

records

Dynamic management products that maintain information regarding project progress.

reduce (risk response)

A response to a risk where proactive actions are taken to reduce the probability of the event occurring by performing some form of control, and/or to reduce the impact of the event should it occur.

registers

Formal repositories managed by the Project Manager that require agreement by the Project Board on their format, composition and use. PRINCE2 has three registers: Issue Register, Risk Register and Quality Register.

reject (risk response)

A response to a risk (opportunity) where a conscious and deliberate decision is taken not to exploit or enhance an opportunity, having discerned that it is more economical to do so than to attempt a risk response action. The opportunity should continue to be monitored.

release

The set of products in a handover. The contents of a release are managed, tested and deployed as a single entity. See also 'handover'.

reports

Management products providing a snapshot of the status of certain aspects of the project.

request for change

A proposal for a change to a baseline. It is a type of issue.

residual risk

The risk remaining after the risk response has been applied.

responsible authority

The person or group commissioning the project (typically corporate or programme management) who has the authority to commit resources and funds on behalf of the commissioning organization.

reviewer

A person or group independent of the producer who assesses whether a product meets its requirements as defined in its Product Description.

risk

An uncertain event or set of events that, should it occur, will have an effect on the achievement of objectives. A risk is measured by a combination of the probability of a perceived threat or opportunity occurring, and the magnitude of its impact on objectives.

risk actionee

A nominated owner of an action to address a risk. Some actions may not be within the remit of the risk owner to control explicitly; in that situation there should be a nominated owner of the action to address the risk. He or she will need to keep the risk owner apprised of the situation.

risk appetite

An organization's unique attitude towards risk taking that in turn dictates the amount of risk that it considers is acceptable.

risk estimation

The estimation of probability and impact of an individual risk, taking into account predetermined standards, target risk levels, interdependencies and other relevant factors.

risk evaluation

The process of understanding the net effect of the identified threats and opportunities on an activity when aggregated together.

risk management

The systematic application of principles, approaches and processes to the tasks of identifying and assessing risks, and then planning and implementing risk responses.

Risk Management Strategy

A strategy describing the goals of applying risk management, as well as the procedure that will be adopted, roles and responsibilities, risk tolerances, the timing of risk management interventions, the tools and techniques that will be used, and the reporting requirements.

risk owner

A named individual who is responsible for the management, monitoring and control of all aspects of a particular risk assigned to them, including the implementation of the selected responses to address the threats or to maximize the opportunities.

risk profile

A description of the types of risk that are faced by an organization and its exposure to those risks.

Risk Register

A record of identified risks relating to an initiative, including their status and history.

risk response

Actions that may be taken to bring a situation to a level where exposure to risk is acceptable to the organization. These responses fall into a number of risk response categories.

risk response category

A category of risk response. For threats, the individual risk response category can be avoid, reduce, transfer, accept or share. For opportunities, the individual risk response category can be exploit, enhance, reject or share.

risk tolerance

The threshold levels of risk exposure which, when exceeded, will trigger an Exception Report to bring the situation to the attention of the Project Board. Risk tolerances could include limits on the plan's aggregated risks (e.g. cost of aggregated threats to remain less than 10% of the plan's budget), or limits on any individual threat (e.g. any threat to operational service). Risk tolerance is documented in the Risk Management Strategy.

risk tolerance line

A line drawn on the summary risk profile. Risks that appear above this line cannot be accepted (lived with) without referring them to a higher authority. For a project, the Project Manager would refer these risks to the Project Board.

role description

A description of the set of responsibilities specific to a role.

schedule

Graphical representation of a plan (for example, a Gantt chart), typically describing a sequence of tasks, together with resource allocations, which collectively deliver the plan. In PRINCE2, project activities should only be documented in the schedules associated with a Project Plan, Stage Plan or Team Plan. Actions that are allocated from day-to-day management may be documented in the relevant project log (i.e. Risk Register, Daily Log, Issue Register, Quality Register) if they do not require significant activity.

scope

For a plan, the sum total of its products and the extent of their requirements. It is described by the product breakdown structure for the plan and associated Product Descriptions.

scope tolerance

The permissible deviation in a plan's scope that is allowed before the deviation needs to be escalated to the next level of management. Scope tolerance is documented in the respective plan in the form of a note or reference to the product breakdown structure for that plan. See 'tolerance'.

Senior Responsible Owner

A UK government term for the individual responsible for ensuring that a project or programme of change meets its objectives and delivers the projected benefits. The person should be the owner of the overall business change that is being supported by the project. The Senior Responsible Owner (SRO) should ensure that the change maintains its business focus, that it has clear authority, and that the context, including risks, is actively managed. This individual must be senior and must take personal responsibility for successful delivery of the project. The SRO should be recognized as the owner throughout the organization.

The SRO appoints the project's Executive (or in some cases may elect to be the Executive).

Senior Supplier

The Project Board role that provides knowledge and experience of the main discipline(s) involved in the production of the project's deliverable(s). The Senior Supplier represents the supplier interests within the project and provides supplier resources.

Senior User

The Project Board role accountable for ensuring that user needs are specified correctly and that the solution meets those needs.

share (risk response)

A risk response to either a threat or an opportunity through the application of a pain/gain formula: both parties share the gain (within pre-agreed limits) if the cost is less than the cost plan; and both share the pain (again within pre-agreed limits) if the cost plan is exceeded.

specialist product

A product whose development is the subject of the plan. The specialist products are specific to an individual project (for example, an advertising campaign, a car park ticketing system, foundations for a building, a new business process etc.) Also known as a deliverable or output.

sponsor

The main driving force behind a programme or project. PRINCE2 does not define a role for the sponsor, but the sponsor is most likely to be the Executive on the Project Board, or the person who has appointed the Executive.

stage

See 'management stage' or 'technical stage'.

Stage Plan

A detailed plan used as the basis for project management control throughout a stage.

stakeholder

Any individual, group or organization that can affect, be affected by, or perceive itself to be affected by, an initiative (programme, project, activity, risk).

start-up

The pre-project activities undertaken by the Executive and the Project Manager to produce the outline Business Case, Project Brief and Initiation Stage Plan.

strategy

An approach or line to take, designed to achieve a long-term aim. Strategies can exist at different levels – at the corporate, programme and project level. At the project level, PRINCE2 defines four strategies: Communication Management Strategy, Configuration Management Strategy, Quality Management Strategy and Risk Management Strategy.

supplier

The person, group or groups responsible for the supply of the project's specialist products.

tailoring

The appropriate use of PRINCE2 on any given project, ensuring that there is the correct amount of planning, control, governance and use of the processes and themes (whereas the adoption of PRINCE2 across an organization is known as 'embedding').

Team Manager

The person responsible for the production of those products allocated by the Project Manager (as defined in a Work Package) to an appropriate quality, timescale and at a cost acceptable to the Project Board. This role reports to, and takes direction from, the Project Manager. If a Team Manager is not assigned, then the Project Manager undertakes the responsibilities of the Team Manager role.

Team Plan

An optional level of plan used as the basis for team management control when executing Work Packages.

technical stage

A method of grouping work together by the set of techniques used, or the products created. This results in stages covering elements such as design, build and implementation. Such stages are technical stages and are a separate concept from management stages.

theme

An aspect of project management that needs to be continually addressed, and that requires specific treatment for the PRINCE2 processes to be effective.

time tolerance

The permissible deviation in a plan's time that is allowed before the deviation needs to be escalated to the next level of management. Time tolerance is documented in the respective plan. See also 'tolerance'.

time-driven control

A management control that is periodic in nature, to enable the next higher authority to monitor progress – e.g. a control that takes place every two weeks.

PRINCE2 offers two key time-driven progress reports: Checkpoint Report and Highlight Report.

tolerance

The permissible deviation above and below a plan's target for time and cost without escalating the deviation to the next level of management. There may also be tolerance levels for quality, scope, benefit and risk. Tolerance is applied at project, stage and team levels.

tranche

A programme management term describing a group of projects structured around distinct step changes in capability and benefit delivery.

transfer (risk response)

A response to a threat where a third party takes on responsibility for some of the financial impact of the threat (for example, through insurance or by means of appropriate clauses in a contract).

trigger

An event or decision that triggers a PRINCE2 process.

user

The person or group who will use one or more of the project's products.

user acceptance

A specific type of acceptance by the person or group who will use the product once it is handed over into the operational environment.

variant

A variation on a baselined product. For example, an operations manual may have an English variant and a Spanish variant.

version

A specific baseline of a product. Versions typically use naming conventions that enable the sequence or date of the baseline to be identified. For example, Project Plan version 2 is the baseline after Project Plan version 1.

waterfall method

A development approach that is linear and sequential with distinct goals for each phase of development. Once a phase of development is completed, the development proceeds to the next phase and earlier phases are not revisited (hence the analogy that water flowing down a mountain cannot go back).

Work Package

The set of information relevant to the creation of one or more products. It will contain a description of the work, the Product Description(s), details of any constraints on production, and confirmation of the agreement between the Project Manager and the person or Team Manager who is to implement the Work Package that the work can be done within the constraints.

Index

Index